Dark Symbols, Obscure Signs

Dark Symbols, Obscure Signs

God, Self, and

Community in

the Slave Mind

With a New Introduction

Riggins R. Earl Jr.

The University of Tennessee Press / Knoxville

LIBRARY OF CONGRESS CATALOGING-IN-PUBLICATION DATA

Earl, Riggins Renal.
Dark symbols, obscure signs: God, self, and community in
the slave mind: with a new introduction/Riggins R. Earl, Jr.
    p. cm.
Originally published: Maryknoll, N.Y.: Orbis Books, c1993
as v. 7 in series: The Bishop Henry McNeal Turner studies
in North American Black religion. Includes bibliographical
references (p.) and index.

ISBN 1-57233-217-4 (pbk.: alk. paper)

1. African Americans—Southern States—Religion.
2. Slaves—Southern States—Religion.
3. Racism—Religious aspects—Christianity.
4. Racism—Biblical teaching.
5. Slaves—Southern States—Folklore.
6. Southern States—Race relations.
I. Title.

BR563.N4 E37 2003
277.3'081'08996073—dc21   2002075083

To the memory of

LOVELENE (LOVE) 1942–1986

Contents

Preface

The last thirty years in America have been decades of tremendous social, economic, political, behavioral, and ideological change. African-American religion has undeniably contributed positively to the social change phenomenon. Fair and honest scholarship recognizes African Americans' positive religious contributions to American public life. Bringing white academicians, however, to recognize African-American religion as a worthy subject of scholarly inquiry has been a greater hurdle to cross. Thanks primarily to the persistent scholarly, as well as political, efforts of James Cone, African-American religion has forged for itself a place of at least marginal existence in the white academy.

James Cone's *Black Theology and Black Power*, published almost twenty-five years ago, has really been the necessary precursor for what I have tried to do in this study. Published as a religious intellectual's response to the Black Power philosophy, Cone's book became the scholarly guide for understanding the political contributions of black religion since slavery. Defying the rhetoric and ethics of the Integrationist philosophy, Cone dared speak of self, God, and community in ethnic terms. In this sense he gave theological legitimacy to the Black Power movement. It was a breath of fresh air for those of my generation who were then pursuing doctorates in the field of religion. Cone's theological affirmation of blackness provoked us to question the primary assumption of the Integrationist philosophy which said: In the body of Christ there are no black or white, male or female, Jew or Greek. This sort of rhetoric presented no problems even for white liberals who, unconsciously if not consciously, assumed that whiteness was normative for all God-talk. Cone's theological challenge helped African-American religious leaders of the Integrationist persuasion to see that they stood to forfeit their own God-given right of ethnic affirmation. It demanded a radical hermeneutical shift in our theological and ethical queries. He dared us to reshape our universal assumptions about traditional European theological and ethical paradigms.

James Cone's theological interpretation of the Black Power movement philosophy, which was antithetical to the Integrationist philosophy, made him the normative interpretive voice in the academy. Spartan demands upon his professional skills and energies have robbed him of the time and solitude that are necessary for taking the discussion of African-American theology beyond the conflicts of the Integrationist philosophy and those of the Black Power philosophy.

This essay makes the case that a critical examination of slave sources is foundational for African-American theological and ethical reflection. Without it, scholarly investigation of African-American religious experience is simply reduced to either a study of the thesis of the Integrationist philosophy or the antithesis of the Black Power philosophy. Consequently, any reductionist interpretation of the African-American religious experience stands to ignore its intricate aspects; the value of the opposites for construing a thesis.

While a Ph.D. student at Vanderbilt University I got the idea for such a study. Despite the passionate desire of my soul to do otherwise, I was enough of a political realist to hold such an idea in abeyance until completing my dissertation. I initiated the research for this project during my last year on the faculty at the University of Tennessee at Knoxville. It became a constant preoccupation when I joined the faculty at the Interdenominational Theological Center, where I eventually organized a seminar class called Foundations of African American Theology and Ethics. This seminar has provided the formal context for querying with students the primary sources that were used for this study. I am ever in the debt of those students who became, so to speak, my academic querying partners.

A decade of research and writing went into bringing this project to the printed page. Now that it is in print I trust that friends and foes alike will temper their criticisms with a spirit of compassion. Those who would dare be pioneers in any area must always risk, in the words of Langston Hughes' poem, "Mother to Son," "going in the dark where there ain't been no light." This expression best sums up what the case has been for me in my exploration.

During these years of research and study a number of awards have helped bring this project to fruition. I wish to acknowledge a study leave from the University of Tennessee of Knoxville. This leave allowed me the chance to deepen my knowledge of such theoretical sources in African-American historical sources, phenomenology and philosophy. Also, I am thankful to the Interdenominational Theological Center and the American Association of Theological Schools for support grants that made possible a study leave during the academic year of 1988-89. A research grant from the Interdenominational Theological Center, in the summer of 1987, enabled me to finish my archival research in different libraries of the country.

Special thanks to my friends Jim Holloway and the members of the Department of Religion and Philosophy at Berea College for their willingness to discuss many of the ideas in these chapters. Their invitation for me to be the Visiting Lilly Professor during the fall semester of 1988 gave me a different audience for testing my ideas. It proved to be a rewarding occasion for several reasons. Here I spent the majority of my time writing the first rough draft of this manuscript. In addition, I met once a week with a seminar group of honor students to discuss the seminal ideas that have been fleshed out in these chapters. Several meetings, also, with a group of faculty members of the liberal arts college contributed to the development and completion of this project. I would like to thank President John B. Stephenson of Berea College who saw to it that my stay at Berea College was comfortable. The hospitable spirit of the Berea College Campus, nestled in the Kentucky mountains, provided therapy for my soul, mind, and body. It was a needed haven where I could slowly allow those internal wounds to heal that had been caused by the death of my wife a year and a half earlier.

Many persons have helped in the course of my research. I am indebted to the directors and staff persons of the following libraries and institutions: The Library of Congress; Mooreland-Spingarn Library of Howard University; Archives of Duke University Library; Schomburg Library; Emory University Library; Divinity School Library; Harvard Memorial Library; Yale Divinity School Library; American University Library; Columbia Theological School Library; Union School of Theology Library of New York; Union Theological Seminary Library of Richmond Virginia; Howard University Divinity School Library (Miss Irene Owen, who at that time was the librarian at Howard, was extremely helpful to me in my research efforts); Vanderbilt University Library; Fisk University Library; and Atlanta University Center Library, where special thanks are due to Mr. Flemister and Dr. Joseph Troutman.

Teachers, colleagues, students, and friends have helped refine the direction of this study over the years. I thank all of those students who have studied with me in the seminar, Foundations of African American Theology and Ethics at the Interdenominational Theological Center. Special thanks to the late J. Kim, former colleague with me on the faculty at the University of Tennessee, for serving as a gadfly when this project was only an idea. Thanks to Stan Lusby, Charles Reynolds, and Jack Reese (former chancellor of the University of Tennessee) for institutional support. Ronald Potter served as an invaluable friend with whom I tested many of my earlier presuppositions. Thanks also to James E. Sellers, Thomas Ogletree, Charles Long, Arthur Dycke, David Shannon, James Washington, the late Robert Williams, Delores Williams, James Laney, and President James Costen of the Interdenominational Theological Center for his institutional support and personal encouragement.

Wayne Merrit, Peter Paris, Jackie Grant, James Cone, Howard Harrod, Ronald Potter, and Gayraud Wilmore have all read portions of the manuscript in its developmental stages and made helpful suggestions. Special thanks goes to Michele Jacques, a former student, for helping get both the endnotes and the bibliography of this study in final form. Completion of this project for publication was made easier because of the editorial assistance of Robert Ellsberg of Orbis Books.

Studies of this nature require a lot of sacrificial time away from family members. Following my wife's sickness and death, the need of help with the children became indispensable. I am eternally grateful for a number of persons' compassionate contributions. Anna Jones, Angelia Clark, and Helen Meadows each, at different times, contributed in a positive way as caretaker of the children, making it possible for me to attend to this project. Most of all I am grateful for Renal, Nathan, and Regina, who have grown up watching me work on this study, for trusting me even when I was unable to be physically present for them.

I dedicate this book to the memory of Lovelene — affectionately called Love by her close friends and family members. Lovelene and I enjoyed the sacred union of marriage for twenty-two years. During that period we mutually shared the challenging roles of spouses, parents, lovers, playmates, and friends. Our relationship deepened my understanding of what it means to be an embodied self for the other. In November 1986, Lovelene, after a battle with breast cancer, made the ultimate transition. Although it seems that her life was cut short in the middle of her song, constant communion with Lovelene's spirit has aided in the researching and writing of this book.

Introduction 2003

In 1993, Orbis Books published the first edition of *Dark Symbols, Obscure Signs: God, Self, and Community in the Slave Mind*. I did not then, nor do I now, see myself doing a formal theology or ethics of the black experience. Academics of theology and religion are not reluctant to posit their scholarly views of what is being said in slave sources. I have sought, during my tenure of professional scholarship, to first identify and explain foundational religio-ethical meaning constructs of the black experience. I have deemed this a prerequisite for developing in the future a more in-depth statement on the theology and ethics of the black experience. I propose methodologically to accomplish this foundational task by doing an interpretive reading of the religio-ethical meaning constructs of selected primary black sources. In my first book, *Dark Symbols, Obscure Signs*, I initially sought to lay the methodological groundwork for this rather challenging task. My operative assumption in this study is that the black scholar's first duty must be to identify and explicate the *religio-ethical* meaning construct of conversion as evidenced in the slave sources. *Dark Symbols, Obscure Signs* investigates slaves' conversion experiences as expressed in their songs, stories, sermons, etc. This critical exploration of slaves' conversion experiences shows how they reconstructed for themselves their own normative vision of God, self, and community. I intentionally call the phenomenon of slaves' conversion experiences a *religio-ethical*, rather than a *Christian ethical*, foundational meaning construct because slaves' perception of God was not limited to their masters' lexiconized understanding. According to their own testimonies, slaves never interpreted their conversion experiences as conditioning them to better serve their masters. On the contrary, under the secret slave community's critical watch, authentic conversion came to mean that God was better equipping the oppressed for communicating with God and each other their innate yearnings for freedom.

In *Dark Symbols, Obscure Signs*, I presumed the methodological task of identifying and explaining slaves' foundational religious experience. I will call it the religio-ethical meaning conversion construct. It will help us in doing the following: (1) exploring how Christian enslavers arbitrarily crafted their own ideologically oppressive catechetical conversion formulae for converting slaves to a skewed version of Christianity; and (2) exploring how converted black slaves creatively crafted a counter conversion language to reflect their new visionary experience of God, self, and community. The study shows that slaves forged out of enslavers' oppressive monological conversion language their own dialogical understanding of liberation. Slave masters undoubtedly perceived slaves' conversion testimonies as being no more than dark symbols and obscure signs. Defiantly, slaves employed their own dialogical language, denounced by their masters as naïve, to nurture in each other a radical hunger and vision for freedom.

Contemporary scholarship must not underestimate the value of seriously study-ing the slave community's sources. I argue in *Dark Symbols, Obscure Signs* that slaves' conversion experience, apart from their masters, was the initial ritualized step toward autonomy that defied their masters' attempt at absolute control. The conversion experience birthed in slaves a critical consciousness of spatial and temporal freedom that exceeded their masters' imagination. Radical experiences of conversion to Jesus afforded slaves the common language for transcending major tribal differences among themselves. Such a discourse on conversion shows that it is a foundational religio-ethical meaning construct of the black experience.

Conversion is not a foundational religio-ethical construct that merely has meaning for understanding its expression in the slave sources, however. It is a foundational religio-ethical meaning construct that manifests itself in the con-sciousness of blacks at every phase of their struggle for freedom and justice.

Dark Symbols, Obscure Signs seeks to ask the fundamental question of the slave sources: How did slaves re-construe enslavers' catechetical conversion language about God, self, and, community for their own liberated conversion experience? An understanding of slaves' re-construal of their enslavers' Christian conversion language depends largely on a careful answer to the preceding question. Slaves believed that the God of their conversion encounters, counter to their enslavers' racist teachings about them, radically transformed them into agents of critical self-awareness.[1] Encounters with this God convinced slaves of the heavenly value of their bodies and souls (contrary to their masters' oppressive ideology). Converted slaves characterized the radicalness of their conversion in life and death metaphors: "struck dead by God and made alive again." Briefly, slaves understood conversion to be a radical death/life transitional experience that par-adoxically concealed and revealed the complex dimensions of their existence. This paradoxical experience of conversion took the convert from darkness to light; from death to life; from sinfulness to righteousness; from slavery to free-dom; from hell to heaven; and from plantation to the mythic promised land. It was in slaves' reconstructed conversion language that they came to a radical theocentric and Christocentric anthropological understanding of themselves.

Readers of this republished edition of *Dark Symbols, Obscure Signs* stand to benefit from a comparative methodological reading of its presuppositions to other black religious scholars' works on the subject. I will seek to make the case for this by doing the following: (1) briefly noting two of the major black social protest movements' impact upon black religious scholars' methodological presuppositions and interpretations of slave sources; (2) referencing some black religious scholars' published works on slave sources and clarifying their different methodological perspectives; and (3) showing the methodological connections of *Dark Symbols, Obscure Signs* to the sequel volumes that I propose on the foundational religio-ethical meaning constructs of the black experience.

BLACK RELIGIOUS SCHOLARS AND SOCIAL PROTEST

Black religious scholarship of the slave sources has been profoundly influenced by two major social protest eras: (1) the integrationist social protest era; and (2) the black power social protest/apologist era.[2] Each era respectively has colored religious scholars' interpretative readings of the slave sources. The emergence, in the last thirty years, of black religious scholars who have dared investigate blacks' contribution to religio-ethical discourse has revolutionized the academic study of religion and theology. This investigative type of bold scholarship is the creative result of what I would term the black power protest/apologist era. Prior to this period was the integrationist social protest era. Black religious scholars of the integrationist social protest era gave very little, if any, scholarly attention to the religio-ethical value of primary slave sources. Scholars outside the field of religion but within the humanities and social sciences who published and republished works on the slave sources in the last forty years undoubtedly jump-started black religious scholars' academic interest in the intellectual value of these materials.[3]

Prior to the black religious scholars' black power protest/apologist era, scholarly interpretations of primary slave sources were produced mainly by scholars in the fields of literature, history, cultural anthropology, etc. These scholars' own published works on slavery, as well as their edited reprints of publications from the previous century on the subject, became increasingly useful in the academy as the protest against racial injustice increased. Black religious scholars who were educated before and during the integrationist protest era were expected to assimilate the white seminary's definitions of normative theological education. This amounted to their being trained *away from* the richness of their own black religious culture. It meant being able to speak in the scholarly vernacular of the white academy to the black church, to express religious ideas and feelings in the philosophical categories of the seminary's most revered German theologians and philosophers. Nowhere did the seminary curriculum reference blacks' practical or theoretical contributions in the history of Christendom. In white liberal seminaries at the time, it was an era of benign neglect. Ironically, the poorest white student of the seminary read church history with a feeling of connectedness through his European ancestry. Such a student could mythically believe himself to be somewhere in the narrative of church history. This in itself provided an incentive for him to study the makers and shapers of the church's story. On the contrary, this was not the case for blacks during the integrationist era. Benignly, blacks were formally considered marginal to the mainstream of the religious history of the American people.[4]

Some black religious scholars of the integrationist protest era faced the constant temptation of desiring to be assimilated into the mainstream of white church culture. Highly educated black religious leadership was expected to reflect the norms and practices of the white seminary and church. Black academics of religion, even in predominantly black theological schools, viewed blacks' religious beliefs and practices with sometimes less intellectual interest than did their white counterparts of the academy. A brief word about the methodological approaches of such black scholars as Joseph R. Washington of the integrationist era and James H. Cone of the black power period may illuminate the above claims.

Washington's Integrationist Methodology

Joseph R. Washington's book *Black Religion: The Negro and Christianity in the United States* intentionally distinguishes between what he calls "black folk religion" and "Christianity."[5] A trained Ph.D. in the Sociology of Religion from Boston University, Washington concludes that the folksiness of black religion prevented it from being authentically Christian and Protestant. Traditional black religion, for Washington, failed to embrace Christian doctrine. Although inclined to overly simplify the truth, Washington rightly notes that the majority of black church leaders did not make their faith applicable to the civil rights struggle. He scurrilously attacks traditional black church leaders' tendency to place their own vested interest over the cause of Christ. Washington admonishes more enlightened blacks to get rid of "their folksy Negro religion," which he notes had its origin in slavery, and integrate with willing mainline white Protestants of the integrationist era. On the one hand, Washington dangerously assumes that white Protestant Christianity unilaterally had everything good to offer blacks. On the other, he concludes that black folk religion lacked any beneficiary value for blacks. Unfortunately, Washington's disciplined scholarly intellect allowed him to see neither the opaque strengths of black religion—as well as its weaknesses—nor the inherent racism of white Christianity. He would later seek to correct this failure in sequel publications.

On the contrary, James H. Cone clearly saw the inherent strength of black religion and became its premier apologetic voice. He must be characterized as the black intellectual scholar who initially forged the link from an integrationist hermeneutic to a black power hermeneutic. As a scholar, Cone became the critical religious voice of the black community, bridging the gap between the integrationist and the black power era.

Cone's Black Power Protest/Apologist Methodology

James H. Cone dared to challenge Washington's thesis about the shortcoming of "Negro religion." Cone's first book, *Black Theology and Black Power*, was published the year following the death of Martin Luther King Jr.[6] It sparked for that period a dynamic interest in the scholarly study of religion and theology. Cone's book gave critical voice to what blacks had felt daily but were unable to express in academic language. Much of this had to do with the fact that the white academy could not conceive of a non-white authoritative voice on such a marginal subject as black religion. Cone's militant published voice filled a critical void in the world of academe. His ideas about blacks and religion made for an invaluable conversation piece for all graduate students in the study of religion. Before Cone, no black scholar of religion had dared to claim that the black experience was a corrective to the misguided assertions of mainstream theological and ethical discourse. Aspiring integrationist religious scholars such as Benjamin Mays and Howard Thurman did not make ethnicity the focus of their teachings. They instead admonished blacks to embrace the values of universal love and justice to triumph over the impediments of race, class, religion, and nationality. On the contrary, Cone projected blackness as the theological and ethical indicator that God was with blacks and against their oppressors. Integrationists presented a picture of God endowing blacks with the capacity to suffer, like Jesus, triumphantly. Cone dared advocate the unpopular belief that God was black and therefore on the side of the oppressed. Cone envisioned a God who had no problem with oppressed people subscribing to Malcolm X's "By any means necessary" liberation ethic. Mays and Thurman would have never drawn such a conclusion about the ethnocentric partiality of God's nature or actions.

Cone, starting his professional teaching career at the birth of what has been termed the black power era, brought his theological training to bear on the existential questions being raised by young blacks of that period: Why has God allowed blacks to suffer so at the hands of whites? Is God a liberator of the oppressed? These questions motivated Cone to search critically for answers in the black community's primary religious and ethical language. It was for this reason that the young professor Cone undertook as his scholarly interest a theological study of the black protest movement as well as spirituals and the blues.

In *Black Theology and Black Power*, Cone boldly notes that blacks, since arriving in America, had embraced a God of protest. Believing that this God affirmed blacks' right to protest, he asserts that blacks chose this God as their liberator. Blacks' perception of God was antithetical to their white oppressors' vision of God. Cone's affirmation of black protest rhetoric demanded a radical shift in the paradigm of theological reflection at the time from a non-violent protest ethic to a "By any means necessary" black power protest ethic.

In his book *The Spirituals and the Blues*, Cone unequivocally expresses his desire, first, "to examine the spirituals and blues as cultural expressions of black people, having prime significance for their community" and, secondly, "to reflect on the theological and sociological implications of these songs."[7] Prior to Cone, what intelligent black would have dared, in the name of theology, make such audacious assumptions about the possibilities of the black slave sources? Cone asserts that certain questions touch at the very foundation of black religion and reflect in the spiritual songs. They couch the very substance of black religion as reflected in the spirituals: "What did it mean 'to steal away to Jesus' when one had been *stolen* from Africa and enslaved in white America? What did it mean to 'work on a building that is a true foundation' or to 'hold up the blood-stained banner for the Lord,' when one had no building to call his own, and one's own blood was stained with slavery? What did it mean to be a 'child of God' and a black slave in a white society?"[8] Methodologically, Cone makes no pretense of doing any objective theological interpretation of the primary slave sources. Instead, he confesses that he is "an unbiased interpreter of the spirituals and the blues."[9] Cone values the impact that the singing of the spiritual songs had on him during his youthful development in Arkansas. He notes that this was the period of the Jim Crow South and demands that the song lyrics of this era must be interpreted contextually to exclude whites. Speaking of the mystical dimension of the songs, Cone proceeds with the idea that there is a "deeper level of experience which transcends tools of objective" historical research. Interestingly, Cone notes that that experience is available only to those who share the spirit and participate in the *faith* of the people who created these songs: "I am referring to the power and energy released in blacks' devotion to the God of emotion."[10] Cone unapologetically concurs with LeRoi Jones that "the God spoken about in blacks' songs is not the one in the white songs though the words might be the same. (They are not even pronounced alike.) But it is a different quality of energy they summon."[11]

Cone makes no claim to be an objective interpreter of the spirituals and the blues. He unabashedly states that his intention is to be subjective in his interpretation. He asserts that the black interpreter of the spirituals and the blues brings a hermeneutic of feeling to the text that those who have not experienced being black and victimized do not. Cone illustrates his assertion by quoting the black spiritual song "Every Time I Feel the Spirit." Seeking to make a case for the difference in perception of what whites hear and what blacks hear when seeking an interpretation, Cone makes the following observation: "To interpret the theological significance of the spiritual for the black community, 'academic' tools are not enough. The interpreter must *feel* the Spirit, that is he must feel his way into the power of black music, responding both to its rhythm and the faith in the experience it affirms. This song invites the believer closer to the very sources of black being, and to experience the black community's power to endure and the will to survive."[12] Cone avows that his purpose in *The Spirituals and the Blues* is "to uncover the theological presuppositions of black music as reflected in the spirituals and the blues, asking: What do they tell us about black people's deepest aspiration and devotion?"[13]

BEYOND CONE'S SOCIAL PROTEST/APOLOGIST METHODOLOGY

Cone's work necessarily prepared the way for the next generation of scholars in religion who would take the academic study of slave sources to the next level. Dwight N. Hopkins and George C. Cummings, both former Ph.D. students of Cone, published a collection of scholarly essays entitled *Cut Loose Your Stammering Tongue: Black Theology in the Slave Narratives*. This collection of essays explores the subject of black theology in the slave narratives. The essays portray the different perspectives of five scholars' (four males and one female) probing of the slave sources as sources for theological and ethical discourse.

Hopkins's Methodological Presuppositions

Dwight N. Hopkins's introductory essay to *Cut Loose Your Stammering Tongue* is very insightful for a brief understanding of the genesis of contemporary black theology. Hopkins asserts that the essays in the volume aim to take the academic study of black theology and religion beyond protest/apologetics.[14] Noting the need for the academic study of black theology and religion, Hopkins calls for "a method of African American theology and black religion where the main resource for black action and talk about God arises out of the lives and words of *poor* black people's faith."[15] Desirous to exceed the contributions of Cone and other scholars such as Gayraud Wilmore, Hopkins proposes that the key methodological question is "how to develop further that foundational framework—the unity and distinction between Christian and non-Christian, church, and non-church, theological and religious resources in African American faith and life."[16] Hopkins undoubtedly was supersensitive to the criticism, at the time, that condemned black theology as being no more than a tar brushing of Eurocentric theological categories. For this reason Hopkins wants a black theology that will, in the words of black slaves, *Cut Loose Your Stammering Tongue*.

Desirous of putting black voices at the center of African American religious scholarship, Hopkins writes that these sources of primary black voices will help free the stammering tongues of black theologians from their Eurocentric speech impediments of class, race, etc. Summarily, Hopkins believes that the slave narratives will tell black theology to cut loose its stammering tongue with at least four "words" of ancestral wisdom:

> First they tell us to hear and heed the life-language of our chained fore-bearers. . . .
>
> Second, black slaves remove obstacles from our God-talk by imbuing us with their unique liberation practice, world-view, language, thought-patterns, and theological common sense. . . .
>
> Third, slaves' language, thought, and practice show us how God presents God's particular self in the constrained, marred lives of a faith-freed, beautiful, black people. . . .
>
> Fourth, the volumes of slave narratives provide a theological abundance of religious experience from non-Christian hearers of God's freeing spirit. . . .[17]

Hopkins presupposes methodologically that there is a difference between slave theology (he means God-talk) and today's black theology and that some of the key elements needed in the constructive task of today's black theology are found in slave theology. Hopkins notes, for example, that "Slave theology verified the intimate link between the church and the community, a connection that does not pit the sacred against the secular, as in certain elements in Euro-American theology."[18] He makes cross-bearing the focus of the slave community's theological understanding.

Cummings's a Priori Correlation Methodology

In "The Slave Narrative as a Source of Black Theological Discourse: The Spirit and Eschatology," George C. Cummings notes that contemporary black theological discourse in the United States is faced with the evaluative assessment of "the values, symbols, and images from the black experience that will empower the contemporary black liberation struggle."[19] For this reason Cummings calls for "engaging the process of utilizing the slave narratives as a source for theological ideas and interpreting the significance of the Spirit and the eschatology in them."[20] He claims that his methodological presuppositions are "defined by an a priori commitment to the struggles for liberation of the black oppressed."[21] Informed by such theoretical presuppositions, Cummings seeks methodologically to "engage the slave narratives with the biblical text in order to establish mutually critical correlations between these sources of theological discourse."[22] His ultimate hermeneutical aim is "the discernment of the community's ongoing struggle for liberation, and the empowerment of the black oppressed so that they might better understand themselves, sustain their hope, and continue the struggle to transform their circumstances."[23] Guided by such hermeneutical presuppositions, Cummings proposes to "describe and interpret the meaning of the experiences of the Spirit testified to in these slave narratives."[24] Cummings reads the slave interviews as "a descriptive/interpretative task" to show "the connections they reflect between the presence of the Spirit of God and the hopes and aspirations of the slave community."[25] Cummings believes that "Close scrutiny of the slave narratives shows that they can provide the raw material for an interpretation of the Spirit and eschatology in the slave narratives."[26] The following quote best summarizes Cummings's understanding of the way that eschatology works in the consciousness of slaves as reflected in their narratives:

> The eschatological expectations shared in the slave testimonies showed that their encounter with the Spirit of the Lord enabled them to evolve a critique of racism and racists, dream a grand vision of freedom, nurture communal relations, fight for freedom, defend each other, affirm their humanity, and hear the melody of the future by acting in the present to create it. "Strangest thing," said ex-slave John Crawford, "is that while Mammy was in her spell of prayin' that a little boy was eight-year old up North who grew up and set the niggers free."[27]

Coleman's Organic Syncretic Methodology

Will Coleman reads the slave narratives with slightly different hermeneutical presuppositions. His essay in *Cut Loose Your Stammering Tongue*, "'Coming through 'Ligion': Metaphor in Non-Christian Experiences With the Spirit(s) in African American Slave Narratives," is rather methodologically instructive for the scholar of slave narratives. Drawing from Paul Ricoeur's hermeneutical method, Coleman assumes that the slave narratives constitute a depository of metaphorical language that describes both slaves' Christian and non-Christian experiences with the spirits and the Spirit. He thinks that slaves created their own unique form of linguistic-poetic discourse. Coleman's investigative concern is to explore "how African American people use metaphors to describe both non-Christian and Christian experiences with the spirits and the Spirit." He thinks, along with such scholars as Albert J. Raboteau, that the historical antecedents to the institutional African American church were traditional African religions and what came to be known as the Invisible Institution.[28] For this reason Coleman reads the slave narratives from what he calls an "*organic syncretic* methodology. It is of an organic syncretic nature in the sense that it enabled slaves to combine their Afrocentric religious beliefs with the Eurocentric ones of their masters."[29] He explains that the result of this merger was a unique form of African American Christianity: "The consequence of this merger was their own unique form of African American Christianity. In many slave narratives that describe 'conversion experiences,' this process was spoken of metaphorically as 'coming through 'ligion.'"[30] Coleman proceeds to expand his methodological procedure of inquiry with the following statement of purpose:

> In this essay I will investigate both experiences of the spirits and the Spirit among African American slaves as recounted through selected narratives. It is primarily a hermeneutical consideration of the ways in which slaves experienced the reality of God, their deceased ancestors, and other spiritual beings known in various ways as ghosts, hants, and spirits. I am especially concerned with the borderline or transitional phase (that of "coming through 'Ligion") between traditional African experience of the spirits (through dreams, visions, and other spiritual phenomena) within the North American context and a more Christian encounter with the Spirit.[31]

To accomplish his goal, Coleman utilizes four hermeneutical insights from the writings of Paul Ricoeur: (1) The task of hermeneutics; (2) the importance of symbolic and hermeneutical language; (3) the function of the narrative genre; and (4) the appropriation of what the text presents.[32] Coleman wants to know what the implications are of non-Christian and Christian African American slave narratives for a black theology of liberation.

Coleman rightly notes that both the non-Christian and Christian testimonies of slave narratives provide radical insights into the total religious life of African American slaves. Continuing to draw from Ricoeur, Coleman proceeds to expound upon this non-Christian/Christian distinction:

> The symbols and metaphors slaves used to express their reality provide the primary articulation of linguistic liberation from both the religious and theological language of their masters. More specifically, I maintain that the slaves' metaphors press against the limits of traditional contemporary African American theologians with an opportunity to explore new possibilities for black theology via metaphors taken from both non-Christian and Christian sources. To this end black theology will be strengthened by drinking from the deep fountain of the total African American religious experience which has been and remains pluralistic.[33]

Coleman notes that dominance of the culture of Eurocentric Christianity makes it difficult to carry out what he proposes that his organic syncretic method accomplishes. He must ponder the difficult question of how to delineate a theology of African American slaves when traditional, Eurocentric Christian theology is by definition critical reflection upon the God who is revealed in the scriptures, especially through the incarnation of Jesus Christ and the work of the Holy Spirit. In reality, Coleman's method calls for the religious scholar of the slave narratives to struggle for clarity about what is actually Christian and non-Christian. He rightly thinks that slave narratives that are not explicitly Christian should be read without "any attempt to Christianize them, or make them comply with our presuppositions of what they ought to be saying. They should be allowed to speak for themselves, from the reality found in the text."[34] Coleman does not tell us how to do that. He does not tell us why slaves see certain spirits as bad. Do they see these spirits as being bad because they are experiencing them through conditioned Christian sensibilities? An additional question is: Does Coleman rely too heavily upon Ricoeur's hermeneutical way of reading the text? I think that Coleman has the right idea hermeneutically when he suggests that we must probe for the world of the text or the autonomy of it. The methodological problem, however, is when do we know that we have been successful? Does not Hans-Georg Gadamer remind us of the problem of trying to enter the world of the text? Coleman does not demand that we wrestle with these essential questions: To what degree can we enter into the world of the slave narrative? Is the world of the slave narrative synonymous with the world of the slave? To what degree can we really comprehend the world of the slave narrative and make it our own? Can the reader enter the horizon of the world of the text without bringing his/her own horizon of meaning? If our own horizon of meaning fuses with that of the world of the text, can we then say that we have entered the slave narrative's world? Coleman might have found Mechal Sobel's work on the world that masters and slaves made together in Virginia very helpful in his argument.[35]

Sanders's Theoretical Methodology

Cheryl P. Sanders distinctly declares in "Liberation Ethics in Ex-Slave Interviews"[36] that she reads the slave narratives in search of liberation ethics. She starts with the presupposition that the slave narratives are the products of ex-slave interviews. Sanders's intent here is to show that the slave narrative has been shaped by the querying voice of the interviewer as well as the responding voice of the interviewee. Her second presupposition is that "The ex-slave interviews provide day-to-day moral data that can be used to analyze the ethical perspectives of the ex-slaves."[37] For Sanders, "conversion" is the transparent concept for identifying and analyzing the ethical perspectives of the ex-slaves' moral data. Sanders understands the ex-slave's conversion experience to have meant a "conscious moral change from wrong to right, involving reorientation of the self from complacency or error to a state of right religious knowledge and action."[38] As a trained ethicist,

Sanders is desirous of evaluating human actions, character, and institutions in terms of good and evil, right and wrong. She presupposes that ex-slaves' testimonies of their experiences of conversion reflect how those experiences influenced ex-slaves' social ethical perspectives in concert with the change in personal morality. Sanders finds ex-slaves' conversion experience data important for investigation although it did not alter a slave's legal status. Three critical questions guide her analytical study: "If conversion causes a significant reorientation of the self in moral terms, what, if any, ethical realignments did conversion produce in the converts' attitude towards slavery? How were the social and religious ethics of the converted slaves related with reference to the problem of slavery? Did the experience of conversion generate a liberation ethic among slaves?"[39] Sanders relies upon the theoretical methodology of Ralph B. Potter to explore and discern the various patterns of moral discourse used by slaves. Sanders notes that Potter's paradigm searches out four essential elements in an ethical statement:

(1) empirical definition of the situation;
(2) affirmation of loyalty;
(3) mode of ethical reasoning; and
(4) quasi-theological beliefs concerning God, humankind, and human destiny.[40]

Sanders selects four ex-slave interviews for special analysis from the thousands of oral histories collected during the 1920s and 1930s. A compilation of these slave narratives was edited and published during the 1970s by George P. Rawick under the title *The American Slave: A Composite Autobiography*.[41] Sanders says that she makes her choice of the ex-slave interviews on the basis of three criteria: "1) an explicit testimony of conversion to Christianity; 2) extensive ethical reflection upon the problem of slavery; and 3) diversity of experience of attitudes toward slavery."[42]

Employing Potter's theoretical method, Sanders provides rare insight into the diversity of different slave conversion experiences and their contributions. Sanders shows how the empirical definition of the problem of slavery in ethical terms reflects a similar degree of diversity.[43] Speaking of the four types of conversion experience, Sanders concludes with a rather instructive summary:

> Frank and Little remember slavery as a good system that worked to their own personal benefit and to the benefit of others; Kelley evaluates slavery as an evil system that worked to the economic benefit of whites at the expense of blacks; and Redmoun, who was oblivious to her slave status prior to her emancipation, assesses slavery as good for some slaves and bad for others. With the exception of Kelley, they tend to view the peculiar race relations associated with the institution of slavery in positive terms and willingly identify with the "quality" and benevolence of their former owners. Kelley acknowledges that her mistress was good in comparison with other whites,

but characterizes the race relations of slavery as enmity between whites and blacks. Slavery is understood by these ex-slaves to be a system of reciprocal obligations between owner and slave, but all four tend to base their empirical definitions of the situation on the practical question of humane treatment rather than on the perception that the system was inherently right or wrong.[44]

Sanders's study is critical for reading slave sources because it values the ethical contribution that conversion made to the slave's remaking of self. Sanders makes the case that the experience of Christian conversion placed the slave in a different ethical stream from that of the slave master. She makes this case despite the fact that conversion did make many slaves more servile. Sanders explains: "The conversion experience did not transform them into adherents of the slave ethic taught and upheld by their oppressors, even if it did make them 'better' slaves by bringing an increased measure of moral integrity and conscientiousness into their lives and labors as slaves. If there is any social ethic at all among the ex-slave converts, it is indeed an ethic of liberation and not one of submission to the institution of slavery or to the bondage of oppressive religious beliefs and ideas."[45]

Goatley's Comparative/Narrative Methodology

David Emmanuel Goatley's book, *Were You There? Godforsakenness in Slave Religion*, is a more recent study of the subject.[46] Goatley does a narrative reading of the slave sources in exploration of what he calls "Godforsakenness." He asserts that "An examination of the theology of African American slaves can make a constructive contribution to the question of where God is amid the experience of Godforsakenness."[47] He thinks that it is necessary to compare Godforsakenness in African American slave narratives with the Godforsakenness of Jesus in Mark's Gospel: "[M]oving toward an understanding of the Markan narrative surrounding Jesus' cry of forsakenness can move one toward a meaningful response to the question about the presence or absence of God for those whose life circumstances prevent them from experiencing God's presence."[48] Goatley delineates his methodology as follows:

> The intent of this book is to employ narrative methodology with regard to slave narratives and spirituals and move toward an understanding of the concept of Godforsakenness. After examining Godforsakenness in slave theology, the Markan account of Jesus' crucifixion will be studied, with special attention to the concept of Jesus' Godforsakenness. In light of the extremity of human suffering currently encountered by African Americans, the crisis of Godforsakenness will be considered from within the context of a community that knows all too well what it means to experience the forsakenness of God.[49]

A BLACK WOMANIST SCHOLAR'S METHODOLOGY

Martin's Theoretical Multi-methodology

Joan M. Martin, starting with the slave narratives, does an incisive analysis of what she calls a Christian work ethic of enslaved women. Professor Martin's theoretical method for reading the slave narratives is delineated in her book *More Than Chains and Toil: A Christian Work Ethic of Enslaved Women*.[50] Her work is a thorough study of the ways that black women struggled to redefine themselves under the reality of forced labor in America. The slave narratives are critical to her study. She posits that African American enslaved women were enslaved on three counts: "as racially black, sexually women, and degraded women."[51] Despite the many studies completed on the slave narratives, Martin rightly notes that "black religious scholars have only superficially explored the theme of work." She says of this shortcoming that "a most enigmatic silence has persisted in religious ethics given that work was a central feature of the life of enslaved women and men."[52] Martin's work is a needed initial exploration into uncharted territory. She notes that her work is the "beginning exploration of the religious moral agency of enslaved women through work and its meaning in their struggle for survival and quest for freedom."[53] Martin makes the "experiential realities in the lives of enslaved women and their social world in the antebellum" her critical starting point:

> Drawing on slave narratives and related sources, the book uncovers and discusses four distinct characteristics of an enslaved women's work ethic. Fundamentally, I argue that the work ethic of enslaved Christian women was different from both the Protestant tradition's understanding of work from the reformation notion of vocation, calling, and work, and the work ethic of antebellum slaveholders. I employ a womanist/black feminist racial gender analysis—integral to my argument—combined with poststructural and political science theory.[54]

Martin devotes the first chapter of her study to the investigation of the slave narratives. She focuses on the enslaved lives of women as encompassed in the world of slavery. In struggling with how one gets to the social world of enslavement, Martin concludes that even the theological dimensions of the social world of enslavement "are best examined through the utilization of women's slave narratives." In this chapter Martin views "slave narratives from the perspectives of sacred text" that "provides a lens that assists in seeing the moral agency of enslaved women in the social world of work."[55]

Chapter one of Martin's work pays specific attention to the contribution of female slave narratives to the analysis of work in the experience of African American women. Martin analytically reads the slave sources from an interrelated race, class, and gender perspective. She makes the case that this methodological approach permits the investigation of several key elements in the lives of enslaved women:

1. the distinct nature of enslaved women's work, life and regimen in relation to the institution of slavery and to the slave quarter community life—family and social;
2. the nature of enslaved women's form of resistance, sabotage, and insurrection for self and community against slavery (without arguing for a predominant form of any of these three activities or categories);
3. the African culturally oriented sensibilities used in enslaved women's transformation and creation of slave culture;
4. the high degree of gender consciousness and the racial solidarity which enslaved black women developed; and
5. the fullness of work creativity in the midst of toilsome labor, and the dreams that African American enslaved women had for themselves and their children, which are reflected in African American enslaved culture, both in its strength and in its weakness.[56]

Martin notes that, similar to the Bible,

the slave narrative is as much a gendered sacred text as it is a historical, political, and socio-linguistic text. That is, the slave narratives are gendered writings which reveal the enslaved ones' thoughts, language, politics, theology, and ethics as women and men wrestling with the social constructions of gender in their times. They are narratives written in voices that are gendered voices and represent real people who suffered the degradation of slavery not only as African Americans, but also as socially defined female and male beings. Those narrative sources produced by and about the enslaved women defined the enslaved experience of the African American community as that experience profoundly affected the nature of womanhood, the understanding of the relationship to God-Jesus-Holy Spirit, and the means and choices discerned by enslaved women in realizing human wholeness and freedom.[57]

Undoubtedly Martin's work must be viewed as an invaluable contribution to religious scholars' interpretation of the slave sources.

WORK BEYOND DARK SYMBOLS

Since the publication of *Dark Symbols, Obscure Signs*, I have continued to identify and interpret foundational religio-ethical meaning constructs in the primary sources of the black experience. These constructs have their genesis in the dynamic expressions of slave consciousness. Since slavery these constructs have structured the religious and ethical concerns of blacks in America and vice-versa. From slavery to the present, blacks have been faced with the religious and ethical challenge of being properly greeted, of being accepted as full citizens, of being recognized as capable of telling the truth, of being in quest of a place free of racial oppression.

A subsequent study to *Dark Symbols, Obscure Signs* has been my most recent book, *Dark Salutations: Greetings, Ritual, and God in the Black Community.*[58] *Dark Salutations* makes the case that the ritualistic act of greeting allows for open-ended creativity between the greeter and the greeted. In the black community since slavery, salutatory greeting has tended to keep alive the hope and promise of being *for and with* God and each other. It has kept alive for blacks, as well, the hope and promise of God being *for and with* them. Black Americans' ethnocentric verbal greetings often dominate their moment of social encounter. For this reason, blacks have created luminously dark metaphors by compounding words like "brother" and "man," "sister" and "girl." These metaphors illuminate the prophetic/priestly nature of the religious and moral consciousness of blacks.

In volume three, which is in process, I am doing a study of the right of *status* as a foundational religio-ethical meaning construct in black consciousness. I am temporarily calling this volume *Dark Status: Blacks and the Right to Be Recognized in America.* Slavery intentionally reduced blacks to less than beggar status. The American Constitution finalized that status. In doing so, white Americans constitutionally refused to recognize blacks as having even beggars' rights to full human and citizenship status. All persons of European descent were recognized, on the basis of their white skin alone, as meriting the unconditional right to full citizenship status. The unquestionable assumption was that God had endowed whites with citizenship rights. Those of African descent were, at best, forced to prove themselves worthy of being acknowledged as fully human. Resultantly, black leadership has often, in response to such negativism, produced a schizophrenic type of rhetoric that has demanded of whites, on the one hand, that they recognize blacks as having been endowed by God with equal rights and equal human capacity and demanded of blacks, on the other hand, that they prove themselves worthy of being recognized by whites. During and since slavery, blacks have been preoccupied with the right of status recognition, and the lack of it, in American society. They have fought to have whites legitimately recognize their embodied presence in America. This has been the case despite the fact that whites' policies have often rendered blacks invisible. Blacks' rocky transitory journey from servile slave status to second-class citizenship status to the right to full citizenship status has been long and tedious. Particular attention will be given to the way in which blacks have legally, morally, and religiously responded to America's formal denial of their human dignity. I will show this by doing a critical analysis of selected United States Supreme Court benchmark civil rights cases, to include: *Dred Scott v. Sanford; Plessy v. Ferguson;* and *Brown v. Board of Education.* A methodological interpretation of these cases will make the case for the argument of the right of status as a foundational religio-ethical meaning construct in black consciousness. The study will explore how blacks have read both the Bible and America's governing documents to arrive at their rhetorical responses to the lack of full status recognition.

In volume four I propose to do a study of the right of *testimony* as a foundational religio-ethical meaning construct in black consciousness. I am tentatively titling it *Dark Testimony: Blacks' Right to be Heard in America*. This is the other side of the right to the free speech argument. What happens when a people can exercise the right to speak, only to conclude that there is no official willingness on the nation's part to hear them? Denying them the right to testify in the court of law, whites legally reduced blacks to the dehumanized status of *inaudible otherness*. Legally imputing upon them a status of inaudibility, whites forced blacks to protest publicly against injustice in the streets of America. The imputed status of inaudible otherness deleteriously compounded what Ralph Ellison would later call the "invisible man" status of blacks in the eyes of whites. This reduction of blacks collectively devalued them of their constitutional right of free speech when it was exercised. It said that whites had no faith in blacks' rational capacity for truth-making and truth-bearing decisions. Both an examination of the racism of the judicial system and the civil rights struggle will be critical to this study.

Volume five proposes to study the right of *black persons in relationship to public space* as a foundational religio-ethical meaning construct in black consciousness. I am presently calling this volume *Dark Journey: Blacks' Right to Place and Personhood in America*. This particular meaning construct will illuminate the religious and ethical ways in which blacks have struggled for full acceptance in America's public space. The notion of segregated public space based on race forced blacks to struggle with the value of person versus space. Methodologically, the study will do a critical reading of Jim Crow laws and practices as well as a study of blacks' response to the public accommodations laws. Primarily, a study will be done of the sources that blacks and whites produced about slave trafficking, runaway slaves, hopeful migrants, black nationalists, and expatriates. The quest for free public space dominates the narrative consciousness of blacks from runaway slaves to promised-land-bound migrants to fiery black nationalists to disillusioned black expatriates.

The basic contention is that the proposed volumes suggested above are foundational for doing a constructive theological and ethical interpretation of the black experience. For me, an interpretation of the black experience without this foundational study is premature. The primary sources of the black experience evidence implicitly and explicitly the religious and ethical value of such meaning constructs as *salutations*, *status*, *testimony*, and *journey*. These meaning constructs invariably shape the way that blacks have understood themselves in relationship to God, their oppressors, and each other.

NOTES

1. For an insightful interpretation of the ideological ways that slave masters used the Bible to justify slavery see Katie G. Cannon's essay "Slave Ideology and Biblical Interpretation" in her book *Katie's Canon: Womanism and the Soul of the Black Community* (New York: Continuum Publishing Co., 1995), 38–46.

2. There have been different eras of black social protests. The most dramatic one was what has been characterized as the Civil Rights movement. Out of the numerous publications devoted to it, Taylor Branch has produced the most comprehensive study of that period. Volume one of his study is called *Parting the Waters: America in the King Years, 1954–1963* (New York: Simon and Schuster, 1988). Branch's sequel volume is entitled *Pillar of Fire: America in the King Years, 1963–1965* (New York: Simon and Schuster, 1998). During the late 1960s there emerged what came to be characterized as the black power era. It blossomed into full efflorescence following the death of Martin Luther King Jr. in 1969. For a rather critical interpretation of that era see Harold Cruse's *Plural But Equal: A Critical Study of Blacks and Minorities and America's Plural Society* (New York: William Morrow, 1987).

3. I mean by non-religious scholars those who are not academically trained in the research and interpretation of the beliefs and practices of religion. Academics in the fields of history, literature, and anthropology have generated invaluable primary sources on the black experience for black scholars of black religion and theology.

4. See Sydney Ahlstrom's book *A Religious History of the American People* (New Haven: Yale Univ. Press, 1972). Ahlstrom's work won the National Book Award in 1973. During the decade of the 1960s, when Ahlstrom was organizing his research, critical black consciousness was being birthed in America. Militant black rhetoric, despite white resistance, forged its way into the mainstream of white America. While he does not include a chapter on the subject, Ahlstrom does acknowledge the black church's origin, development, and constructive moral contributions in America.

5. See Joseph R. Washington's book *Black Religion: The Negro and Christianity in the United States* (Boston: Beacon Press, 1964).

6. James H. Cone, *Black Theology and Black Power* (New York: Seabury Press, 1969).

7. James H. Cone, *The Spirituals and the Blues* (New York: Seabury Press, 1972), 3, 9.

8. Ibid.

9. Ibid., 4.

10. Ibid.

11. Ibid., 5.

12. Ibid., 5.

13. Ibid., 6–7.

14. *Cut Loose Your Stammering Tongue: Black Theology in the Slave Narratives*, ed. Dwight N. Hopkins and George C. Cummings (Maryknoll, N.Y.: Orbis Books, 1991).

15. Dwight N. Hopkins, "Introduction," *Cut Loose Your Stammering Tongue*, xiv.

16. Ibid., xv.

17. Ibid., xvi–xvii.

18. Dwight N. Hopkins, "Slave Theology," *Cut Loose Your Stammering Tongue*, 44.

19. George C. Cummings, "The Slave Narrative as a Source of Black Theological Discourse: The Spirit and Eschatology," *Cut Loose Your Stammering Tongue*, 46.

20. Ibid.

21. Ibid., 47.

22. Ibid.

23. Ibid.

24. Ibid.

25. Ibid., 54.

26. Ibid., 59.

27. Ibid., 61.

28. Will Coleman, "'Coming through 'Ligion': Metaphor in Non-Christian and Christian Experiences with the Spirit(s) in African American Slave Narratives," *Cut Loose Your Stammering Tongue*, 68.

29. Ibid.

30. Ibid.

31. Ibid.

32. Ibid.

33. Ibid., 69.

34. Ibid.

35. Mechal Sobel, *The World They Made Together: Black and White Values in Eighteenth-Century Virginia* (Princeton, New Jersey: Princeton Univ. Press, 1987).

36. Cheryl P. Sanders, "Liberation Ethics in the Ex-Slave Interviews," *Cut Loose Your Stammering Tongue*, 103–36.

37. Ibid., 103.

38. Ibid.

39. Ibid.

40. Ibid., 104; see Ralph B. Potter, *War and Moral Discourse* (Richmond: John Knox Press, 1969), 23–24.

41. George P. Rawick, *The American Slave: A Composite Autobiography* 1 (Westport, Conn.: Greenwood Publishing Co., 1972).

42. Sanders, "Liberation Ethics in Ex-Slave Interviews," *Cut Loose Your Stammering Tongue*, 104.

43. Ibid., 107.

44. Ibid., 114.

45. Ibid., 132.

46. David Emmanuel Goatley, *Were You There? Godforsakenness in Slave Religion* (Maryknoll, N.Y.: Orbis Books, 1996).

47. Ibid., xiii.

48. Ibid.

49. Ibid., xiv.

50. Joan M. Martin, *More Than Chains and Toil: A Christian Work Ethic of Enslaved Women* (Louisville, Ky.: Westminster John Knox Press, 2000).

51. Ibid., 4.

52. Ibid., 5.

53. Ibid.

54. Ibid., 6.

55. Ibid.

56. Ibid., 18–19.

57. Ibid., 28.

58. *Dark Salutations: Greetings, Ritual, and God in the African American Community* (Harrisburg, Penn.: Trinity Press International, 2001).

INTRODUCTION

Revaluing the Slave Experience

The overall objective of this study is to examine critically slave masters' responses and slaves' counterresponses to the former's false definition of the latter's anthropological nature. Slave masters anchored their beliefs about their slaves' anthropological nature in biblical scripture. The depth and breadth of such a complex study is necessary for understanding the foundational implications of slaves' counterresponses to their masters' spurious interpretations of the Bible for African-American theological and ethical reflections.

The methodological approach of this study is threefold. First, it critically examines slave masters' misconstrual of biblical scripture to justify their enslavement of Africans. This objective will be accomplished by studying the instructional resources (e.g. sermons, catechisms, addresses, and so forth) that slave masters produced to teach slaves Christianity. Second, it critically examines the various genres of counterresponses that slaves made to their masters' spurious interpretations. The latter objective will be accomplished by studying the varied genres (e.g. conversion testimonies, spiritual songs, ex-slave autobiographies, and trickster stories) that slaves used to make their counterresponses. Four foundational notions of the African-American self can be derived from these different genres of response. Third, the study critically examines the foundational implications of the different types of counterresponses for constructive African-American theological and ethical reflection.

Folk sources of African-American slaves have long been viewed with suspicion by academic historians. One reason given for their suspicion is that most of the folk sources of the slave community were from the oral sources that were placed into written form mainly by white interviewers. This process of knowledge transmission provokes at least two questions. First, how honest were elderly ex-slaves during the 1930s in revealing their knowledge of slavery to white interviewers? How objective were white interviewers in reporting what they actually heard slaves say? James Blassingame acknowledges this problem when he writes of the value of slaves' testimonies: "If scholars want to know the heart and secret thoughts of slaves, they must study the testimony of the blacks."[1] Blassingame makes a case equally as strong for why scholars ought to compare these slave folk sources with the literary sources of the white master class. He writes: "But since the slave did not know the heart and secret thoughts of masters, they must also examine the testimony of whites."[2]

The basic assumption in this study is that neither whites nor blacks had a monopoly on the truth. Again to cite Blassingame, neither "had rended the veil cloaking the life of the other, or seen clearly the pain and the joy bounded by color and caste."[3] Our assumption for using the slave folk sources in this study is that they best reflect what the anthropologist Clifford Geertz has called "the public mind."

In no sense is this intended to be a historical study of sources produced by slaves or their masters. I readily leave such projects to professionally trained historians. They would obviously be more interested in such issues as the precise dating of documentary materials, the identity of their creators and their point of origin. Instead, my interest is of a more philosophical nature. First, I am concerned about the foundational constructs inherent in the primary literary sources themselves. This means that I recognize these sources to constitute what my friend, professor Ronald Potter, has called "the religio-moral language of the African American experience."[4] Second, I am concerned about the methodological implications of these foundational constructs for the constructive task of African-American theology and ethics.

INTERPRETATIONS OF PRIMARY SOURCES

Numerous interpretations have been done of primary slave sources in the last generation by some of the leading scholars of history, political science, and religion. One of the more exhaustive and comprehensive studies of slavery as a cultural phenomenon has been done by the cultural historian Lawrence Levine. Levine's provocative book drew the cultural correlation between slaves' experience and contemporary black consciousness.[5] Levine has thoroughly investigated black songs, folk tales, proverbs, aphorisms, verbal games, and the long narrative oral poems known as "toasts." He argues that the value system of African Americans can only be understood through an analysis of black culture. Radical in his theoretical assertions, Levine characterizes his historical study of *Black Culture and Black Consciousness* as being the history of African-Americans' thinking rather than the history of their thoughts.

Mechal Sobel, a white Jewish historian of Israel, has made a rare contribution to interpreting the primary sources. He has combined the historical, cultural, and social approaches to arrive at his own conclusive study of how slaves influenced each other.[6]

For the last twenty years Eugene Genovese's interpretation of the slave experience has dominated the field of historical scholarship. Employing the Marxist method of analysis, Genovese has shown that such variables as culture, politics, social behavior and economics are at work in the world of slavery.[7] He saw a direct correlation between the paternalistic class systems of the old South and the distinct system of racial subordination. The two appeared to be a single system. Genovese shows in his extensive analytical discourse how these two structures complemented each other functionally. He writes that:

> Paternalism created a tendency for the slaves to identify with a particular community through identification with its masters; it reduced the possibilities for their identification with each other as a class. Racism undermined the slaves' sense of worth as black people and reinforced their dependence on white masters. But these were tendencies, not absolute laws, and the slaves forged weapons of defense, the most important of which was a religion that taught them to love and value each other, to take a critical view of their masters, and to reject the ideological rationale for their own enslavement.[8]

Genovese's theory of comparative analysis has contributed significantly to my own method of interpretation.

Also, I have no intent here to try and prove that African-American slaves' beliefs and practices of Christianity have their antecedents in the African worldview. Scholars of history and cultural anthropology have been better trained to do this than I.[9] Instead, the twofold objective of our study, that we named above, might be delineated in the following way. *First*, the study focuses on how slave masters purposefully misinterpreted the biblical teachings of creation and redemption for their own self-interest. It will be a critical examination of the way slave masters used the scriptures as an ideological tool for the devaluation of the sacredness of the slave's body and soul. *Second*, the study examines how slaves ingeniously reconstructed their masters' fragmented teachings of the Bible to arrive at a more creative understanding of salvation as spiritual liberation of the embodied self. This is specifically seen in what we have termed as slaves' "conversion-story language." *Third*, it focuses on how slaves' reconstruction of their "conversion-story language," which described God's activity in their lives, morally shaped their responses to one another as children of God. *Fourth*, it focuses on how slaves' reconstructed modes of religio-moral discourse (autobiographies and Brer Rabbit stories) to affirm themselves as the endowed agents of God. And *fifth*, it focuses on the possible foundational implications of the meaning structures derived from these sources for the constructive task of African-American theology and ethics.

I have given approximately ten years to this project of researching and interpreting the primary sources used in this study. It has been a pedagogical exercise of asking a lot of simple, but basic, questions about the latent and manifest presuppositions in the readings themselves. Thanks to the challenge of Howard Harrod,[10] during my tenure as a graduate student at Vanderbilt University, I started to explore the value of social phenomenology[11] for reading slave folk sources. Since then, I have read critically in the areas of psychological, social, and hermeneutical phenomenology.[12] This reading has undoubtedly informed my critical evaluations of the primary sources under investigation. What I have done here, however, must not be read as a pure phenomenological study in the technical sense. Professional students of phenomenology will readily recognize both the limitations and the possibilities of describing the constitutive elements of a given social phenomenon.[13] Moreover, I am professionally trained in the discipline of ethics and theology. Postdoctoral study in 1980–81, while in Boston, permitted me to take reading seminars with philosophers Hans Gadamer and James Findley.[14] These rare scholarly experiences deepened my appreciation for the varied ways of reading and interpreting primary philosophical texts. I learned from each scholar the value of seeing how the text itself, as well as its worldview, might provide its own hermeneutical clues. Since that time I have learned to approach the task of reading all kinds of primary texts as a challenging labor of love.

Interpreting primary literary sources always offers the interpreter the opportunity to play with the possibility of their implied and explicit meanings. For instance, what might the writers have had in mind in the composition of the texts? In the process of playing with the possibilities of implicit textual meanings, the interpreter's mental horizons are expanded. According to Gadamer, a fusion takes place between the horizon of the text and that of the interpreter.[15] Despite this awareness, the temptation to draw premature theological and ethical conclusions about these sources has been very real.

PRIMARY INTENTIONS

It will be my basic intent throughout this study to identify and describe the fundamental theological and ethical problem — soul-body dichotomy — of slave masters and slaves during institutional slavery. This will be done by showing how slave masters intentionally misinterpreted biblical anthropology to justify the enslavement of Africans, and how slaves responded in a variety of creative ways. The primary materials of slave masters manifest their own implicit and explicit meaning constructs, all of which have informed my own method of interpretation. They embody slave masters' basic theological and ethical problems regarding slaves' nature. I have referred to it as basic for several reasons. First, because it was slave masters who reasoned theologically and ethically that God had called them to be both slave owners and Christians. These slave masters and their church leaders were unable to drown out either the external voices of abolitionists or the inner voices of their own consciences. It would be a gross misrepresentation of the historical fact to say that all white southerners saw slavery as purely an economic enterprise exempt from the judgment of God. Biblical doctrine was conveniently misinterpreted to try and prove that institutional slavery was ordained by God.

Given our claim above, we will first conceptually identify the problem's structural manifestation in the minds of slave masters and their preachers. This will take place in the first two chapters of the study. Shelton Smith's book, *In His Image, But . . . ,*[16] is one of the most thorough studies of the masters' religious beliefs. Smith, who was a historian of southern church history, has looked critically at the complexities of the proslavery arguments. The intent in chapter one is not to duplicate Smith's invaluable interpretation, but to show that whites' intentional misinterpretation of the slave's anthropological nature constituted the core theological and ethical problem of slavery. Two antithetical ideal type[17] responses, as the literature reflects, were at the heart of this problem. The first response is what I have termed theoretically the *soulless-body type of response* (also termed the naturalist type in chapter one). Advocates of this position contended that slaves of African descent, unlike their white masters, were absolutely void of souls. This view prevailed among this group despite efforts by some of its more moderate members to modify the claim. Using a false method of theological reductionism, these slave masters intended to reduce the slave's anthropological nature (body and soul) to mere body for their own economic advantage. A descriptive analysis of the primary literary sources of these slave masters clearly reveals that advocates of the soulless-body type skewed the scriptures to justify their racist ideology. Also, the slave masters saw that it exonerated them of all claims of responsibilities before "God or man." The soulless-body type provided a needed ideological canvas against which to contrast the responses of Christian apologists of slaves' souls.

The second response is what I theoretically call the *bodiless-soul type* (or the Christian master type in chapter one). It reflects the view of those white Christian ministers and plantation owners who were of the conviction that God created Africans with souls. However, all those of this persuasion were not of the same opinion as to slaves' nature and gradation. These masters believed that their acts of Christian benevolence toward their slaves would satisfy the law of God. They were so convinced of this belief that they became intellectual and social prisoners of their own misguided interpretations of the Bible. First, this manifested itself in their belief in the fallacious doctrine of manifest destiny—a belief that God had called white men to enslave the bodies of black men for the purpose of saving their souls. This meant that Christian masters had to deny the very biblical principle that they affirmed theoretically—that God made the slave with both a soul and body. However, in practice, they had to relate to the slave's body as though it had no relational value to his or her soul. Christian masters, understandably, would have been obligated to emancipate their slaves if they had behaved toward them as sacred embodied souls. These masters compromisingly believed that they could save the souls of slaves and keep them socially categorized as "the least of these" in the sight of God and themselves. Ironically in the worship service, Christian masters professed to have valued slaves as souls of God's creation; however, on the auction blocks and in the fields, masters actually valued slaves' bodies only for their utility. Slaves were seen as mere means to an economic end.

Preachers and missionaries of the plantation sought to make the case that conversion to Christianity stood to enhance slaves' market value. They argued that conversion to Jesus Christ converted slaves from the status of being wild Africans to that of meek servants of their earthly masters and God. Given that the practice of slavery contradicted biblical principles, these religious leaders literally tried to please two masters — "God and man." Incontestably, these ministers and missionaries, due to their economic dependency upon slaves, did more to please masters in this case than God. However, many of these religious leaders were unable to escape the judgment of their own paternalistic theological beliefs. They taught that masters would have to stand before God on the Day of Judgment and give an account for slaves' souls. Such leaders of the South came to constitute what might be termed a minority class of Christian conscience.

Chapter two explores the primary literary sources produced by white preachers and missionaries of the South. Troubled by consciences that, in their words "had been sprinkled by the blood of Jesus," ministers and missionaries of the plantation created a corpus of proslavery literature. These sources comprised sermons, pastoral letters, catechisms, and addresses. These materials were produced intentionally with at least three objectives in mind: to inform slave masters of their biblical responsibilities to slaves; to provide slave masters with pedagogical materials for orally instructing slaves in Christianity; and, to provide slave masters with the needed rational arguments for countering abolitionists' disclaimers of slavery. These materials became crucial in the hands of those slave masters who wanted to satisfy both the law of the spirit and the law of the flesh. The basic thesis in this chapter will show that white divines of the plantation South used their literary skills to prove that slaves' souls must be valued at the expense of their bodies.

The soul-body dichotomy is foundational to the theological and ethical problem because it inevitably affected the way that slaves saw themselves in relationship both to God and their plantation masters. The nature of slavery itself would not allow slaves to escape the ideological influences of their masters. This was definitely the case since Christian masters believed that God held them responsible for teaching slaves Christianity. Slaves' own creative response to this foundational problem will be discussed in chapters three, four, and five where a description is given of the folk genre of slaves' conversion stories, spiritual songs, ex-slave autobiographies, and Brer Rabbit trickster stories. The primary thesis in this section is that slaves, out of the different genres of their folk religion, countered the negative view of their spiritual and physical nature. The Brer Rabbit stories and ex-slave autobiographies show how the community countered what really became a mind and body problem.

Chapter three will show how slaves reconstructed conversion-story language in response to the body-soul problem. Slaves' creative responses to this problem produced what I will term foundational meaning structures that are necessary for the constructive task of African-American theology and ethics. Chapter three will show that slaves produced their own method of determining what constituted the radical transition to a status of new being in God. It will show that slaves understood being converted by God to mean something radically different from what whites intended. Whites had defined it to mean that God had changed slaves for a role of submission to all whites. Conversion for slaves meant that God had freed them to be self-assertive. God freed "the real hidden self" to come forth out of "the old enslaved self" by "striking the old enslaved self dead." When this happened the converted slave would remember his or her "newly revealed self" being able to look down upon "the old dead self." This constituted a spiritual source of double consciousness in the mind of the slave. "The old dead self" must be seen as symbolizing that version of "the self" that was considered the property of the master.

Chapter four shows that corporate conversion must be interpreted to mean God's empowerment of the individual authentic self to become a member of the new social body of salvation. Slaves who experienced this divine miracle knew that they had been delivered from the false theological and ethical separation that masters made between their bodies and souls. God had freed converted slaves to see themselves from God's perspective with the result that converted slaves came to value themselves as embodied sacred selves.

Chapter four will show that slaves formalized personal conversion rhetoric into what I have termed "lyricized conversion language," referring to those spiritual songs of the slave community that make specific reference to the conversion theme. "Lyricized conversion language" reflects the way in which converted slaves addressed the pedagogical needs of both potential candidates for conversion and novice converts. This song language shows how converted slaves helped others make the rite of passage from converted individuals to full members of the converted community. "Lyricized conversion language" became the ritualistic means of creating "we-consciousness" in slaves, providing them with the means to counter that false notion of individualism that the master's conversion rhetoric was designed to foster. The notion of community in "lyricized conversion language" is informed by such organic symbols of the body as hands, feet, and heart. These natural somatic symbols organize the slave community's sense of social identity.

Chapter five of this study makes the case that, while the body-and-soul problem attributed to slaves was a Southern phenomenon, ex-slaves presented a mind-and-body problem that was peculiar to white Northern abolitionists. Ex-slave storytellers always ran the risk of having white abolitionist publishers, editors, and writers reshape their stories about plantation experiences for the benefit of white readers. White Northern abolitionists' primary objective for wanting to have such a paternalistic control over ex-slaves' stories was to convince their readers that slaves had normal minds. They thought that such concrete examples would demonstrate that slaves, if allowed to be free, qualified mentally to be first-class citizens. These examples would counterattack Southern slave masters' degrading claim that Africans were created with inferior minds. Abolitionist sponsors of ex-slaves' autobiographies insisted that they, in the telling of their stories, speak less of their felt experiences as slaves and more of their objective remembrances of them. The dominant thesis of this chapter is that ex-slaves, in defiance of their abolitionist sponsors, used the genre of autobiography to prove to Northern readers that they were endowed with both mind and body. Ex-slaves used the genre of autobiography to prove that they were embodied minds capable of thinking and feeling for themselves.

Chapter six, drawing upon the literary genre of the Brer Rabbit trickster stories, describes slaves' creative responses to the mind-and-body problem that they encountered on the plantation. Since white masters were intimidated by the slaves' strong black bodies, plantation slaves wisely used the small fragile body of the rabbit through which to project their tough-minded radical ideas about plantation life. Brer Rabbit became the animal symbol through which slaves found creative expression as embodied social selves. Via this method, slaves devised an innovative way of holding the mind-and-body phenomenon in creative tension in the face of the dehumanizing structures of slavery.

Chapter seven will identify what I will term the foundational elements necessary for a constructive theology and ethic of the African-American folk experience. I will show here that each genre of the folk sources produces its own conceptual paradigm for looking at the fundamental ideas of *self, God, and community.* These conceptual ways of viewing self, God, and community have been foundationally critical to the formation of African-Americans' identity collectively and individually. Also, they have been foundationally instructive for how African Americans have dealt with the question of ethical duty as Americans. Finally, these foundational constructs clearly show that African Americans, since their genesis in America, have understood them*selves, God,* and *community* in complex terms. Hence, it is a misnomer to say that any one notion of self, God, or community represents the normative way all African Americans have thought or believed.

CHAPTER I

The Slave: A Child of God?

The Foundational Problem

It took generations before history scholars concluded that slaves created an authentic body of knowledge that was reflective of themselves, God, and community. Until a generation ago, white scholars of slave history had concluded that only the records of slave masters were of any rational value for interpreting slavery. Eugene Genovese, using the Marxist method of analysis, has clearly demonstrated the slaves' positive use of the Christian teachings of their masters. Eugene Genovese, a contemporary historian, has carefully reconstructed a new way of understanding how slaves and masters acted and reacted toward each other. His study allows us to see how slaves, using their masters' fragmented teachings of the Bible, spiritually resisted their masters' reduction of them to mere puppetry status. This fact made it very difficult for masters to gain absolute control over their slaves. Genovese was the first prominent white historian to recognize the scholarly value of the oral sayings of slaves. He used them to illustrate his theory of the necessity of mutual compromise between both masters and slaves.[1] Genovese acknowledged that slaves extracted from their masters' Christianity a radically alternative vision of themselves, God and community.

Stanley Elkins was another major white historian, prior to Genovese, whose published conclusions about the master/slave relationships established a precedent. His primary thesis was that masters had unilateral power in shaping the slave's personality. The very nature of this uncontestable power created a pathological kind of paternalism between masters and slaves. This relationship of dominance depersonalized the slave to a stereotypical Sambo-type status. It produced illusions of grandeur on both sides of the pathological relationship: In the slave it produced a false sense of absolute dependence upon the master; in the master it produced a false sense of absolute self-sufficiency. Elkins drew a direct analogy between the relationship that existed between the guard and the prisoner of the Nazi concentration camps of World War II to illustrate his claim about master/slave relationships.

Genovese would later refute Elkins' analogy on the grounds that it reinforced the stereotypical view that slaves were mere pawns in the hands of their masters. It was Genovese's position, also, that Elkins' thesis disregarded the emotional needs of the slave master. At the heart of Elkins' thesis was the belief that the Sambo personality type was normative among slaves. This belief informed Elkins' reading of the slave sources. It was a dominant part of the southern lore:

> Sambo, the typical plantation slave, was docile but irresponsible, loyal but lazy, humble but chronically given to lying and stealing; his behavior was full of infantile silliness and his talk inflated with childish exaggeration. His relationship with his master was one of utter dependence and childlike attachment; it was indeed his childlike quality that was the very key to his being.[2]

A clearer understanding of this master/slave relationship phenomenon has been of no less interest to theologians and ethicists in recent years. This has been the case primarily because the relationship phenomenon provokes profound questions about masters' perceptions of what it meant to "be" and "do" in the world toward their slaves and vice versa.

This chapter will identify whites' varied responses to the question of whether the African was created in the image of God. All whites of the South did not hold a common belief about the African's nature or what the duties of master ought to be toward the slave.

Whites seemed unequivocally certain in their belief that God had created them superior to those of African origin. Ensconced with this notion, literate whites spend much time and energy debating the theological question of the nature of the slave's being. At the very heart of the master/slave relationship, masters had to face the question of whether the African American was created in the image of God. This question required more than a simple "yes" or "no" answer in a society that affirmed the Christian worldview as being normative. It is apparent in the literature, that those masters who took seriously the moral teachings of Christianity continued to struggle with the metaphysical and ethical questions about the slave's being. What this meant, in fact, was that Christian slave masters could never be content to see the enslavement of Africans as being a mere economic or political issue, despite the fact that slave trade and slave labor comprised the backbone of the economy of the Christian. Slavery was a social problem that required their ethical and theological engagement.

I will make the fundamental point that two types[3] of ideal responses to the question of the fundamental nature of the slave are deducible from reading what students of history have classified as the proslavery literature. First, there is what might be called the naturalist response; second, there is what can be termed the Christian-master response. These two types of ideal responses are described in the following section.

THE IDEAL RESPONSE TYPES

The Naturalist Type

The naturalist type response is evident in the proslavery literature of the antebellum South. Naturalists assumed that all questions of whether slaves were created in the image of God were totally irrelevant. They were of the opinion generally that slaves of African origin were mere animated bodies without souls. Naturalists claimed to be the scientific authorities of their day on the theory of creation and the human races and they were intent on proving that the slave of African origin was inferior to white people, both mentally and physically. In order to prove this claim, they spent time and energy studying the physical attributes of those of African descent. The size of the slave's brain as well as the body structure became the object of scientific inquiry. The naturalists commonly concluded that the African's status of natural inferiority gave the slave only utility value on an agrarian labor market.

Most naturalists classified the slave with the lower species of primates such as the orangutan. Only a few naturalists could concede, at best, that the slave could possibly be endowed with even an inferior soul. One fallacious reason that was given for this explanation was that "Africans had lived for unknown centuries in a primitive state" on the mother continent without ever having been exposed to what whites termed "higher civilization." Christian practitioners, although willing to concede the point about civilization, were of the opinion that institutional slavery could elevate slaves spiritually and morally to a competitive level with their white masters. The more cynical of the naturalist type noted, however, that a beast could not be elevated higher than its created potential. It was believed that all attempts would be contrary to God's created plan for the beast of burden. Naturalist ideologues such as Morgan Godwin went against the majority opinion of his day and questioned the presupposition "that slavery had the power so as to unsoul man." The danger of this position, he noted, was "that every great Conqueror might at his pleasure make and unmake souls."[4] Godwin favored the hypothesis that the slave's nature was more a consequence of the conditioning process of slavery than that of divine ordination.

Naturalists of the majority opinion, such as John Evrie, posited what was termed the "different species theory," meaning that slaves were lesser beings with "different bodies, minds, and different natures."[5] The "different species" theory, however, did not satisfy those who were of the unequivocal persuasion that slaves were mere animated bodies. Some cleverly refuted this theory on the grounds that it implied that God possessed both a double nature and image. They also noted that it was in direct conflict with the Bible's anthropological claim that God "made from one blood every nation of men to live on the face of the earth" (Acts 17:26a).

Joseph Washington's contemporary assessment of proslavery literature serves to illuminate the rationale for the naturalists' position. Washington concedes that this literature must be conceptually understood. He calls for making a distinction between what he terms "antiblackness" and "anti-blackness." The former denotes the way in which the primordial notion of blackness manifested itself in the consciousness of the English Puritan mind for three centuries 1500-1800. Washington means by the term "primordial," the qualifier, the symbolism of black as evil as opposed to the symbolism of white as good. He notes that a classical example in the consciousness of the Puritan is the image of the black devil in contrast to the image of the white angel. He makes the conceptual demarcation between "antiblackness" and "anti-blackness" by defining the former as:

> antiblackness is the ancient, historical, primordial (even natural and all but inevitable, as fear at midnight in the cemetery follows sheer delight in high noon) culturally determined, frame of reference, which (in some cultures more than others) develops out of a curious association with the selected strangers of differing hue, as either sheer fascination (attraction), or, morbid repugnance (repulsion).[6]

Washington further notes that:

> If . . . preconscious antiblackness [people] a learned response which, when embellished with religion, can recede into the permanent condition of an antiblackness correspondent with the laws of nature, only through the process of unlearning combined with the dereligionization.
>
> The negative power of antiblack does not reveal itself in the illusion, as it is wont to be named, but in the delusion of anti-blackness (refusal to affirm black people) wherein it can only be understood as a religion or spirit of malevolence.[7]

Literature of the proslavery argument affirms the validity of Washington's claim. Thus, it is understandable that the slave was viewed often as "a beastly savage, without a god, law, religion, or common wealth." The negative power of this sort of teaching upon slaves was in its purportment that God designed and willed the inferiority of the African. This meant that slaves did not only experience slavery as physical subjugation, but as mentally and spiritually oppressive. It meant, Joseph Washington observed, that "the religion of antiblackness was the raison d'etre of our English Puritan Fathers."[8]

The Opaque Body Question

Whites were of the persuasion that physical blackness was a definite sign that slaves were created inferior by God. How else could the sable body of the slave be explained? What was even more evident was the fact that the external blackness of the body was thought to be indicative of the internal depravity of the soul. This was another way of saying that the interior dimension of the self was equally as inferior as its external dimension.[9] Naturalists equated the transparent nature of white skin with both the spiritual, intellectual, and physical superiority of white men and women. Factors such as transparent skin, expressiveness in facial features, and the broad forehead of the white race were all used as physical evidence of the white man's superior status.[10]

The opaque face of the slave, it was believed, revealed the true characteristics of his or her inferior nature. This notion was based on the ancient belief that the higher qualities even of animals were written in their facial features. The face was thought to be

> the window of the soul where may be read the sweet and most exquisite emotions of a sensitive and delicate nature, or as sometimes happens, the gross and sensual thoughts of a depraved and perverted one.[11]

False logic of this sort was used to show that the lack of transparent skin only proved that the slave had no soul. It was thought that the African's dark face signified the impossibility of God revealing anything through her or his soul. How would it have been possible for God's revelation in the soul to have been imaged in the ebony face of the slave? When compared to the soul of the white human being, it was concluded that the African American's black face had no epiphanic value, meaning that the best that the slave could expect in the society of white America was to be a good imitator of his or her master.

The Imitator Theory

Being a good imitator of what was said to be "the noble virtues reflected in the face of the master" was tantamount to being a good slave. Slaves skilled at imitating their masters had to assume the moral and intellectual posture of a child in relationship to the master. Favored slaves of the master were given, despite age, a child's place of permanency in the patriarchal family of the plantation master. It was noted above that Elkins took for granted in his study "a widespread existence of the Sambo image."[12] Elkins attributes one reason for this being the failure of the Protestant church in North America to protect the family and thereby protect the personality. A marked difference has been seen in the way the slave's personality was shaped in the ethos of a Catholic country. It was the closed system of slavery in North America that went unchecked by the Protestant church that produced the Sambo type personality myth.[13] Elkins recognized that there was "a great profusion of individual types," and it was Elkins' intention to show that the classic Sambo type embraced the majority of the slave population.

Genovese's study helps us put the Sambo theory in proper perspective. It identifies the ideological conflict that masters created for themselves. The inevitable conflict being that masters ideally wanted their slaves, like Sambo, to be docile, humble and dependent; but they also wanted them to be diligent, responsible, and resourceful. In the words of Earl E. Thorpe, masters wanted slaves "to give an efficient and adult-like performance."[14] This says in effect that slaves had to be more than imitating Sambos. The sheer need to survive required that they, as much as humanly possible, maximize the use of the game of flattery with their masters. Masters were equally, if not more, reliant as their slaves psychologically upon this practice of self-deception. This was a clear indicator that masters could not rely upon raw physical power alone to control their slaves. Slaves were not oblivious to the psychological tension that existed between themselves and their masters. The relationship, instead, was one that generated everlasting tensions, punctuated by occasional conflicts between combatants using different weapons.[15] The master at best was often only one of the significant others in the life of his slaves. He was not the sole author of the "role," or "roles," that they played. Kenneth Stampp, the historian, has been conclusive on this point:

> Finally, I would suggest that plantation slaves encountered significant others in their own families and communities; that dissembling manipulation, dissociation, role conflict, and lack of clarity were important ingredients of slave behavior; and that plantation life enabled most slaves to develop independent personalities—indeed, provide room for the development of a considerable range of personality types.[16]

Those of the naturalist persuasion were definitely inclined to overlook this fact and thereby fail to see how a Nat Turner could emerge and threaten the master/slave relationship model. Nat Turner was born a slave in Southhampton County, Virginia.

> He inspired what was perhaps the most widely discussed insurrection in the ante-bellum South. It began on August 21, 1831, and resulted in the deaths of some fifty-five whites and two hundred blacks, though perhaps only twenty or thirty slaves were involved in killing whites. Turner eluded capture, thereby adding to the hysteria that spread throughout the South. On October 31, 1831, he was placed in jail at Jerusalem, the county seat. . . . [and] went to the gallows on November 11, 1831, unrepentant.[17]

How could this be so if the slave was a perpetual child of nature? This question is implied in the formal responses of southern whites to Turner's rebellion. Editors of southern newspapers could not bring themselves to characterize Turner's rebellion as the work of a rational man with spiritual capabilities comparable to their own. Had they done so, whites would have conceded that Nat Turner was equally as competent as his white counterpart John Brown to organize and execute a rebellion against the white power structure. Stereotyping Turner's rebellious behavior and that of his men as being beastly in nature made it easier for whites to deal with their own consciences. Newspaper accounts of the day characterized Turner and his men as being no more than beastly imitators of white men: "monsters, a parcel of wretches, black brutes pretending to be men."[18] It was better to operate under this illusion about Turner and his men than go counter to the white man's canon of reason and admit that slaves had the capacity to be self-determining moral agents. When used in reference to Turner, the word intelligence was assigned a negative connotation. One account depicted him as: "being intelligent and shrewd of intellect" while in the same breath, it denounced his behavior as: "being [that of] a coward who was actuated to do what he did from the influence of fanaticism."[19] The implication is that even if he had some degree of marginal intelligence, Turner would not have had the moral courage to do this on his own. It had to be a case of him being influenced by a white man's fanatical influence.

Turner, despite all of the caricatures of him, spoke of himself as a Christian minister called by God. He believed that God had, through a vision, called him to rebel violently against slavery and its masters. Turner became the living proof for many of the naturalist persuasion that it was dangerous to share Christianity with slaves. It was even more dangerous to make them literate Christians. Slaves such as Nat Turner made it even more difficult for those Christian masters who believed that it was their God-given duty to bring the soul of the slave to the saving knowledge of Jesus Christ. Such a view was seen as being ideally impractical in the real world of slavery.

The Ideal Christian Master Type

The ideal Christian master type response — soul versus body — comprises the other half of the proslavery literature. It seems to have prevailed in the proslavery literature for several reasons. First, it was the best weapon that slave masters had to use against their antislavery adversaries of the North. Second, it was more consistent with the Christian worldview of the South. It was the theoretical, if not always the practical, belief of the Christian master that the slave of African origin was created "in the image of God, ... but. ..."[20] It was the unchangeable blackness of the slave's body, which signified the demonic, that left the ideal Christian master type unwilling to assert theologically that the slave was made in the image of God. At best this type of master could only say *theologically* that the slave's soul was created in the image of God. In no way could this belief change the master's *ethical* understanding of the nature of the slave as body. A physical body was perceived as having only utility value for the master's economic end. This meant that the Christian master, in practice, could only accept the slave's soul as having sacred worth in the sight of God.

The Christian master of this type response separated the relationship between the slave's soul and body in his mind. This false dichotomy constituted a theological and ethical Gordian knot that became more difficult for the master to untie with the evolution of institutional slavery. The only way around this problem was to skew the interpretation of biblical anthropology when it came to slaves. Ideal Christian-type masters believed that the souls of slaves satisfied the norm of biblical anthropology, but at the same time had ambiguous concerns about whether the slave's body, because of its blackness, met these same norms. Thinking that an African slave could change his blackness of body was tantamount to believing that the leopard could change its spots.

The blackness of the African slave's soul, of course, was not assigned a state of immutability since it was the theological conviction that Jesus' blood could make it "white as snow." Implied in this conviction was the idea that the soul of the slave, having been washed in the blood of Jesus, had the potential of being elevated on a spiritual level to a similar status with that of the master's soul in God's sight. That this could happen on a social and political level was thought to be an absolute improbability. Whites readily concluded that the dilemma of the external blackness of slaves' bodies gave them the right to be God's viceroys of slaves' souls and ultimately the rulers of their bodies on earth. It was conceded that while the blood of Jesus could not change the blackness of the slave's body, it would transform the status of the slave's soul. This alone, it was thought, would improve the slave's market value.

An examination of selected statements from the writings of four ideal Christian-types for the advocacy of the Christianization of slaves' souls illustrates this thesis. Readers will readily note that the authors were primarily concerned to prove that slaves' souls possessed the potential to be redeemed by the blood of Jesus Christ. A close reading of the four documents further shows theoretically that Christian masters, because of their ethical dilemma, had to see the slave as a soulless body.

Four Respondents' Responses

The material of these respondents was produced mainly in the Colonial period of American history. An examination of it allows us to see that slave masters of the antebellum South obviously benefited from the instructive value of these published discussions. While each of these persons, undoubtedly, produced more than one written source for the purpose of this discussion a representative writing from each will suffice to illustrate our thesis. The first makes a narrative response; the second a sermonic response; the third an essay response; and, the fourth makes an epistolary response. These different styles of responses are indicative of the fact that both proslavers and antislavers used varied forms of literary genre to communicate their ideas on the issue of slavery. Appreciation for their different types of responses ought to give us a greater feel for the complexities of the minds of those who taught slaves Christianity.

An English minister's contrived dialogical response. Near the end of the Colonial period in the United States, Leigh Richmond, an English minister, wrote and published a pamphlet to American slaveholders titled *The African Servant*. Richmond was Rector of Turvy, Bedfordshire, England and a missionary to the slave population in the American colonies. He took pride in the fact, by his own admission, that his materials were used by plantation owners to tutor their slaves in the "fundamentals of Christianity."

In this pamphlet, *The African Servant*,[21] Richmond creates a pedagogical resource for slave owners to teach their slaves Christianity. Concerned to teach masters how to tutor their slaves, Richmond presumed to structure the pedagogical logic of the pamphlet in the form of a master/servant dialogue. It is in actuality, however, the master's monologue projected upon the servant and echoed back to the master. This is a classical example of the mythic master, Sambo-type relationship. Richmond's primary objective was to prove that the slave's soul and behavior were transformable by the blood of Jesus Christ. It was Richmond's intent that his publication serve as an incentive for masters to work expeditiously for the conversion of their slaves to Christianity.

Richmond gives the indication that the incident in the pamphlet is based on his personal experience with slaves. Apparently this was done to enhance the appeal of his publication in the eyes of his readers. A second reason for this might have been to make his own experience a model lesson for masters and white ministers of the slave population. There were certain questions that every novice, minister or missionary, ought to ask the master about the servant's behavior and knowledge when called upon to teach Christianity to his slaves. Richmond highlights three, among many, that were crucial: "Does he know anything about the principles of Christianity? Does he behave well as a servant? Was he always so well behaved?"[22] Richmond's presentation of the owner's commentary on the servant's behavior, before and after enslavement, reflects the prevailing Christian attitude of the day that said "the enslavement of the African was the will of God." The slave owner in the dialogue makes the following observation regarding the servant's behavior since his two-year period of enslavement: "He is as honest and civil a fellow as ever came aboard a ship, or lived in a house." The contrary was the case when the master first met the servant: "He was often very unruly, deceitful, but for the last two years he has been quite another creature."[23] Here was the verification of the theological assumption that God ordained white masters to enslave Africans for the purpose of elevating them to a higher level of civil and moral awareness. This was the preparatory stage necessary before exposing them to the teachings of Jesus Christ. Slavery was God's means of bringing Africans to Jesus Christ.

Another aspect of Richmond's contrived master-servant dialogue is that he has the African servant use white people's condemning stereotypes of slaves. First, this happens when the African servant makes a negative assessment of his own spiritual condition and knowledge of God before having been captured and taken from Africa. Before this episode, the African servant's attitude toward his spiritual welfare was one of ignorance and indifference: "me no care for my soul at all before then. No man teach me a word about my soul." Second, Richmond has the African servant buy into the white man's hermeneutical circle of double theological self-denigration, that is, to be deemed of worthless value in body and soul before master and God. The job of the white minister-missionary was to convince the slave to think of self totally in a self-denigrating way. The servant must say: "Me think no good, nor do no good." Primarily, this became an act of double self-denigration because it demanded that slaves see themselves interiorly and exteriorly in a worthless light before God and master. This meant that they were solely at the mercy of white people and their God. It was the blood of the white man's Jesus that could whiten the black soul. This severity of the African servant's interior and exterior condition would require God's extra salvation power to save her or his soul. The servant is made to say: "Me believe that Jesus Christ came into the world to save sinners; and though me chief of sinners, though me be only poor black negro."[24]

An English minister's sermonic response. Thomas Bacon was an Anglican cleric who served in the Maryland province during the Colonial period under the auspices of the Society of the Propagation of the Gospel. During his tenure of ministerial service in the Maryland province, Bacon wrote and preached sermons that were reflective of his theological belief about slaves' anthropological nature. In four of these published sermons he delineated a theological rationale for masters' Christian duties toward their slaves.

Bacon's literary greeting of slaves as "my dear black brethren and sisters" sounds rather strange to the ears of the modern reader. Despite this expression of affection, Bacon does not escape the temptation of his generation to falsely dichotomize slaves' anthropological nature of body and soul. This fact of falsification must be seen in Bacon's refusal to recognize the slave's soul as having sacred value. Bacon admonished slaves to "serve God because he made you." What then was the rationale for slaves serving their masters? Bacon's answer was that: "God made servants and slaves to work for the masters and mistresses that provide for them."[25] Since it was thought that slavery was ordained by God, slaves who were cruelly treated were told to trust God's compensatory justice.

Contrary to his peers, Bacon warned masters that their slaves were justified in disobeying them when they encouraged them: "to steal, to murder, to set a neighbor's house on fire, to do harm to anybody's goods, or cattle, or to get drunk, or to curse or swear, or to work on Sundays." In short, Bacon concluded that disobedience to the master was permissible on the part of the slave if the master ordered the slave to go against anything that God ordered.

Bacon believed that slaves shared coequality with their masters on spiritual grounds only. Planters were persuaded to recognize that their slaves had an inalienable spiritual right to be taught the gospel of Jesus Christ. Bacon warned naturalists of the eternal danger of classifying slaves as no more than beasts. He reminded them that skin color must not be the criterion for deciding who has souls. His reason was that the spurious criterion of color "would disqualify such persons as Tertullian, Cyprian, Augustine, and other primitive African members."[26] This by no means meant that Bacon was ready to concede that slaves ought be acknowledged as social and political equals with whites. They were always to be looked upon as being inferior because they were black of body.

A former English planter's essay response. Richard Nisbet, once an owner of slaves in the West Indies, changed from being a rabid defender of the slave's beastly nature to becoming an advocate of the slave having been created in the image of God. A native of England and a graduate of Oxford, Nisbet became a member of the elite planter class in the West Indies. Here Nisbet became an arch enemy of those who believed in the humanity of slaves, characterizing them as "beastly in their customs and grossly stupid" in their actions. He noted with others of his generation that slaves were inferior by nature and culture. Borrowing the words of his intellectual mentor, Dave Hume, Nisbet said "that nature designed the total absence of any symptoms of ingenuity" in every living black person.

Such scurrilous attacks upon slaves provoked Benjamin Rush, an American physician, to upbraid Nisbet for having

> charged the father of Mankind with being the author of the greatest Evils to his children, and unworthily traduced the whole of your brethren, the poor Africans, and attempted to sink Creatures, Formed like yourself, in the image of God, and equally capable of Happiness both here and hereafter, below the rank of Monsters and Barbarians, or even the Brutes themselves.[27]

Plantation failure and mental problems forced Nisbet to move to America where he underwent psychiatric treatment at the University of Pennsylvania Hospital. Ironically, Rush, Nisbet's critic was engaged in psychiatric research at the same hospital.[28]

Nisbet wrote his book, *The Capacity Of Negroes For Religious And Moral Improvement*, as a correction of his rabid vilification of blacks. Joseph Washington says that Nisbet "moved to the more Anglican pacification position." In diametrical opposition to his earlier position, Nisbet affirmed the slave as a co-equal with masters only in the spiritual sense. He believed that slavery was a needed institutional corrective for elevating slaves spiritually and culturally to an equal level with whites. Slavery was viewed as "a school of chastisement" that was necessary for the spiritual elevation of slaves. Nisbet was against slavery being used, however, for any other means than the enhancement of the souls of slaves. Those who claimed to be created in the image of God were expected to do no less for their slaves who, also, were said to be made in God's image.

A transatlantic epistolary response. The letter was another literary form that was used by both proslavers and antislavers to convey their opinions both publicly and privately. One of the more provocative letters defending privately slaves' spiritual capacity is titled "A Letter to an American Planter from his Friend in London."[29] It consists of an anonymous Londoner writing to an unnamed American friend, who is a slaveholder, in response to a conversation that they had during the American's previous visit with him in London. The letter's scholarly value is that: It shows that written and oral conversations were shared on the subject of slavery even by friends on separate continents; and, it shows that a certain degree of hearty confession and intellectual struggle took place between friends, although separated by the ocean, over this very controversial subject of slavery.

The Londoner unapologetically intercedes on behalf of slaves' souls despite his American friend's claim that slaves were idolatrous by nature and practice. It was the Londoner's belief that to ignore the slave's soul amounted to the slaveholder "placing worldly advantage over the principles of God." The Londoner, in defense of the slave's body, appealed both to the interest of Christ and that of the master. The Londoner makes no mention of the need for his friend to respect the slave's body for its own intrinsic worth. He does reprimand his American friend, however, for making a false correlation between the blackness of both the slave's body and of the soul. The Londoner, in defense of Africans' status in the created order, asked his friend: "Are they not Transcripts of the same Divine original? Have they not the same capacities for immortality with our own?" In the name of the christological principle of inclusiveness, the Londoner asked his American friend: "And did not the same redeemer who died for us die for them also?" God, the Londoner reasoned, has created a common body of spirituality between the slaveholder and slave so that they might be mutually instrumental in promoting each other's felicity: "that whilst they, by the Labour of the Body promote your temporal Interest, you in Return, might promote the spiritual eternal Welfare of their precious and immortal souls."[30]

The Londoner writes, following the American slaveholder's visit with him, that his American friend was from *"this new Land of Promise."* The Londoner forthrightly reminds his American friend that *"its Divine Province hath blessed you with a comfortable habitation, an extensive fruitful Estate amply stocked with a large number of healthful negroes."* He challenged his friend to admit that his possession of *"a large number of healthful negroes"* must account for his having become rich in this new land. This, more than anything else, accounted for the fact that it was a *"new Land of Promise"* for him. Apparently in an earlier encounter serious disagreement had taken place between the two gentlemen over the subject of the value of Christianity in the life of slaves. The Londoner makes the point that he had sought to convince the American, during the former meeting, that Christianity was the planter's *"best means of reconciling his slaves to their state of Servitude."*

Finally, the Londoner delineates his American friend's rationale for not teaching slaves Christianity:

(a) *that no time* can be spared from the daily labor for their instructions; (b) that some slaves had been known to misbehave after baptism and (c) some imported slaves seemed entirely corrupted and depraved . . . their very nature seemed sunken into ignorance, ferocity and brutality.[31]

Such reasons were denounced by the Londoner as being very poor excuses. Denying slaves the right to worship God on the Sabbath amounted to a flagrant violation of the law of God because it was considered a day for spiritual restoration. The charge of the bad behavior of slaves following baptism was dismissed as trivial since many whites were guilty of the same. On the subject of the slave's anthropological nature, the Londoner warned the American of the danger of placing limitations upon God.

The Basic Fact

Undeniably, ideal Christian masters' interpretations of African slaves' anthropological nature was more complex than masters of the naturalist-type response. The reason being that the former dared assert unequivocally that slavery was all a part of the providential will of God. Ideal Christian master types could not let the naturalist type have the last word about the African slave's anthropological nature for at least two fundamental reasons. First, naturalists' anthropological theory would play right into the hands of their abolitionist adversaries of the North. Second, naturalists' anthropological theory was feared by the ideal Christian type because it was believed to be antithetical to the teachings of the Bible. Those of the ideal Christian master type were ever haunted by the biblical belief that "to whom much is given much is required." They lived with an almost incurable anxiety that God would require of them, on the final Judgment Day, an honest account of their Christian stewardship of their slaves. Subsequently, ideal Christian master types produced a corpus of pedagogical literature that focused primarily on the duties of Christian masters toward their slaves and vice versa.

Ideal Christian master types failed to realize that their theological interpretation of the African slave's anthropological nature had negatively implicated them with their slaves. Subsequently, ideal type Christian masters became the victims of their own hermeneutical circle of double negativity.

THE HERMENEUTICAL CIRCLE OF DOUBLE NEGATIVITY

Christian masters' contradictory theological understanding about the blackness of the African slave's body in relationship to his and her soul left them in a moral quandary. The ideal Christian's quandary—body versus soul—is reflected in the following question: Can we teach slaves to think of themselves as being absolutely worthless before God without being guilty of thinking of ourselves more highly than we ought before God? This was a theological issue at its core; it constituted a hermeneutical circle of double negativity. To teach slaves that they were "black of body" and "blacker of soul" was to teach them the theory of double self-negation. It required that slaves think of themselves as having only negative value both before their masters and God. This truth is illustrated by the following prayer lines of a white missionary preacher composed for plantation masters to teach their slaves: "*O Thou great God, the Maker of all creatures, I, a poor black sinner, black in body and still blacker in sin . . .*"[32] These lines required slaves to denounce themselves interiorly and exteriorly, body and soul, as being worthless in God's sight. Requiring slaves to ritualize their own inferiority in these prayer lines, masters were affirming their belief that white skin made them superior in the sight of God. Such spurious interpretation contributed to whites' false sense of divinely ordained preeminence over those of African origin.

These erroneous theological concepts make it clear as to why even the more sincere white Christians of the time willingly compromised the sacred worth of the slave's body in the name of the soul's salvation. Even the prominent evangelist, George Whitfield, while it seems unbelievable today, was guilty of compromising the sacredness of the slave's body for the salvation of the soul. He counseled an American Colonist, who was apparently in a moral quandary over his ethical obligation to the physical abuse of the slave, that: "Enslaving their bodies, comparatively speaking, would be an incontestable evil, as proper care taken for their souls."[33] Some whites were so troubled over the slave's blackness of body and soul that they lived in the eschatological hope that God would make the souls of slaves permanently white in the world to come. The following quote from a memorial rendered to a slave named Caesar, who lived during the early American period is a case in point:

In Memory of Caesar

Herein lies the
best of slaves

Now turning into dust:
Caesar the Ethiopian craves
A place among the just.
His fled soul has fled
To realms of heavenly light
And by the blood that Jesus shed
Is changed from black to White.
Jan. 15, he quitted the state
In the 77th year of his age
1780.[34]

We have identified two ideal types of responses that slave masters made to the slave's anthropological nature. One was what we called an ideal naturalist type response; the other was what we termed an ideal Christian master type of response. The former saw the slave as being no more than a bodiless soul while the latter saw the slave as a soulless body. Our next need is to examine critically the pedagogical resources that ideal Christian masters used to instruct slaves orally in their duties to God and themselves.

CHAPTER 2

Duty, Bondage, and Pedagogy

Most white clerics of the antebellum South believed that they were bound by God to share the gospel of Jesus Christ with slaves. They predicated their belief on the biblical principle that God created slaves with souls for whom Jesus died. This minority group of divines was careful to interpret the scripture so as to accommodate slave masters' economic interests. Much of this had to do primarily with the fact that southern divines were hired by slave masters. Southern divines learned the importance of helping anxiety-ridden masters to see the direct correlation between converted slaves and obedient ones. In short, they taught that conversion to Jesus actually made better slaves. These divines designed the theological and moral blueprints of what ought to constitute the right relationship between a Christian master and his slaves. Ministers of the plantations believed it was their responsibility to do the following for the perpetuation of right relationships between slaves and masters: to teach and convert slave masters to the idea that their slaves possessed souls; to convince masters that converting slaves to Jesus Christ actually made them better servants, enhancing the value of their bodies on the trade market; and, to create adequate pedagogical resources that would facilitate the instruction of slaves in the knowledge necessary for Christian conversion.

We will accomplish the above task by analyzing the sermons, pastoral letters, addresses and catechisms, produced by missionaries and preachers of plantations. These materials reflect the practical responses of Christian apologists of slavery to the master/slave relationship dilemma. Under the sacred canopy of Southern culture, these white ministers preached and taught that all masters must answer to God, on the great Day of Judgment, for the mistreatment of their slaves in this world. The second part of the chapter will be a descriptive analysis of the body of pedagogy that missionaries and pastors wrote for masters. These divines intended that masters study it for the purpose of learning what constituted right Christian duties to their slaves and vice versa. Two objectives, among the many, stand out as to why the divines of the South wrote these materials. First, they believed that these materials would arm masters with the needed Christian apology for defending institutional slavery against rabid abolitionists' attacks. Second, it was believed that these teachings about master and slave relationships and duties would enable masters to better prepare their slaves for a servile Christian role. Their ultimate hope, however, was that this material would better prepare masters and their slaves to live with God in the eschatological world.

BONDAGE AND CHRISTIAN DUTY

White missionaries and preachers of the antebellum South concluded, from their readings of the scripture, that masters and slaves were spiritual sisters and brothers. Their reasoning was that God's acts of creation and Jesus' acts of redemption had made this possible. Missionaries and preachers warned masters uncompromisingly of the divine retribution that they would face on God's Judgment Day if they failed to convert their slaves' souls. These divines, by their own admission, willingly sacrificed the freedom that is bequeathed from the "love of Christ" for the bondage that is imposed from an understanding of the "law of Christ" alone. In doing this, all of those who professed to be Christians lost sight of the New Testament's message of dialectical freedom that is at the heart of Jesus' message of liberation. Inevitably, many missionaries and ministers of the antebellum South became servants of the notion of duty for duty's sake. Nowhere in the literature are there any attestations on the part of whites made to relate to the slave as an embodied equal before God. These divines, given the economic power of slave owners, had to accent law over the slave's personhood. An arbitrary notion of loyalty to the concept of duty often placed white ministers and missionaries, in relationship to the white master class, in a marginal position morally and theologically. It created informally, if not formally, a marginal servant class of white ministers and missionaries in the South.

The Marginal Servant Class

Some ministers and missionaries actually were justified in believing that masters, because of their loyalty to Jesus Christ for the salvation of slaves' souls, recognized these divines as having only marginal status in the plantation's class structure. The more suspicious religious leaders rightly concluded that invariably a tension existed over what it meant to be faithful to the mission of Jesus Christ while being employed by the plantation master.[1] Many masters contributed immensely to the notion of a marginalized group by insisting that these divines be the living embodiment of what was commonly called the "humble missionary" philosophy. Primary teaching sources used by the missionaries often indicate the hardships—even ill-treatment at the hands of cruel masters—that they thought it necessary to endure sharing the gospel of Jesus Christ with the slave population. Some missionary/preachers chose to live a marginalized existence for the sake of the slave's soul. Some considered it a badge of honor to describe themselves in servile terms:

> Servant of slaves literally treated as inferior by the proprietors, as hardly equal to the overseers, half starved sometimes, suffocated with smoke, sick with the stench of dirty cabins and as-dirty negroes sleepless for the stings of ... musquitoes [sic] and all in the very centre ... of the kingdom of disease.[2]

One preacher paralleled his own life of suffering, for this cause of ministering to slaves, to the persecution Paul suffered for taking the gospel to the Gentiles. After years of having preached to slaves on a certain plantation, the preacher noted in the waning years of his life that:

> I have come to say my last to you. It is: None but Christ. Three times I have had my life in jeopardy for preaching the gospel to you. Three times I have broken the ice on the edge of the water and swam across the Cape Fear to preach the gospel to you and now, if in my last hour I could trust to that, or anything else but Christ crucified, for my salvation, all should be lost, and my soul perish forever.[3]

Subscribers of this humble missionary philosophy believed that they were mandated by God to "teach the living how to live and, the dying how to die, while trusting the merits of the blood of the Lamb shed for the redemption of the whole human race."[4] They were haunted by at least two threatening realities: primarily the agitating abolitionists of the North, and the belief that they must answer to God for their responsibilities to slaves on Judgment Day. They were unequivocally certain that the Bible supported their beliefs about their Christian duties toward slaves. They were successful in pricking the consciences of a few masters to the extent that some masters experienced what might be termed the "wrestling Jacob" syndrome.[5]

They lived in conscious conflict, on the one hand, with an acute awareness of the rightness and wrongness of slavery. On the other hand, they could not ignore the exemplary model that the humble missionaries presented. Clearly many missionaries and ministers dared not take lightly their sense of duty for the salvation of slaves' souls. This is echoed in Bishop Meade's soul-searching moment at the end of his tenure of ministry to the slaves of a particular plantation:

> I asked myself had I tried to fulfill my duty since I had come to these perishing souls, to teach them the way, the truth and the life?[6]

Meade exemplifies those missionaries who were consumed by the belief of having God-given duties to both slaves and masters. Meade and others of his ilk resolved that the highest reward attainable for working among slaves was to hear the inner voice of God's approval.

Christian Apologists, Conscience, and Duty

Missionaries and preachers used the teachings of the book of Genesis to inform their anthropological theories about the nature of the African slave. Circumscribed by the closed ideology of the slave society, missionaries and preachers of the antebellum South often wavered in their rationale for Africans' inferior nature. Some said the African was created inferior in every way to whites. Others said that the African was created equal to whites but disobeyed Noah during the flood and experienced a state of twice-fallenness. Just how the African's spiritual, moral, and physical defacement took place was a question of perennial debate.

All white Christians of the ideal type were not fully comfortable with the general assumption that God had made them, as a group, to rule over the African slave for the mutual good of humankind. Some could see that such an assumption raised serious theological questions about God's nature. For example, why would God suffer the degradation of a whole race of people merely for the purpose of giving the white race a challenging Christian mission? Concerns of this nature required that whites methodically search the scriptures for answers. A common answer that whites derived from this biblical inquiry was that slavery must inevitably be seen as God's moral school of discipline that was necessary for the African. Discipline was thought to be the necessary moral means for slaves to be good servants of white people while on the earth. It was also believed to be the best means of conditioning the souls of Africans to serve God in heaven.

This preparatory theory of slavery was based on the presupposition that it would be better to mutilate the African's body in order to save the soul. This barbaric means of attempted control was deemed "to be indispensable for the attachment of the greatest possible good" in the temporal order. The more articulate Christian apologists of slavery conceded that mutilation of the body stood to improve both the character of masters and slaves. Primarily, the apologists reasoned that slavery cultivated in the master such virtues as: "Forbearance, self-control, justice and benevolence." Secondarily, they claimed that slavery instilled in the slave such virtues as: "patience, humility, fidelity and deference to God's will."[7] Slavery was understood as an institution that was ordained by God and was therefore "perceived as being a natural rather than as an artificial evil, introduced by the imperfect state of mankind."[8]

In addition to the scriptures, Christian apologists of slavery cited what they termed "natural history," as well, to make the case for the Africans' inferior status in the created order. "Natural history," as opposed to "sacred history," was that body of information about human existence that was not recorded in the Bible. Biblical information about human existence was referred to as "sacred history" under the sacred canopy of the ante-bellum South.[9] The expectation was that both types of history would allow for the hermeneutical retrieval of all ethnic groups' historical and cultural antecedents. John Fairly concluded that the entire African continent was void of any trace of positive historical antecedents. Along with this absolute negative assessment, Fairly further cautioned that it was the duty of "the white church to carefully examine the religious history of the Negro race, before making it cotrustee of the things committed by her All wise Founder to the keeping of the Caucasian race."[10]

Some Christian apologists of slavery, convinced that slaves had souls, drew heavily upon the biblical stories of the Creation and the Flood to buttress their argument. They, even by doing so, often found themselves hard pressed to explain the African's relationship to Adam in the Genesis story. The so-called progressive-minded reasoned that slaves were of the same Adamic origin as was the white man. They, however, were haunted by their opponents' perennial question: "If God created them, what has accounted for Africans' underachievement collectively and individually in the hierarchy of civilization?" One of the most prevailing explanatory theories, which proposed to answer this question, was based on the account of Noah's fall in the book of Genesis. It posited the claim that Noah was the common father of the white and the black races. He was the "preacher of righteousness" who taught "the ancestors of the Negro the same religious instructions that were imparted to his white brethren for three hundred years after the flood."[11] This theory begged several questions: First, in what way did the African's knowledge of God reflect Noah's egalitarian instructions? Second, what happened to the Godlike image that was presumed to have been in Africans during the Noahian age?

Whites, in their attempts to answer these questions, measured every aspect of the African's being by their own definition of humanity. Their primary conclusion was that they as whites had retained more of the image of God following the episode of the Adamic fall than African slaves. These whites believed that Godlike characteristics of the white human being were evident in what was termed humanity's "marvelous works of industry and art"; as well as "the written record of the mighty works of God and his dealings with the children of men."[12] The belief that whites were both the documenters and keepers of the revealed actions of God gave them a sense of uncontested superiority over the African. This false belief led whites to believe that they qualified to be, on God's behalf, both stewards and tutors of what they called "the inferior African." Whites thought that the lack of empirical evidence about the African continent supported their claim of stewardship rights. According to John Fairly, there was "no clearly distinctive reference to the African in the Scriptures," and "all missionary reports from black Africa portray the negro as almost nude, and presenting every characteristic which distinguishes the pure negro of equatorial Africa." Also, "the negro had, within five hundred and fifty years, lost the knowledge of God, as taught him by his ancestor, Noah, and had already lapsed into savagery."[13]

The Theory of the Twice-Fallen

Some Christian apologists concluded that the major theological difference between themselves and the African was that the latter existed in a twice-fallen state. Their notion of the twice-fallen theory was that humankind had fallen once as a result of Adam's sin in the garden of Eden. Moreover, the African fell a second time because of being disobedient to Noah's instructions following the flood. This disobedience amounted to the African disobeying the primal parent of the human race. Whites reasoned that in the Adamic fall episode the African fell into history, of which they understood themselves to be the interpreters and keepers. Then it was claimed that in the second fall episode, the African fell into a barbaric state of nature over which white humanity perceived itself to be a master. A white theologian of the time said, of the African, regarding the second fall:

in every instance; after being brought to the knowledge of God; the negro race must have lapsed, more or less speedily into absoluter savagery; losing totally that knowledge, and all sense of responsibility to any God. [14]

The theory of the twice-fallen provided the theological justification for making slaves out of Africans. It was viewed as the biblical explanation of why God needed whites to enslave Africans. The assumption was that the consequences of twice-fallenness reflected itself in Africans' lack of rational faculties to govern themselves or form any elevated standard of conduct and character. Those who held to the twice-fallen theory easily concluded that Africans, by their disobedience of Noah's instructions, were the makers of their own servitude.

Biblical Authority and Duty

A minority of Christian apologists of slavery advocated that God created masters and slaves with souls. They asserted that the New Testament required that masters fulfill their God-given duties to slaves. Apologists of this persuasion refused to exempt masters from the demands of the law of God, which they believed were presented with explicit clarity in the scriptures. Partly because of this belief, ministers and missionaries developed a tome of pedagogical and inspirational resources delineating the duties of masters to their slaves and vice versa. Living paradoxically as it were under an eschatological cloud of hope and anxiety, similar to that of New Testament believers, these missionaries and preachers invoked the biblical language of divine retribution against insensitive masters. They warned that God would summon all masters to stewardship accountability on the Judgment Day. These divines of minority status felt bound by the gospel mandate to preach the gospel to every creature including slaves. It became a kind of moral arsenal in the hands of some missionaries and preachers of plantations. Charles C. Jones, preacher-missionary and an owner of slaves himself, summarized that masters' misuse of authority could jeopardize them temporally and eternally in both "their moral values and high civility in this life," and "their souls forever on the day of judgment." Jones labored zealously to convert other masters of their Christian duty to the slave population of the South. Having few moral equals in this matter, Jones warned masters, himself included, that

> [we] by the providence and word of God are under obligation to impart the word of God to our servants. It may be added, that we cannot disregard this obligation thus divinely imposed, without forfeiting our humanity, our gratitude, our consistency, our claim to the spirit of Christianity itself.[15]

Jones, subscribing to the permissive will of God doctrine commonly appealed to during his day, believed that: "It was by the permission of the Almighty God, in his Inscrutable providence over the affairs of men, that Negroes were taken from Africa and transported to these shores.[16] He did not, however, in his writings, address the notion of Africans' mythic beginnings. Jones, instead, devoted his energies to helping masters understand what their obligations were to slaves and vice versa. He said that "in the providence of God we were constituted masters, superiors; and constituted their guardians."[17] This was the theological cornerstone in Jones' doctrine of white supremacy.

Jones summarized his belief that the moral imperative of the Word of God was inescapable in this statement: "The gospel is the gift of God to men, and those who possess it are bound to bestow it upon those who do not."[18] Jones believed that the command to "Go ye into all the world and preach the gospel to every creature" comprised the core message of its inclusivity. It was a clear demonstration that "God recognizes men not as a particular nation or color, but collectively, as the intelligent and accountable creatures of God."[19] For Jones this was the God who "made of one blood all the nations of the earth." Jones prophetically reminded the white church and its leaders that it had no choice but to fulfill the gospel command on behalf of slaves: "We cannot dare, we dare not, neglect them and turn to others."[20]

In addition to the "one blood, one race" theory, Jones told white masters that they were duty bound by the "love thy neighbor as thyself" moral commandment of the Bible. It constituted the moral prism through which masters were admonished to see slaves' humanity. For Jones this meant that masters could not live oblivious to the physical suffering of their slaves and claim to be Christians.[21] Jones reasoned that neighborly rights of slaves to masters were based upon both the natural and civil structures of human existence. This erudite southern churchman noted that the principle of natural law ought to have taught masters that "slaves were members of the great family of men." Jones challenged all whites to see that the civil laws of the slave South made "slaves members of our own communities and parts of our very household."

Moreover, Jones invoked the biblical moral injunction of "do unto others as you would have them do unto you" to warn masters of their Christian duties toward slaves. He noted that the Bible taught masters that: "All things whatsoever ye would that men should do unto you, do you even so unto them." Under this moral injunction, Jones believed that slaves must be recognized spiritually as human beings. He even granted that this biblical moral principle gave slaves the right to complain against cruel masters. Jones warned that masters who disregarded this principle stood to forfeit their "claim to the spirit of Christianity itself which is love," and the "rightful claim of God's love for themselves."[22] Ultimately, they stood to lose, in fact, their assumed savior status of being the salt of the earth.

Jones, along with other benevolent slave masters of his day, was the creator of his own moral conundrum as it related to slaves. He, along with his colleagues, wanted to be exemplary models of Christian slave masters. Because of their desire they searched the scriptures in a sincere attempt to give divine sanction to their behavior.

Jones cited Paul's biblical injunction "masters render unto your servants that which is just, and equal, knowing that ye, also, have a master in heaven" as the normative text for pricking the consciences of slave masters. Bishop Meade of Virginia warned that masters could not neglect the souls of their slaves without doing negative damage to themselves spiritually. He confessed for the masters of his day: "In reality we are guilty of the most criminal neglect, by withholding the spiritual instruction and discipline which would infinitely outweigh every temporal blessing that could be lavished upon them by the most indulgent master."[23] It was a mystery to Meade how masters, who believed they had been given their positions of authority by a wise and gracious Providence, could fail so miserably in their Christian duty toward their slaves.

The best Calvinist architects of theological interpretation, such as Jones and Meade, summoned defiant masters to repent for having dreadfully failed in their God-given responsibility toward slaves. Masters who refused to heed such prophetic teaching were viewed as being abusers of the power given them by God. They were seen as using it for self-gain rather than the glory of God. Often missionaries and preachers of the plantations relied heavily on the rare opportunity to warn masters of the coming Day of Judgment that was spoken of in the Bible. Generally the use of this biblical rhetoric was the most efficacious weapon of moral persuasion that preachers and missionaries had at their disposal.

Judgment Day Principles and Subordinate Principles

The Judgment Day principle entailed four subordinate moral principles: the debtor principle; the common parent principle; the exemplary Christ-servant principle; and the witnessing slave principle. All of these were drawn from the biblical accounts in the New Testament. It was taught and believed by some that the Master in heaven would invoke these principles, on the Day of Judgment, as the criteria for testing the works of slave masters. An examination of each of these principles is in order.

The debtor principle. Most Christians of the religious South were rhetorically active in citing the Bible's "do unto others as you would have them do unto you," moral debtor principle. It was perceived as the norm for regulating behavior both among equals and unequals of the social order. Missionary-minded clerics were generally uncompromising in their conviction that slave masters were not exempt from the judgment of this principle. They believed master and slaves exerted a mutual moral influence on each other that would last into eternity. This meant that master and slave could hinder or help each other's welfare for the next world. The principle of social proximity, required by plantation life, was one explanation given for the mutual influence slave and master had upon one another from the cradle to the grave. Bishop Meade noted that beyond the grave they were destined "to sleep in the ground side by side and return to the dust."[24] The Bishop conceded that the artificial distinctions of this world, such as those based on somatic differences between slaves and masters, would be of no value in the other world. The single issue would be whether masters had dutifully given slaves the gospel of Jesus Christ. Placed in the form of a question it would be: "To what degree had masters been almoners of God's grace to their slaves?"

The common parent principle. Most plantation preachers asserted uncompromisingly that God was the common parent even of slaves' souls. They could not easily dismiss the biblical assertion that God had designed Christianity for the benefit of all classes, races, and nationalities. Despite the fact that slavery called for the physical subjugation of African Americans, these preachers could not ignore the spiritual implications of the biblical principle that said: "out of one blood God had made every nation of the earth." If God was presented as the common parent of all humankind, Jesus was presented to slaves as the common brother of all humankind. Masters were challenged to make Jesus' life and teachings the norm for relating to their slaves. Jesus was characterized as the authentically embodied demonstration of the "one blood, one race" theory.

Even James Thornwell, a Presbyterian minister and the South's premier theologian of slavery, unequivocally admitted that God was the common parent of slave and master. He told the master class of the southern white church "that the Negro is of one blood with ourselves."[25] In addition, Thornwell noted that slave and master shared equal ontological status as sinners just as they had a common need for redemption before God.[26] Ironically, Thornwell would only concede on theological grounds that the slave was inferior to whites. He refuted scientific claims, made by the likes of Voltaire, that linked blacks with the brute. Because Thornwell believed that slaves' humanity was grounded in the image of God, he told his hearers: "We are not ashamed to call him [the slave] our brother."[27]

The Christ-servant exemplary principle. Plantation clerics, such as Bishop Meade, presented Jesus to slave masters as the servant-of-servants, the leadership model to guide them in relating to their slaves. This notion was intended to be equally liberating for both masters and slaves. Jesus was presented to masters as having freely chosen his servant-of-servants role. Meade notes that Jesus: "chose the form of a servant and became the servant-of-servants, illustrating its blessed doctrine by his own meek, patient, suffering life."[28] In this role, Jesus submitted to the law of adaptability in "all his precepts and promises and doctrines to the poor, and those who were in bondage." He was believed to be faultless in word and deed toward those who were in bondage. Jesus was portrayed as the servant-of-servants to masters for the purpose of theologically legitimating their sense of authority over slaves. The same notion, on the contrary, was presented to slaves for the purpose of theologically legitimating in them a sense of their having been ordained for bondage. Slaves were taught to perceive Jesus as a genuinely passive and humble servant of the master class. Masters were expected to understand Jesus as the aggressive leader of the established order who voluntarily chose the role of the servant-of-servants to gain absolute power over the social order.

Christ as the moral judge principle. The biblical account of the judgment scene, heavily utilized by white preachers, was invoked as a moral deterrent to insensitive masters. Preachers used it to warn them that they must stand on the Day of Judgment and be judged by "the servant-of-servant's Christ." It would be the day of dramatic status reversal when the servant-of-servant's Christ would become the judging Lord of slaves and their masters without respect of person. All masters would have to answer the judging Lord of history for their treatment of their slaves. Threatening images of the Day of Judgment must have been sobering for those masters who were very much influenced by biblical literalism. They were challenged to anticipate this scenario on that day: Christ is seated on the throne with eternal judging power and every slave they had owned, in this world, will be brought on the witness stand. Christ will require the master's relationship to his slaves to be replayed before him. The voice of the judging Lord of history might be heard to say on that day:

These were your servants on earth. They labored for you ten, fifteen, twenty, thirty years. They wore out their lives to supply you with food, and raiment, and conveniences, and luxuries for your mortal life. You had them wholly at your disposal. You had my gospel in your hands. I made you the almoners of my grace to them. Did you remember their never dying souls?[29]

Such rhetoric of moral persuasion was very much a part of the teachings of a small group of plantation preachers.

The witnessing slave principle. While they sided with masters that slaves had no legal rights in the everyday world, plantation clerics, such as Meade, posited the notion that slaves would be witnesses "against" or "for" their masters in the high court of heaven. Masters who were inclined to ignore this warning, because they believed that slaves were property, were challenged to: "call them before you; look on the countenance of each; mark them well and remember that you will meet them again, and they will be strong witnesses either for or against you."[30] The reader readily notes in Meade's words of warning the epiphanic power that he assigns to the slave's face on the Day of Judgment. Recall that one means that masters used to dehumanize slaves was to deny them, at will, the right to look them in the face. Thomas Bacon, Anglican rector of colonial Maryland, noted that all cases before the judging Lord of history will be impartially heard:

Complaints will be impartially heard; where Masters and servants shall one day appear Face to Face; and where strict justice will be done them, without the least Favor or Affection.[31]

Those masters who were persuaded by such rhetoric of moral persuasion must have lived anxiously in anticipation of that dreadful day. The master would not only have to answer for his own soul but the souls of his entire household, which included his slaves. It was such religious leaders of biblical eschatology that led masters to conclude that "to whom much is given much is required." Deep-rooted anxiety derived from the anticipation of the moral challenge of this day caused some clerics, such as E. T. Baird, of the South to lament publicly: "Fearful brethren are the responsibilities of the master."[32] What southern clerics called "that day and hour of fearful reckoning" hung over the heads of masters like an ominous cloud. This made it all the more imperative that missionaries and clerics be unequivocally clear in their pedagogical instructions to masters.

DUTIES AND METHODS OF PEDAGOGY

Having made a theological case for the eternal value of the slave's soul, white preachers had to help masters overcome two fundamental phobias. One fear was that the Christian conversion of slaves would make them rebellious to earthly authority. A second fear was that teaching slaves to read, which was deemed necessary to make them Christians, would further enhance their potential for insubordination against their masters. Since such fears were real in the minds of masters, the burden was upon plantation preachers to disprove the rationale upon which they were based. The intellectual elite of the clergy produced a body of pedagogy (consisting of sermons, pastoral letters, catechisms, and addresses) to make African Americans both good Christians and good slaves. A descriptive analysis of at least three basic themes in the literature will illustrate our claim.

Conversion to Christ and a Model Slave

Plantation preachers used the following rationale to support the claim that conversion to Christ would make model slaves: (1) The theological and ethical proof that God had ordained slavery as a moral means of preparing the African for the introduction of Christianity. God had suffered the white humanity to enslave Africans to bring their souls to a saving knowledge of Jesus Christ. (2) The soul salvation of the white Christian was invariably intertwined with the soul salvation of the slave. White Christians believed that God had made them stewards of the sacred scriptures for this express purpose. Failure to do so would mean, as we have shown above, that whites would not be able to stand in good conscience before the judging Lord of history. Motivated by this fact alone, a group of intellectual elites of the plantation clergy set forth to prove by precept and example that conversion to Christ would make model slaves.

Their first task was to show that there was always a demonstrable difference in the slave's behavior following conversion to Jesus Christ. One way this was proven was for the missionary to show, through accounts of slave conversions, that the message of the gospel had the power to transform the slaves from their wild African nature. Conversion stories were told of recently arrived Africans who were catechized and converted to Jesus. A common description of such a slave's identity before conversion was that: "He was from Africa and totally ignorant of spiritual things." Such phrases as "totally ignorant" became a literary device for writers making a comparative judgment between the unconverted and the converted slave. It demonstrated the difference between the slave's state in Africa and the new one in the land of Christianity. As one missionary observed about that difference: "in their country they had all heard of the devil, but none had ever heard of the other one of whom I had told him, Jesus the Christ."[33] The objective of the missionary was to show that the African, despite a background of spiritual depravity, had a natural disposition for being taught the Bible: "He took my advice and began to call upon the name of the Lord of enlightenment and mercy."[34] Implied in this description is the notion that the greater the spiritual ignorance was among Africans the more receptive they were to instructional preparation for the gospel.

It was common, also, for the missionary to show that converted slaves could be instrumental in leading their unconverted masters to salvation. Missionaries were careful to show masters, who feared that it might make slaves lazy, that Christian conversion actually motivated slaves to be better workers. In one account a missionary notes, following conversion, that the slave's behavior the next day conformed with the plantation's work ethic: "he went to the field as one of us." Missionaries also showed that the slave might even influence an unconverted master to become converted. One missionary described the actions of an elderly slave toward his master following conversion. The slave's compassionate actions toward his master proved that conversion actually bonded him to his master and Jesus:

> The old African dropped his hoe and ran at once to meet his master, telling him in his broken way of the Jesus he had found, and entreating him also to seek the blessing which Jesus could only give.[35]

That Jesus could transform the life of a "pure African" was proof that Christianity could make a "bad nigger" good.

The belief that conversion to Christianity would make a "bad nigger good" was the antithesis of the philosophy that the slave must be a "good nigger" before qualifing as a catechumen. It appears, from reading the primary sources, that those who used the sermons and other sources were never free themselves of this contradiction. Missionary/preachers were certainly uncompromising in their conviction that the slave must be morally good, according to the master's definition of goodness, to be even worthy of Christ. Had they conceded otherwise, masters and preachers would have left room for the rebellious slave type, such as Nat Turner, to be saved Christians. A missionary's account of the conversion of a slave named Friday was used as a model lesson. Friday is described as "a genuine African, not so long from his native wilds and greegree worship that shadows of them do not hover about him."[36] Conversion gives Friday a new self-awareness of the dark places in his life caused by his African origin. The narrative account portrays him as being almost idolatrously grateful to the missionary for bringing him the gospel. Friday's gratuitous response is perceived by the missionary as being reflective of his idolatrous African ways: "he came near to drifting back toward the dangerous shoals of his old idol worship by setting up to himself an idol in the flesh."[37] Despite Friday's "wild dark African nature," which was believed to be both internal and external, the missionary portrays him as a model exhibit of what Jesus Christ could do for those of savage origin:

> In the clear, peaceful light of the gospel that had come upon him, he was a living illustration of the power of Jesus to tame and make as new creatures his savage race.[38]

In short, the word to anxiety-ridden masters was that the gospel of Jesus Christ would save the soul of the slave, as well as increase his economic value as a tool of labor in the slave market.

The missionary position above makes more sense, perhaps, when it is understood that unconverted slaves were stereotyped as being "deficient in the three cardinal virtues of veracity, chastity and honesty."[39] Some missionaries believed that conversion to Christianity would raise slaves to the moral level of their white counterparts; others were not as idealistic. One argument that was used by idealists to counter the pessimists about slaves' conversion potential was the biblical reminder that: "Where little is given little is required."[40] Idealists about slaves' spiritual nature would not compromise their conviction that conversion to Jesus Christ had the transforming power to change the African's savage nature. They were unequivocally convinced that "it had left him a new creature in Christ Jesus." In the same manner they eagerly awaited what it might yet do for him.[41] Slaveholders were not troubled by the variable of this unknown as long as it could be shown to be in their favor, and not undermine their authority. That is to say as long as it could be proven that Christianity would transform what they perceived to be the "sly, rebellious, trifling, untrustworthy, sexually promiscuous" African into a model of "humility, sincerity, simplicity, integrity, and consistency." It was expected that Jesus would make the slave a lover of law and order as defined and implemented by the master. The slave was expected to perceive work as a joyful lot, which it had pleased God to give him.

Despite these optimistic instructional accounts by missionaries, the question, Was it absolutely possible to bring black bond persons to Christianity without bringing about a concomitant spirit of rebelliousness in them? continued to haunt the anxious master. Rather than face the question directly, white clerics rationalized that Christianity would dignify the slave's status as a socially inferior servant in the eyes of God. White clerics claimed that Christianity would "raise obedience, humility, patience, and recognition to the level of high virtue"[42] in the slaves. Given this objective, it is understandable that many plantation owners required that the preacher to slaves "be a man of unquestionable piety; should be humble, dedicated and self-sacrificing; he must not accept popular applause."[43] This meant that these preachers, as we have shown above, often were required to assume a kind of marginal identity to their employers.

If preachers saw themselves as Christ's servant of the slave class, it stands to reason that they would portray Jesus as the exemplary servant-of-servants. They declared that this Jesus founded a religion that was "the pillar of society, the safeguard of nations, the parent of social morals, which alone has the power to curb the fury passions, and secure everyone his right."[44] This law-and-order Jesus blessed "the social order to the rich, the enjoyment of their wealth; to the nobles, the preservation of their honors; and to the princes, the stability of their thrones." Jesus was unequivocally opposed to "insurrection, anarchy and bloodshed-revolts against masters, or treason against states."[45] Slaves were admonished to imitate, in their own conduct, this Jesus who went about doing good, healing the sick and teaching people to repent of their sins. This law-and-order Jesus was "despised by the greater part of men, and the wicked Jews, and Pontius Pilate mocked him and put him to death." Advocates of the law-and-order Jesus told slaves who suffered mistreatment from their masters that: "Jesus had done no crime for which he was put to death; he committed no sin."[46]

Slaves were instructed to view Jesus as their great moral pattern who was worthy of their emulation in daily relationships with their masters and one another. It was made clear, of course, that Jesus chose to be an exemplary servant-of-servants. Many masters favored those slaves who consented to be Christlike in their servile status over unconverted slaves. If they chose to be like Jesus, slaves were expected to understand themselves as God's innocent sufferers of history, to be led as sheep to the slaughter, enduring the cross and despising the shame. Slaves were told to practice the hospitable spirit of Jesus that typified his life. In their actions, slaves were to love their enemies, to feed them, to give them drink, and to make them their friends by love and kind treatment. The primary objective of such a prescriptive ethic was to bind the slave to the will of the master in the name of Jesus Christ. It meant, in actuality, that slaves could only be saved according to their master's definition of "good works." In order for slaves to know what constituted their master's definition of "good works," it was necessary to teach them with the right method of pedagogy. This pedagogy was designed for oral instruction, since it was illegal to teach slaves to read.

Oral Instructions and Christian Servility

Given that it was a violation of the law to teach slaves to read, preachers and missionaries relied upon the method of oral instruction alone to educate slaves. Possibly very few, if any, of the clerics saw themselves compromising with evil when they accepted that it was a sin to teach slaves to read. Cooperation with masters, and not confrontation, was the rule since missionaries and preachers of the plantations were employees of the planter class. These divines defended the oral method of instructing slaves on the following grounds. It made possible the teaching of illiterate and intellectually inferior slaves; it amplified the effectiveness of the proof-texting process used to reenforce the slaveholder's unquestioned authority; it was effective in exciting the mind, awakening thought and keeping the attention of the slave alive; it created a social bonding between slave and master by bringing them into a face-to-face encounter with each other; and, it reenforced the slaves' need of organic dependency upon the master.

Pedagogical methods for accomplishing these objectives took two significant modes of instructional discourse. The first was what we will term the catechetical mode. Literate preachers of the master class were cognizant of the fact that the Greek verb *katechein* meant "to resound, echo" or "to hand down." Catechesis as an "oral re-echoing was a teaching technique of the early church, where it was understood as a verbal exhortation to live a moral life."[47]

Southern preachers, who wrote the catechetical materials, intended to make slaves merely the re-echoes of their masters' interpretations of Christianity. This method, at best, temporarily mollified many anxiety-ridden masters. It was inadequate for any permanent abatement, however, of whatever legitimate fears the masters must have had. The fear, for instance, that the slave might one day recognize the autonomous power of his or her own voice and substitute it for the master's instructed re-echoes. It must have been analogous to the ventriloquist's fear that the dummy, the re-echoer of the owner's voice, might one day speak out—rebelling against the need of the owner to speak through the dummy. This "banking" approach to Christian instruction might be interpreted as having been the mere postponement of an inevitably explosive problem. It could not rescue the slave from what whites termed a "helpless state of moral degradation"[48] without provoking the slave to raise questions and seek answers beyond the parameters of the catechism.

The second mode of instructional discourse was the sermon, written for what was described as "the childish mind" of the slave, that was designed for masters or preachers to read from when they assembled slaves for worship. Sermon writers for the slave population generally wrote with the following objectives in mind: (1) to make unnecessary the use of those preachers who might stir up the spirit of rebellion among slaves; (2) to enable the preacher, or reader to put oneself in sympathy with slaves, by using similar language with which they were familiar; and (3) to supply the master with the resources necessary for carrying out a system of household instruction.[49] A. F. Dickson, a Presbyterian minister, reasoned that the simplified version of sermons that he wrote for slaves would "give them a favour" in the view of blacks that belong to no other address. It was his impression that slaves "love the sermon; they love to recall and talk over the text of the sermon."[50] As a selling point for his specially written sermons, Dickson reminded pious masters that:

> Those who are accustomed from week to week to call together, the servants of the field or the house, to read, converse, and pray with them, or to instruct them from the catechism will find a valuable auxiliary in this volume.[51]

Among Presbyterian and Episcopalian clergy, sermonic and catechetical modes of discourse were viewed as foundational for preparing slaves to be Christians. This mode of discourse was the prerequisite for what might be termed postdiscourse expectations.

Postdiscourse Expectations

Among the cleric elite, Presbyterians and Episcopalians, the sermon and the catechism interfaced with each other in the liturgy for slaves. Depending on the preference of the worship leader, the sermon followed the catechism or vice versa. In either case, the preacher would query the audience to see if the hearers had comprehended the intended theological and ethical objectives of the catechetical or sermonic instructions. The following is a summary example of the way that the preacher utilized both the sermon and the catechism in the same worship service:

> The congregation rising in response to the preacher would repeat after him line by line the Apostle's Creed. Then came explanatory questions, which were readily answered. The commandments would next be repeated, and then the repeating of the Scripture, which was always carefully explained. After that a hymn was sung, a prayer offered, and the sermon began.[52]

Since it was deemed that slaves were highly emotional creatures by nature, primary emphasis was placed on preparing the slave's mind and heart for Christian conversion. This approach of the clerical elite was somewhat antithetical to that of the camp meeting revivalists, mainly Methodists and Baptists, who were great arousers of human feelings through both their techniques of preaching and singing. In order to counteract the emotional emphasis, J. B. Adger, a Presbyterian, called upon the church of the South to "thoroughly imbue [the slaves'] minds with the principles and the precepts of the Bible, and store their minds with facts and narratives of its history."[53] Preachers and teachers were admonished "to watch over [slaves] as far as possible both directly and indirectly and by means of class leaders, as a faithful shepherd watches over his sheep."[54]

In order to accomplish the paramount objective of the slaves' profession of Christianity, great emphasis was placed upon short sermons and brief catechisms. Short expositions were given on subjects that were pertinent to daily living such as: "the lying tongue," "the meaning of Christmas," "Good Friday," and "Easter Sunday." Moral lessons for the slave's daily living were drawn from the parables and the stories of Jesus' healing ministry. Dickson was adamant about the need, however, for the slave to learn biblical doctrine. He contended that it would better equip the slave for executing her or his duties in daily life. The presupposition was that if the slave knew what was expected by the master, the slave would do it.

The Catechism and the Slave's Mind

Interestingly, these leaders of the church had no theological problem with the idea that God was the Creator of the slave. They taught slaves, as a matter of fact, through their sermons and catechisms, that they were made in the image of God. The catechizer asked the slave: "Who made you?" The slave was told to answer: "God made me." The conflict came in the subsequent question: "For what purpose did God make you?" The master's answer in the slave's mouth became what might be termed the catechizer's ethical imposition upon slaves: "to please both my earthly and heavenly masters." Joseph Washington has noted in his study of the anti-blackness mindset of English religion that catechisms designed for slaves exceeded traditional theological questions. It is for this reason that he says that catechisms "were unadulterated mind control devices in the form of Christian indoctrination."[55] The following is a case in point:

Q. 37 When Negroes become religious, how must they behave to their masters?

A. The scriptures in many places command them, to be honest, diligent and faithful in all things, and not to give saucy answers; and even when they are whipped for doing well, to take it patiently and look to God for their reward.

Q. 39 Which do you think is the happiest person, the master, or the slave?

A. When I rise on a cold morning and make a fire, and my master in bed; or when I labour in the sun, on a hot day, and my master in the shade; then I think him happier than I am.

Q. 40 Do you think you are happier than he?

A. Yes: When I come in from my work; eat my hearty supper, worship my maker; lie down without care on my mind; sleep sound; get up in the morning strong and fresh; and hear that my master could not sleep, for thinking on his debts and taxes; and how he shall provide victuals and clothes for his family, or what he shall do for them when they are sick—then I bless God that he has placed me in my humble station; I pity my master, and feel myself happier than he is.

Q. 41 Then it seems every body is best, just where God has placed them?

A. Yes: The Scriptures say, if I am called, being a slave, I am not to care for it; for every true Christian, is Christ's free man, whether he be bound or free in this world.

Q. 41 How can you be free and bound both?

A. If Jesus Christ has broke the chain of sin, and freed me from the curse of the law, and the slavery of the devil, I am free indeed, although my body and services may be at the command of another.

Q. 48 Is there the same heaven and hell for white and black?

A. Yes: There will be no difference there, but what more holiness or more sin makes.[56]

Sambo and Toney: The Stereotypical Dialogue

Another mind-controlling technique used by white ministers was for them to create literature that portrayed slaves dialoging with each other about their souls' salvation. Such literature was prepared for white masters to show them that knowledge of the mind of slaves was important for leading them to Christ, and a pious Christian slave on the plantation could be instrumental in leading the unconverted to Christ. Edmund Botsford, a Baptist minister of South Carolina and Georgia, perfected imaginary dialogue among slaves to an art in his book *Sambo and Toney: A Dialogue Between Two Slaves*. According to Richard Furman, a prominent Baptist minister of that generation, the book was very popular among the reading audience of the antebellum South. Furman noted, in his words of tribute to him, that Botsford's objective for publishing the dialogue was for "the religious instruction of negroes, in a manner suited to the general capacity of that people."[57] The dialogue commences with a serious conversation between two slaves of different plantations on the subject of Christian conversion. Sambo initially expresses grave concern to Toney that, despite their deep friendship, death will separate them forever, since Toney has not been converted by Jesus Christ. Sambo is made to typify the converted slave who was supposed to be the envy of every master; Toney typifies the unconverted slave who was perceived as the liability of every master. A more detailed analysis suggests the author's intentions. First, Botsford intended to show that the converted slave was a needed alter ego for the unconverted slave. Sambo is portrayed in the dialogical construction as Toney's alter ego. Botsford presents Toney as a typical procrastinating slave who thinks that his youthfulness allows him plenty of time in the future to think about "the God question" and his soul. Prophetically, Sambo notes that slaves who wait until they are old to come to God are of very little utility value to his ministry, just as old slaves are of little value to their earthly masters.

Sambo's technique is first to provoke Toney to confess openly his private thoughts about God; second, Sambo interprets Toney's thoughts for him. Toney confesses that the extent of his experience of God was limited to a dream that he had. It was while in this state of dream consciousness, Toney remembered having experienced the travel of his soul into the "outer world," where he encountered an angry God who had the power to strike him "headlong into hell."[58] In the dream he heard an alter voice tell him: "Toney you have lost your soul; you can't repent; you needn't pray; God won't hear such a wicked man; you may as well go on your old way and get all the pleasure you can."[59] Sambo explains that this was the deceptive voice of the devil.

Botsford's second intention was to show the priestly influence of a converted slave patriarch upon unconverted slaves on the plantation. Following a provocative session with Sambo, Toney is troubled by the prayer that he hears Uncle Davy praying. Presenting him as a model Christian, Botsford summarizes the nature and purpose of Uncle Davy's prayer:

Uncle Davy prayed for master and mistress and the children; he prayed for the Lord to convert young master's heart, and he thanked the Lord for opening master's heart to let minister come and preach to us; and he prayed the Lord to bless the gospel on the plantation; and then he thanked the Lord for revealing Jesus Christ to him, a poor sinner; and then he prayed so heartily that he and all who were baptized might be kept from sin and might live peacefully and quietly together, and be honest and faithful servants, and remember that the Lord was always looking upon them; and then he prayed so earnestly that if any poor creature on the plantation was in trouble for his sins, the Lord would carry on the work in his poor soul until he found rest in Jesus; and a good deal more like that.[60]

Here Botsford presents the slave patriarch as a model of pious Christian servility whose words and deeds were intended to influence positively sinners such as Toney. Uncle Davy is portrayed, also, as the priestly patriarch in the slave community who makes intercessory prayer on behalf of his unconverted master and his household.

Botsford's third intention was to show how conversion, according to the master's definition, transformed Toney's behavior toward his master. Botsford's narrative takes us through Toney's preconversion crisis period to his confessional surrender of being: "a poor sinner worse than any other sinner in the world besides." The converted Toney is made to speak words of profound gratitude for salvation: "I now thank and praise God for sending his Son to die for me."[61] He confesses to his alter ego, Sambo, of how he felt initially when he realized he was being saved: "I was too happy; I say Glory, glory, glory to my God for ever and ever. I tell most every body I meet how good I feel."[62] Toney was first motivated, according to Botsford, to share his experience of transformation with his master:

I went to my master and fell on my knees, and said, Oh, my master, I've been a bad servant; I've been cursing and lying and stealing, doing every bad thing; I hope you will forgive me; I trust I shall never do the like again; I trust the Lord has pardoned me.[63]

Botsford gives us a stereotypical case of the plantation South's perception of what ought to have constituted the normative slave conversion. The converted slave was expected to be forgiven by his master in order to be forgiven by God.

Baptism as the Final Rite of Passage into Servitude

The final rite of passage that the slave had to go through to be considered a model servant was that of baptism at the hands of the white minister. This ceremony was designed to assure the master that the slave was a safe slave in the hands of Jesus Christ.

Baptism symbolized both theological and ethical legitimation of the slave into Christian servitude. It took place once the slave had done the following: (a) been instructed in the practical knowledge and the application of Christian doctrine; (b) received the consent of their masters with a good testimony and proof of their honest life and sober conversation; (c) repeated orally the covenant of consent, written by a white preacher, at the baptismal ceremony.[64] In some cases the slave's spiritual sponsor, generally the master or mistress, was expected to stand in the slave's stead until he or she reached the age of accountability. Spiritual sponsors, at the baptismal ritual, were expected to speak favorably of the slave's moral fitness for baptism. The fact that slaves were required to repeat the covenant of consent at their baptism, clearly showed the power and authority that whites assumed over slaves' bodies and souls. The following is an example of the way that the covenant of consent read:

> You declare in the presence of God and the Congregation that you do not ask for the Holy Baptism out of any design to free yourself from the duty and obedience you owe to your master while you live, but merely for the good of your soul and to partake of the graces and blessings promised to the members of the church of Jesus Christ.[65]

Another requirement was that the slave's name be changed to a Christian one at baptism. This signified that the slave had been made a new social, as well as, spiritual being. New names were given neophyte Christians from biblical characters, or, verses of the scripture by the godparent.[66] The slave was to acknowledge, when questioned at the ceremony, the gift of this new name.[67] The sponsor was also expected to stand as a buffer between the helpless one and the devil who was characterized as the "Accuser," "Tempter," "Serpent," and "the Wicked One."[68]

Slaves were not to interpret baptism, although it meant "the renunciation of the pomp and vanities of this wicked world," as a call to an ascetic life style. This would conflict with the work ethic of slavery. Baptism was to be understood as a symbolic indication that slaves had repudiated all signs and symbols of their African heritage such as witchcraft, drums, and dance.[69] Witchcraft was defined as being sinful because its practitioners pretended to "know and do only what God can."[70]

The slave was expected to be Christlike in deportment toward all superiors and other slaves. This was the genuine sign that God had truly converted the slave from the old African nature. The slave was to "love and pray for the master more than ever," as was demonstrated by Uncle Davy in the Sambo and Toney dialogue. Such a slave demonstrated to skeptical masters that Christian conversion was the best insurance policy against the rebellious slave. It undermined the teachings of those skeptics who said "that religion is of no use, has no good influence, does not make a people better."[71] This Christlike suffering servant slave was expected to live by the following creed:

To order myself lowly and revertly to all my betters; To hurt nobody by word or deed; To be true and Just In all my dealings; To bear no malice nor hatred in my heart; To keep my hands from stealing, my tongue from evil speaking, lying and slandering; To keep my body in temperance, and soberness and chastity; Not to covet nor desire other men's goods; but to learn to labour truly to get my own living, and to do my duty in that state of life unto which it shall please God to call me.[72]

Ironically slaves were expected to be model servants to those defined as their "betters" meaning "the governors, teachers, spiritual pastors, patrols and masters of the social order."[73] Those, so characterized for the slave, were said to be "wiser, higher, older, and more religious than himself."[74] Slaves were told that satisfying their "betters" was the earthly means to a heavenly end. It was in satisfying their "betters" on earth that they were made: (1) satisfiers of God's justice; (2) compassionate sufferers; and, (3) a perfect moral pattern after Christ. Missionaries and preachers always held up to the slaves, Jesus as the exemplary teacher who came to instruct the oppressed, as well, about heaven, hell, and salvation.[75]

CHAPTER 3

The Self in the Self Response

If white ministers' objective of their conversion language was to dehumanize slaves, how did slaves reconstruct a humanized view of themselves? How did they deduce from the misconstrued conversion language of the plantation divines a liberated notion of themselves? Slaves believed that God had transformed them into new beings with a radically different mission in the world — a mission that required them to live counter to plantation values. First, converted slaves believed that their status of new being in Jesus interiorly distanced them from the psychological abuse of slavery. It gave them the needed transcendent means of getting a critical perspective of both their masters and themselves. Second, slaves believed that their definition of conversion gave them a radical sense of God having disengaged them from the world for the purpose of calling them to radically engage it. This twofold perspective of new being and purpose gave the slaves a sense of divine worth in a world that negated their self-worth.

Of all of the language that slaves used to characterize the rite of conversion, none of the phrases made any reference to the blackness of the slave's own body. Occasionally, objects of slaves' visions such as Jesus, God, and angels were characterized as white. Slaves, moreover, saw the Devil in their visions as being black. Hell was imaged as being populated with the devil's black imps. They also made references to the white things of nature such as snow. Given this reality, it will be helpful if we do the following in this chapter. First, to show how the slave community retold the Creation story from the book of Genesis for the purpose of critiquing the white man's myth that God made white skin superior. Second, we will show how the community reconstructed the conversion language to address the metaphysical issue of the social self. A right perspective of the social self fortified slaves with an interior self capable of coping with the realities of a racist society.

A brief analysis of the slave community's use of creation language might illuminate the possible disjunctions between it and the conversion language. The slave community's stories of the Creation explicitly address the theme of skin color and function to demythologize the negative value given to black skin. Yet slaves gave practically no attention to the factor of their own skin color in their personal conversion stories. Among hypothetical reasons might be that white recorders of these stories as told by ex-slaves might have had very little interest in what blacks thought about color during the 1930s when most of the interviews of ex-slaves took place. Furthermore, given the hostile racial climate of the thirties, many blacks might have been reluctant to openly discuss the issue of race with white interviewers.

A few stories, however, about God and skin color were collected and preserved as part of the African-American folk tradition. Descriptive analysis of several stories will show that slaves did critically address the myth that God created white skin superior to black skin. The first story addressing the issues of hair and skin color, recollected by Charity Moore, is the biblical Creation story with Adam and Eve portrayed as black. A second story is based on the idea that at one time people lived in caves and there was no sun. The suggestion is that in some mythic time and place, when everyone had black skin, color was not an issue. A third story suggests that black people were created by the devil, while white people were created by God.

CREATION STORIES OF THE SLAVE COMMUNITY

Adam and Eve

A South Carolina slave by the name of Charity Moore retold a story told by his father Isaiah Moore, that highlights the color myth. Charity Moore, interviewed by W. W. Dixon, said that his father was "the Uncle Remus of the plantation." Charity recalled that his father, designated as the plantation's storyteller, told Bible tales to the slave children that he never told white children of the plantation. Charity claimed that his father "knew the catechism from cover to cover, and from the back to the startin' end."[1] Whites had rewarded Charity's father with a Bible for answering every question in the catechism. The catechism that Charity produced for the interviewer was published in 1840. One of the stories that Charity remembered being told for slave children only was that Adam and Eve were both black.

The story notes that *"the first man, Adam, was a black man. Eve was Ginger cake color, wid long black hair down to her ankles."* Adam's only worry in the garden was his *"kinky hair."* It was his state of dissatisfaction that worried Eve. The more Adam played in Eve's hair the higher his anxiety level rose when he remembered that she could not do that with his hair. During all of this the devil had been sitting up in the plum bushes observing the uneasiness taking place between Adam and Eve over Adam's lack of long straight hair. In the meantime Eve's hair was growing longer and longer. Adam stopped taking the usual walks with Eve. Noticing this difference in their relationship, *"the devil took the shape of a serpent, glided after Eve, and stole up and twisted hisself up into dat hair far enough to whisper in one of them pretty ears."* It was what the devil said that is of note: *"Somebody's got something for to tell you, dat will make Adam glad and like hisself again! Keep your ears open all day long."* Following this the serpent dropped to the ground and "crawled up into the apple tree, close by the fountain." According to the storyteller the serpent knew that Eve was going to the fountain to bathe. The devil knew that Eve was grief stricken over Adam's discontent with the status of his hair. Between the apple tree and the fountain *"the devil changed himself into an angel of light, a male angel."* It is Satan's actions as an angel of light that is worth noting in detail:

He took off his silk beaver hat, flourished his gold headed cane, and low: "Good morning! Lovely day! What a beautiful apple, just in your reach too, ahem!" Eve say: "I's not been introduced." "Well," said de debbil, "My subjects call me Prince, 'cause I's de Prince of light. My given name is Lucifer. I's at your service, dear lady." Eve 'flected: "A prince, he'll be a king some day." Then de debbil say: "of course, one of your beauty will one day be a queen. I seen a sadness on your lovely face as you come 'long. What might be your wory?" Eve told him and he low: "Just git Adam to eat one bite out dat apple 'bove your head and in a night his hair will grow as long, be as black, and as straight as your'n." "Us dare not tech it, lest us die." Then Satan stepped a distance dis way, then another way and come by and say: "Gracious lady! Dis tree not in the midst of the garden. De one in the midst is that crabapple tree over younder. Of course the good Lord didn't want you to eat crabapples." De debbil done got her all mixed up. De apple looked so good, she reached up, and quick as you can say "Jack Robinson," she bite the apple and run to Adam wid de rest of it and say: "Husband eat quick and your hair will be as long, as black, and straight as mine, in de mornin'." While he was eatin' it, and takin' de last swallow of de apple, he was 'minded of the disobedience and choked twice. Ever since then a man has a Adam's apple to 'mind him of the sin of disobedience. Twasn't long befo' de Lord come alookin' for them. Adam got so scared his face turned white, right then, and next mornin' he was a white man wid long hair but worst off then when he was a nigger. Dere was more to that tale but I disremeber it now.[2]

Charity's fragmented story, that he remembered from his father, of the Creation of the first man and woman reads almost like tragicomedy. The following things ought be noted about the story in relation to our discussion: According to this story the original man and woman were of an African hue. What this says, perhaps, is that there was a time when slaves of African descent saw the darkness of their skin as being natural and good. This was undoubtedly at a time before Africans encountered whites. Perhaps Charity's father is alluding to mythic time. It was the difference that Adam noted between the texture of his hair and Eve's that caused him angst. Hair in most cultures has been thought of as a symbol of both pride and vanity. It is the role that the storyteller gives the devil in the story that immediately demands our attention. The devil, by taking the form of a serpent, uses Eve's hair to get to her ear. But what is even more exciting in the story is the fact that the devil has self-transforming power. According to the storyteller, he transforms himself from *"a serpent"* into an *"angel of light."*

The devil cleverly sees that Eve, because of her worry about Adam's unhappiness, is a vulnerable candidate for eating the fruit of disobedience. He suggests that Eve give Adam the fruit that will transform his hair texture and length. Adam, who lacks self-transforming power, eats the fruit of self-transformation. Ironically, the story says nothing at all about the forbidden fruit changing Eve's physical appearance. This could be because she had expressed no dissatisfaction of the way that God had made her. It says, however, that a part of Adam's physical body was changed when he choked on the apple. This happened when he remembered, in the very act of eating, that he was being disobedient to God. Subsequently, the "Adam's apple" in the throat is a reminder of Adam's act of disobedience. The story makes it clear that the source of Adam's sin is that of ingratitude for the natural way that God had made him.

Fear derived from disobedience to God transforms the fearful's physical appearance into an unnatural one. It is the last sentence of the story that becomes the hermeneutical key for understanding it as having had the power of tragicomedy in the slave community: *"Adam got so scared his face turned white, right then, and the next mornin' he was a white man wid long hair but worse off than he was when he was a nigger."*

The story must have been used in the slave community to remind those slaves, who hated themselves for being black, of the terrible consequences of self-hatred. But the greater destructive consequence is that self-hatred can be the consequence of disobedience; disobedience produces the deformation of the physical self. It is for this reason that the storyteller says that Adam, who was transformed overnight into a white man, was in a worse condition than when he was a black man. One wonders does the storyteller have reference to Adam's ontological condition as well. Why was he "worse off" than before? Was it because he had fallen from favor with God? Or was it because he was a white man? Better still, was it because his desire to be the transformer of himself had placed him in the same sinful status with the white man? These are the kinds of questions with which the slave community must have struggled.

The Cave Story

An equally fascinating story in the slave folk tradition was told by slaves about a day when all people were black. It was a time, according to the storyteller when all people lived in caves and there was no sun. The people complained constantly to God about not being able to see each other in the dark. After a series of complaints from the people about being without light, God finally conceded to make the sun. God's one condition was that all persons be on time for the great cosmic event. The story has it that those who slept in the door of the cave got there first and were turned white. Those who slept closest to them where turned yellow. Those who remained in the remote parts of the cave, because they did not get there on time stayed black. It is clear in the story that the notion of white skin only has reference to the phenomenon of "time and space" since once upon a time everyone was black. The suggestion is that in some mythic time and place, when everybody had black skin, color was not an issue.

During the storyteller's narration of the story, a slave named John questions the storyteller about what he meant by the phrase *"all black people being plum black."* This phrase is the pivotal hermeneutical key for understanding the story because it challenges whites' presupposition about who is authentically white or black. Also, the phrase implicated the way that masters had muddled the biological boundary lines between themselves and their house slaves through their libertine miscegenational practices. The story makes a subtle attack upon the licentious behavior of these masters. Uncle Alford, the storyteller, provides an insightful clue to the narration when he observes: *"When Gawd made the sun, dem whut wuz sleepin on the backside of the caves didn't get no light a-tall en dey stayed black."* Here both the elements of subtlety and surprise are at work in the story. There is more at stake here than the stereotypical assertion that God made blacks to work for whites because the blacks are lazy by nature. Rather there is the subtle critique here of the spacial and temporal relations between masters and their slaves. This accounts for John's inquiry about *"slaves on the plantation not being plum black."* The latent message is that the closer slaves were to the master the more likely they were to resemble the master's skin color and features, and to assimilate his value judgments about time and space. The phrase in the story *"those on the backside of the cave"* undoubtedly had reference to field slaves. Also, there were slaves who ran away from plantations and spent years in the woods and caves. These slaves, more than likely, had not been affected by the white "sun" of miscegenation.

The "sun" in the story is the symbol of the white miscegenator. Note that the "sun" does not darken the subjects in the story. It, instead, lightens the color of their skin. Listen to the narrator of the story: *"Dem wut closer t' de do' got more light, en dey wuz lighter-colored than what was on the backside."* The historical fact was that yard servants were definitely tended to be of a lighter skin complexion than those who were field servants. Slaves who worked in the plantation house might be as white as the master himself. The storyteller clenches this point when he says: *"dem whut wuz sleepin' right in the do' mo wuz yaller."* Hence is the story a critique on the immorality of slaves' laziness? Or, is it a critique of the immoral behavior of the white miscegenator? White miscegenators failed to see themselves as the desecrators of the sacredness of slaves' beings.[3]

The Black Body as the Devil's Work

There is evidence that African Americans struggled with the question of whether the blackness of their bodies was the creation of the devil. Possibly the mythic question was: Why did God create whites to reinforce the notion of inferiority in those of African descent? A reported story from African Americans who lived far from white people's teachings and influence is very revealing. They believed that God was the Creator of the white race. These blacks thought that, according to the recorder, the black body was the handiwork of Satan. It was their belief that this making of a human being *"contra to the commands of God"* was the sin for which the devil, once an angel of high degree, was flung from heaven. The recorder of the story recorded it this way:

> Flung into hell en dar he be now tied ter de wheel er de chariot er fire! Chained ter de turnin' wheel er fire; en dar he gwine stay twel de great Risin' Day. The devil succeeding only in forming the shape of a man and without the soul, became as it were, a creator of death, but there come no life, dar come no breaf! But de Lo'd he feel's sorry for the dead man dat he gin him breaf en er soul same as er white man.[4]

The folklorist who recorded this story characterized it as an "uncouth legend." Why would blacks even entertain such a ludicrous notion that the devil would create a black body? Could it be that what we really have here is the African-American community's subtle attack upon the white community's flagrant disregard for the natural sacredness of their bodies? Was it not the objective of slavery to de-soul the body of the slave? All of this must have been viewed by the slave community as being *"contra to the commands of God."*

Satan's inability to create the positive out of the negative becomes the key theological issue in the story. The storyteller says of the devil's futile actions: *"He blew en blew, but dar came no life, no breaf!"* Note that while the Satan is given credit with being able to create a human form, the body, it is void of divine substance. Satan is recognized as having only the power to mimic God's actions as Creator; Satan is powerless to be an original creator.

The theological climax is reached in the story in God's response to Satan's colossal failure as creator. It is the status of the dead man, symbolic of Satan's failure, that provokes God to act: *"But the Lo'd he feel's sorry for the dead man dat he gin him bref en a soul same as he did de white man."*

Here we are given a clue of the slave community's profound theological understanding of what it meant to be created in the image of God. They understood their own creation as the result of the mercy of God. Despite all of the attempts of the satanic forces of slavery to make them into that which was less than human, only God was recognized as having the power to make the black body sacred. Satan is portrayed in this story as a monistic creator. God is portrayed as the only being with the power to create the great dialectic of spirit and flesh; of life and death.

CONVERSION AND TRANSCENDENCE

In the conversion sources slaves are in search of a vision of self that transcends the physical. It is for this reason that these stories must not be viewed as purely escapist language. Rather, they must be seen as dialectical language necessary for helping slaves deal with the complex relationship between the spirit and the flesh, between the religious and the social.

At least five elements are identifiable in the language through which the slave community expressed the normative conversion experience. An analysis of these elements is invaluable for understanding the slave's conversion experience.

The slave community formulated its own criteria for distinguishing between what it perceived to be an authentic conversion experience from one that was unauthentic. All claimants of the authentic conversion experience must have: "felt the power of God"; "seen the travel of his or her soul"; and "tasted the love of God."[5] This formula constituted the transitional phases that anyone, who claimed to have been born of the Spirit of God, must have experienced. The structure of normative visionary conversion language of the slave community is based on these three phases—*feel, see, and taste.* Individually and collectively, this language was internalized. It created a covenanted understanding of what actually constituted being converted by the Spirit of God. It was through this mode of language that slaves experienced having their ontological status radically changed.

Reconstructed conversion language allowed slaves to make the transition from the status of being the master's property to that of being authentic members of the family of God. This process was accomplished by God making slaves both *witnesses* to and *participators* in God's spiritual transformation of their lives. Slaves who had been defined and perceived as mere objects of their master's gaze could now enjoy subject-object awareness independent of the master's authority. God gave each convert significant partnership rights in the dialogue, which was a vital part of the salvation drama, that took place between God and the individual.

We will apply our thesis, first, to a particular conversion story of a slave named Morte. Second, insights from Morte's story will shed light on the notion of conversion as a death = life dialectic in the slave community's conversion language. Slaves understood that conversion took place when the power of God called the "new self" out of the "old dead self" ("dead" symbolizing the enslaved self) at what they termed "hell's dark door." Third, we will examine the notion of hell as the negative symbol of the eternal timeless place. Fourth, we will examine the notion of heaven as a positive symbol of the eternal timeless place. Finally, we will examine the value that conversion language gives to interpersonal relations.

I approach the slave sources with the presupposition that they implicitly bear the community's hermeneutic. Although greatly influenced by the leading thinkers of history, phenomenology, and hermeneutics,[6] I have tried to be faithful to the reading of the text as well as the slave's worldview.

Certain repetitive phrases in the conversion stories illuminate what must have constituted the slave community's normative visionary conversion language. The converted community formalized this pilgrimage rite of passage experience into what they called the "dying the sinner's death" phenomenon. Those who had this experience verbally defied the power of physical death over their future existence. Each of them victoriously testified to having experienced the gift of death-proof-status in Jesus. Confessionally each could say: "I have done died one time and I a'nt gonna die no more." Internalization of this sort of language helped slaves to overcome what we earlier termed the theology of double self-negation ("black of body and blacker of soul" consciousness) taught by white Christian leaders. It did this by giving slaves the spiritual sense of belonging to God as an embodied soul, that is, God's spirit possessed the whole self.

Slaves emerged to such a radical new consciousness of themselves by making the death/life dialectic of Jesus' "death" and "resurrection" the critical tenet of their faith-stance. This transitional process is identifiable in the constitutive elements of the slave community's normative conversion language formulas. It comprises the invaluable hermeneutical key of our inquiry and interpretation.

Slaves were made authentic members of the family of God in a world that refused to recognize them as being authentic selves. One primary belief of the slave community was that the spiritual travel of the soul to the timeless places of heaven and hell was mandatory for those who had been "struck dead" by the Spirit of God. The metaphorical language of having been "struck dead" by the Spirit of God really described the state of dream consciousness that only those experiencing the conversion of their souls might experience.

Dream consciousness was believed by the slave community to be a metaphysical gift from God that had placed the one experiencing conversion outside of the temporal self for the purpose of turning the universe of oneself and one's fellow human beings into objects of contemplation. Given the oppressive nature of slavery, it is understandable that the visionary world of slaves' conversion experience became normative for critically evaluating the social world of slavery. The community was confident that this gift from God — to transcend the oppressive structures of institutional slavery gave all persons the necessary critical insight for coping with the daily inequities of this world.

Perceived as a gift of God, slaves assigned preeminent value to the dream-consciousness experience. They prioritized it over both the master's liturgical and pedagogical instructions. Methodologically, dream consciousness made possible an interactional mode of communicating with God. It gave slaves a radically alternative awareness of being able to communicate with God. It empowered them with transcending power over the oppressive master-slave model. Freeing them temporally from the hegemonic world of the master, this mode of dream consciousness gave slaves a critical perspective of double consciousness that originated from a spiritual encounter with God. It gave them a vision of the greater Other; it took place in their own metaphysical world beyond the master's reach.

A second characteristic of the dream-consciousness experience was that only God could initiate it. Slaves rejoiced in the knowledge that they themselves did not know "when" or "where" God might decide to "strike them dead." In their rejoicing, slaves affirmed God's absolute freedom and power to act in the lives and events of human beings. Moreover, it mirrors the community's awareness of God's freedom to create and implement God's own liberation agenda. Affirmation of this fact gave slaves the needed sense of spiritual independence from the oppressive paternal authority of their masters.

Morte's Conversion Story

We know nothing about Morte's life other than his conversion story. He received God's gift of witness-participator during the course of his conversion experience. He came to experience God directly as his Creator and Redeemer when God brought the new Morte out of the old Morte. The old Morte is the passive object of the conversion experience and the new Morte is the witness-participator of it. God makes the new Morte a dialogical partner in the salvation experience to the point that Morte can raise questions about the different stages of the experience. It is the gift of dialogical freedom that is seen in the slave community's "call and response" communication structure. The freedom of inquiry into the actions of the Creator and Redeemer of his soul gives Morte a radically new sense of what it means to be given the status of agency in the world. Encounters with God made dialogical freedom possible for Morte. On the other hand, Morte's inevitable confrontation with the master disallowed the possibility of dialogue between the slave and master since the dialogue presupposed mutual trust. A mutual understanding for the need of dishonesty on the part of slave and master was often necessary for the relationship to work.[7] An interpretative analysis of the constitutive elements of Morte's conversion story, according to the conversion sensory formulas—feel, taste, see— illustrates our claim.

Feel the Power of God

The slave community believed that the revelatory power of God could only be experienced by the individual when God initiated the process of self-disclosure. It was believed that this happened to every individual only as a result of "God opening up his understanding and revealing his mighty works to him."[8] God initiated this transformation process in Morte's life while he was plowing in the corn field on his master's plantation. Hearing what he takes to be his master's voice, Morte dropped his plow and ran, fearful of being whipped. In the midst of flight Morte recognized that the voice of God was calling him both to judgment and mercy. First Morte hears God's call of mercy: *"Fear not my little one for behold! I come to you a message of truth."*[9] God's call of judgment is heard in the imperative to Morte: *"You got to die and can't live."* In other words Morte must experience the death rendering power of God that can only radically dissociate him from the untruthful structures of plantation time and space.

Morte reported that the power of God rendered him physically helpless: *"Everything got dark and I was unable to stand any longer."* The darkness undoubtedly symbolized for him the fixed boundary between the world of plantation space and time and that of timeless existence. This is indicated in Morte's confession: *"I looked up and saw that I was in a new world."* Again, Morte hears God's voice of trusting mercy in the new world: *"My little one, I have loved you with an everlasting love."* Morte cannot appreciate this language about God's faithfulness toward him personally until God has placed him in a new self-transcending position where he can see what the precarious state of his being was: *"I saw my old body suspending over a burning pit by a web like a spider web."* God made Morte both the witness-participator of his spiritual transition.

The God of visionary conversion rhetoric shows Morte both who he was and who he has become: *"a chosen vessel unto the Lord."* According to this statement, the new Morte is under God's ownership. Nowhere in any of the storytellers' accounts of slaves' conversion stories do they ever say that God recognizes them as being property of masters. Now under his new owner, Morte is empowered with the gift of agency that comes with this gift of "everlasting love." That is to say, Morte is now a free agent within the parameters of God's love. God's affirmation of this fact can be heard in the moral imperative and promise: *"Be upright and I will guide you unto all truth."* Morte is now free to choose God because God has chosen him. What must be seen here is that God's gift of agency and the gift of a human-divine working partnership (*"I will guide you in all truth"*) constitute an inseparable faith package.

It is very clear in the story that God relates to Morte on a different value system than does his slave master. The master relates to Morte on the basis of his former behavior under the slave work ethic that made good behavior on the slave's part a prerequisite to salvation. Prior to the vision, Morte had violated the slave work ethic by plowing up the corn. In the vision, the mistake-conscious Morte is being sent to work in God's field of labor under a new working arrangement or contract. On the plantation his master watches him work; in the vision God promises to work with Morte as both his *"guide and helper."* This new working arrangement of radical partnership with God is heard in the directive: *"Go and I will go with you. Preach and I will preach with you."*[10]

As God's working partner, Morte is placed under the work ethic of grace. He is told by God that: *"My grace is sufficient for you."* Under the servile work ethic of slavery, Morte is whipped for his mistakes; in God's field of labor, he is assured that his mistakes are covered by grace. What God's grace ethic gives Morte, that the slave system does not, is the gift of self-confidence as a laborer. Morte hears this in God's admonition regarding his new identifiable status of being for others: *"You are henceforth the salt of the earth."*

The temporary world of conversion dream consciousness, however, does not exonerate Morte from the reality of the everyday world of slave labor. *"Coming to his real senses"* is the phrase that Morte uses to show that he understood the difference between the world of dream consciousness and that of plantation reality. In the world of his *"real senses,"* Morte discovers that he *"has plowed up more of the master's corn"* than he had before he entered the world of conversion dream consciousness. How would the visionary rhetoric of Morte's experience help him negotiate his mistakes in the real world of his master? This became the inescapable test question for Morte. It must have been the case for every slave who professed to having had the visionary conversion experience. This must have epitomized the crisis moment in the slave's consciousness when God's absolute authority, that had been experienced in the conversion vision, actually conflicted with the authority of the plantation master.

Morte is sobered by his master's unwillingness to accept his alibi that God actually plowed up the corn.[11] In one sense Morte is right in his interpretation since it was God who struck him dead; it was God who carried him off into the world of dream consciousness. However, it is an answer that has no negotiable value in the master's world. Morte's answer indicates that he has not been converted by the Spirit of God to the point that he is willing to take full responsibility for his actions. He has not internalized God's promise, heard in the visionary rhetoric, of being with him, because he is still fearful of his master's power to punish physically. While enroute from the field to the barn, to receive his due physical punishment, Morte is succumbed in a vision for a second time by the power of God.

In the second conversion vision Morte experiences all three phases of the visionary conversion formula. He *feels* and *sees* and *tastes*, the power of

God in a radically new way. God's messenger, Gabriel, objectifies his sins to him as a great mountain, symbolic of his *"stammering tongue and his deaf ears."* The moment of liberation is experienced when Morte sees them rolled into hell. He is then commissioned by the heavenly voice to: *"Go in peace fearing no man."* The messenger assures Morte that the sign of his new liberation is in his heavenly gift of new speaking and hearing skills: *"I have cut loose your stammering tongue and unstopped your deaf ears."* It is important to point out here that what usually constitutes sin in the conversion stories is the "fear of being" in general. The allusions to the white Protestant evangelical understanding of sin as "drinking," "smoking," "gambling," and "dancing" are all symptomatic conditions of this "fear of being" in general. The convert is never told to stop these activities, but is told to: *"Be strong and lo! I am with you even until the world shall end. Amen."*[12]

See the Travel of the Soul

The theme of visionary soul travel is at the heart of Morte's conversion experience. It constitutes his radical dissociation from what he termed the *"world of his real senses."* The touch of God's power frees him from this world and takes him to the timeless visionary worlds of hell and heaven. Visits to both places make it possible for Morte to compare himself as a changed being to the preconverted self. It is God's power that takes Morte from the master's corn field, where he was working, to these timeless visionary places. God shows the newly converted Morte, at *"hell's dark door,"* just how insecure the unconverted Morte really was *"suspending over the pit of hell on a spider web."* God makes Morte a witness-participator in the vision of his own conversion experience. As witness, Morte sees his soul being liberated from "hell's dark door" and taken to heaven; as participator, he shares dialogically with God's messengers and God in the liberation process.

Visionary travel to heaven assures Morte that God has prepared him to be an agent for God's cause in the *"world of his real senses."* The message implied in God's deliverance of Morte from "hell's dark door" is: if God can deliver Morte from the devil and his angels, God can deliver Morte from the fear that he has of his master. This comes through very clear in God's directive that Morte return to the world of his master and be God's salvation agent. Such directives speak both directly and indirectly to Morte's fears of his master: *"Go in peace and fear not for lo! I will throw around you a strong arm of protection." "Neither shall your oppressors be able to harm you."* The term *oppressors* stands out in this directive because it rarely occurs in the tradition of the conversion stories. The phrase that appears most commonly is that of "your enemies." We might speculate that slaves sensed that the phrase "your enemies" was less threatening politically than that of "your oppressors." In the timeless place of heaven Morte is told by what means God used to save him: "I have saved you through grace by faith, not of yourself but as the gift of God."[13] This is a reminder to Morte that God must be the source for his strength and courage.

Taste the Love of God

Having "tasted the love of God," a common theme that runs through all of the conversion stories, is a metaphorical description for having ingested God's love. This is Morte's testimony when God transports him from the world of visionary consciousness back into the everyday world of slave labor. Motivated now by God's love, rather than the fear of his master, Morte has the needed faith and courage to tell his master what this God of his conversion vision rhetoric has commanded him to do: "to preach the gospel to all men." This charge takes precedence over his master's power. No amount of physical abuse from the master can deter Morte from his mission. The moment that Morte makes this confession he experiences the same feeling of liberation in the "world of his real senses" that he had known in that of his vision: "I felt a great love in my heart that made me feel like stooping and kissing the very ground."[14] It was a direct experience of having internalized God's perfect love that exonerated him from the fear of all mortal persons, even his master. Morte is now empowered with a dignified sense of humility that negated his old controlling spirit of servile humility that constituted the character of his unconverted nature.

Morte believed that the master was so affected by this new gift of love, emitted from his new self, that he was able to preach his first message to the plantation family. This gave Morte the opportunity to explain how God's power had worked upon him in the conversion vision: "I told them that God had a chosen people and that he had raised me up as an example of his matchless love." In addition, he had the courage to tell the master and his family that: "they must be born again and that their souls must be freed from the shackles of hell."[15] Morte understands that God's conversion power has placed him in the rare position to analyze his master's moral and onto-logical shortcomings.

An Embodied Soul Experience

The birth of embodied soul consciousness, as reflected in the slave community's interpretation of the conversion moment, was experienced as both a radical exterior and interior transformation of the self. The slave community expected each convert to be able to cite the "I looked new" formula that went: "I looked at my hands and they looked new; I looked at my feet and they did too." Newness of being was the consequence of the individual having "been born of the spirit of God, felt his power, tasted his love and seen the travel of his soul."[16] Slaves likened their experience of this rite of passage to having been "struck dead . . . ; killed dead by God and made alive." This death experience, ironically, was characterized as both a life-taking and life-giving phenomenon.

The most dramatic moment of the conversion experience, according to the narrators of it, was when slaves were overwhelmed by the Spirit of God at some unprecedented time and place. One might be working in the field, cooking in the kitchen, or lying across the bed when such dramatic moments of spiritual transformation occurred.

Slaves never mentioned, in these accounts, of being converted in the church of the master. This apparently was done intentionally to show that their conversion experience was in no way connected to the master's definition of religious reality. Slaves had experienced this "new reality" dimension of their existence over which no earthling, not even the master, had any definitive claim. They had, in fact, experienced the true source of freedom. The following signs were deemed true indicators of the subject having undergone the radical experience of spiritual transformation: *"A feeling of malaise; a vague feeling of depression or sickness that the individual was unable to rationally explain."* It often became the prime motivational factor that made a seeker of God out of a former sinner. The victim, rendered totally dysfunctional of motor skills, might speak of his or her condition as being analogous to *"some great weight"* pressing down. In addition, all verbal skills were generally lost momentarily, making natural responses such as laughing and crying impossible. A typical response was: *"I tried to cry and move but was unable to do either."*[17]

This feeling of paralysis generally signaled the preparatory moment for the candidate's radical dissociation, by the Spirit of God, from the routine assignments of the everyday world. Another true indicator of the power of God's seductive spirit over the candidate was the lack of communication skills. The subjective formula for describing this experience was: "I could neither speak nor move for my tongue stuck to the roof of my mouth; my jaws became locked and my limbs were stiff."[18] In addition, the individual often recalled having been fearful for no known reason, a "fear of being" in general.

Those seduced by the power of God told of having experienced *"being overwhelmed by darkness at high noon; hearing thunder, and seeing the flashing of zig zagging lightning; seeing the moon drip away in blood and feeling old hell itself shake on her foundations."* These catastrophic signs, borrowed from the apocalyptic language of the Bible, provided slaves with the means of making the radical transition to what became for them the world of visionary reality.

Hell's Dark Door

The new reality dissociates the visionary from all earthly reality, taking the self to the timeless places of both hell and heaven. Hell became a powerful symbol in the conversion stories of slaves, because it was the dreadful place from where God saved them. They were told by the divine messenger that they were fugitives from it. Hell is portrayed in their visions as a literal place of burning fire — the abode of the devil and his angels. It was the symbolic place opposite of heaven.

Hell in the conversion stories must be seen paradoxically both as the place of "no exit" and that of "the exodus." It is the marked place in the vision of the converted where God rescues the self from the deadly grasp of the devil. Hell is where the one seduced by the Spirit of God becomes the witness of and participator in the miraculous transformation of the self. The "traveling self" is taken in the vision to what she or he metaphorically calls *"hell's dark door,"* symbolizing the place of no exit! God tells the death-stricken one that she or he must wait here at *"hell's dark door"* for his or her transformation and *"orders to travel."* The following quotation is a descriptive account of how this transformation was understood to have taken place:

> I saw old satan and his hell-hounds. He set them after me and as he did I saw myself come out of myself. I was a little angel and I began to fly. I sailed along just high enough and fast enough to keep out of their reach. I looked to the east and saw a man standing looking at me as I flew. He sounded a trumpet and the hell-hounds tucked their tails and left off from running after me.[19]

In this description, slaves make analogies between experiences encountered during the rite of spiritual transformation, while at *"hell's dark door,"* to those on the plantation: *"being tracked down by Satan's hell-hounds"*; *"being chased by Satan with a lethal instrument"* such as a pitchfork. The more profound insight must be heard in the slave's account of being transformed into a new self. He sees himself, as spectator and experiencer, come out of himself. The self that came out was *"a little angel."*

This description provokes some interesting theological questions about how some slaves, if not all, understood the conversion experience. If the slave sees his newly changed self come out of his old self, what does this say about some slaves' understanding of the doctrine of original sin? Does it indicate that slaves did not fully buy into the white man's theological instruction of total depravity? The theological description *"I saw myself come out of myself"* might suggest that slaves were conscious of being possessed with some degree of intrinsic goodness all along. Slavery had undoubtedly forced the *"angelic self"* into submission. Another message implied here, perhaps, is that the slave cannot evolve into his *"angelic self"* until he flees from both his oppressor and the place of oppression itself.

Another common phrase that the convert used in describing his or her conversion was *"and I stood looking down on old me . . . lying at Hell's dark door."* The conversion experience, as depicted here, denoted the birth of positive double consciousness. It projected, as well, a dialectical understanding of the self as a body and soul phenomenon. The implicit idea of the *"exalted self"* looking down on the *"old dead self"* is that the former comes out of the latter. It, also, affirms the converted as witness-participator of God's transforming power. Slaves would have the chance, out of this dialectical experience, to see themselves both as objects and subjects of their own spiritual transformation. They were able to see, through the eyes of their newly transformed selves, the old servile selves from which they had been liberated. The converted often spoke of seeing his or her *"new self"* in a triumphant position over the *"old servile self."* The experience is expressed in a variety of ways: seeing the old self at *"hell's dark door";* dying and seeing oneself having a temporal and spiritual body; as experiencing the self as *"a being in a being, a man in a man";* having seen *"one of ones' spirits washing the feet of the other spirit";* and, seeing the newly transformed self standing adjacent to the old servile self *"at the brinks of hell."*

Hell and the Sinner's Death

Hell is where one *"dies the sinner's death."* The visionary sees and hears all those who did not escape hell groaning and suffering there. Its victims are heard to cry: *"Woe! Woe! Woe!"*[20] Those who die the sinner's death might request to be taken to see hell before being allowed to see heaven, suggesting that there was a need for them to make their own comparison between the two places.[21] Hell is characterized as the place of death and chaotic destruction: *"human souls are piled up on top of each other";* *"ravenous beasts, ready to devour their prey, fill its deep chasm";* *"people are seen roaming and staggering along in utter chaos."*[22]

Hell and Slavery

Many slaves made analogies between their slave experience and hell itself, calling slavery *"hell without fires."* The bitter experiences of slavery undoubtedly made many slaves believers in hell.[23] It was at *"hell's dark door"* that the slave said of his spiritual transformation that *"my dungeon shook and my chains fell off."* All of the metallic body paraphernalia, associated with the slave experience, were left in hell: *"My sin heavey as lead came off and fell in the bottomless pit of hell."* A clear indication of liberation was when the liberated would see *"the sparks fly up"* from the sinful metal trappings that imprisoned the body. Another phrase commonly used for leaving the *"old servile self"* in hell was *"done been shuck over hell."*[24] The colloquial term *"shuck,"* commonly used by the harvesters of corn crops and seafood crops might provide an additional insight to what slaves meant by the converted self phenomenon. Shucking has to do with a stripping away of the outer layer, which is generally considered worthless, from the inner source. Was the slave community saying that conversion happens when God places the individual over hell and strips the unreal self off of the real self and leaves the former to hell's destructive consumption?

There was also a notion among some slaves that hell was really more metaphysical than concrete. This is illustrated in the story of an African American who told of his spiritual experiences of wandering through the realm of lower darkness before seeking church membership. During one exploration, he reportedly asked his guide: *"Brother, whar's de fire?"* Before replying, the guide stopped, turned to his questioner, opened up his heart — *"same as a cook-'oman opens a stove door,"* and all within his bared breast the horror-stricken seeker beheld a rolling, whirling sea of flame. The guide said lamentingly: *"for, oh, my brother, . . . hit's widin, — de fire is widin!"*[25]

Hell as the Home of the Devil and His Angels

Hell is the home of the devil and his angels. A story in the black American folk tradition credits the devil with being the original bringer of fire to the world:

De first fire was brung to de worril from de devil; hit's long been quench fer ourns usin', but dat left wid de devil, hit ain't never done been quench, and never is ter be.[26]

Satan, in his abode, is characterized in the conversion stories as the great tempter of the one who has been transformed by the Spirit of God. The devil and his angels are noted for such shenanigans as: *"Sticking out their tongues and making motions as if to lay hands on the fugitive from hell and drag him into the pit"*; *"Growling with anger at the fugitive"*; *"Hotly pursuing the candidate for salvation"*; and, *"throwing metal balls at the fugitive."* It is only when a heavenly agent intervenes in the spiritual traveler's behalf that Satan and his angels are forced to retreat back into the pit of hell.

Satan is depicted also as having a physical disability: *"a club foot as red as fire."*[27] He was said in some of the stories to have a *"club hand."* His face was portrayed as *"black as it could be and his eyes as red as fire."*[28] He is even seen *"sitting in the middle of the smoke of hell with his eyes wide open staring at his prey."*[29] One of the most terrifying images was for the fugitive to see Satan, similar to the way that the master did, coming after him on a black horse with a pronged fork in his hand.[30] Despite all of the similarities that can be made between Satan's behavior and that of the malevolent plantation master, narrators of the stories never explicitly make mention of the white master.

The Timeless Place of Heaven

Heaven and Its Liberator

Heaven is portrayed in the visions as the home of Jesus, the liberator. It is the ultimate home of the new convert. In the visions, the heavenly liberator is given such titles or names as *"an angel,"* *"Jesus,"* *"Gabriel,"* and *"a voice from God."* The true mark of the liberator is always known by his reassuring words to the fearful such as *"Be not afraid!"* Other phrases that made up the formulas of reassurance were some of the following: *"My little one, I have loved you with an everlasting love"*; *"You are this day made alive* and freed from hell"; My grace is sufficient for you"; "You are a chosen vessel unto the Lord"; "My little one be not afraid"; "I am God Almighty I freed your soul from death and hell"; "I am with you an everlasting prop."[31] Those who were sick and confused were told: "I am a doctor that cures all diseases."[32] The lost and confused are told: "Follow me. I am the Way, the Truth and the Life and the very door to my Father."[33] These consolatory words were confirmed by "shouts and amens" from the angelic hosts surrounding the throne of heaven.

Converts were given a tour of heaven that, actually, gave them a foretaste of joy divine. After being rescued from hell, the transformed self is taken in the vision to the new home for a temporary tour. Heaven is depicted as the place of eternal joy, where one sees all loved ones who have preceded in death. The culminating joy of heaven is to commune with those of the heavenly community. Here, one has an opportunity to see: his or her name written in the Lamb's book of Life; God sitting in deep contemplation on the throne; members of the heavenly family in holy communion with each other. All these experiences are indicators that the witness-participator has been liberated from "hell's dark door." While on the heavenly tour the traveler might even be baptized by Jesus and consecrated for earthly service at the heavenly altar. Such ritualistic initiations that took place in the visions indicated, undoubtedly, that slaves of this mind-set wanted to radically dissociate themselves from the white church's definition of religious purification.

Heaven as a Dialectical Symbol of Timeless Space

Slaves found the notion of heaven to be nutritious spiritual food for their oppressed imaginations, as have many other oppressed groups through the ages. They thought of it as a timeless place where the converted anticipated living eternally with God and God's host. Heaven is a complex rather than simplistic notion in the conversion stories. It might be asserted theoretically that heaven had dialectical implications for experiencers of conversion in the following sense. On the one hand, it was perceived as the ultimate place of destination where the redeemed would receive from God their compensatory reward for having been faithful in this world. On the other hand, God took the candidate for conversion there temporarily for spiritual empowerment that made coping responsibly with the immoral world possible. Visitation of heaven by the candidate for conversion was to be understood only as a brief visionary experience. In the visionary experience, heaven was where the candidate celebrated, with the heavenly family, God's redeeming power. Two basic symbolic descriptions of heaven stand out in slaves' portrayal in their conversion story accounts: First, the symbolic description of the route to heaven. Second, the symbolic description of the hospitable nature of heaven's denizens.

The "little path" to heaven metaphor. Great self-discipline was required of all earthlings whom God had saved from "hell's dark door" for the heavenly journey. This is symbolized by the *"little path"* that the convert claims to be placed on following deliverance from *"hell's dark door."* The convert recalls being turned by Jesus from the *"big road into a little path."*[34] These contrasting images of structured pilgrimage, the *"big road"* and the *"little path,"* undoubtedly reflect the plantation landscape of the slave's everyday world. In the spatial arrangement of this world, the plantation mansion stood at the end of *"big road";* slave quarters were at the end of the many *"little paths."* What the slave did in the conversion story accounts was to invert the spatial metaphors of plantation topography in the description of going from hell to heaven. Heaven is at the end of the *"little path";* hell is placed at the end of the *"big road."*[35]

The *"little path"* might require that the converted one go *"through the fire,"* which is symbolic of the structured self-sacrifice that the traveler had to go through in order to reach heaven.[36] Another description for this narrow path of travel was a *"little white path."*[37] This might have been symbolic of the path of the Milky Way that slaves used as a planetary guide for travel at night when they took the Underground Railroad route to the North. In one account, the convert said that: *"through the spirit I came to see the meaning of the thicket briars, the snakes, the dogs and the cows. They were my enemies."* These were the natural obstacles that slaves had to encounter in their attempt to flee from the plantation to freedom. Jesus was perceived as the freedom guide who counseled against fear, *"be not afraid,"* and who promised eternal guidance: *"I will ever be thy guide."* The *"little path"* metaphor in Jesus' instructions might be likened to the fine print on a contract. One might fail to read it at a great personal risk. It was for this reason that the convert had to always be attuned to Jesus' exhortation to: *"Keep thy feet in the straight and narrow path and follow me and all the demons in hell shall not be able to cause you to stumble or to fall."*[38]

The place of hospitality. On the tour of heaven the traveler was assured by the heavenly host that it was a place of eternal rest from the many trials and tribulations of this oppressive world. This was affirmed by showing the traveler: (a) A customized seat in heaven, symbolizing very-important-person status that God has for the weary traveler upon victorious arrival. Converts, during their temporary visits to heaven, told of having seen and sat in their VIP seats. Individuals said jubilantly: *"I also saw my seat and sat in it."*[39] (b) One's name written in the Lamb's book of life, signifying that his or her soul had been protected by God's ultimate sacrifice in Jesus.[40] (c) One being greeted by a special welcome committee, signifying his/her very-important-person status.[41] (d) One being dressed up by his/her heavenly mother and told *"Everything just fits."*[42] (e) One being baptized and commissioned by Jesus.[43] (f) One being given a freedom ticket, with one's name written on it, from hell to heaven, signifying the personal dimension of salvation freedom.[44] (g) One being shown one's special bed to sleep in that awaits the convert's final arrival.[45]

On the other hand, slaves understood heaven as the timeless place where

God commissioned the converted to be a moral agent in this world. The slave's radical understanding of agency grew out of his or her dialogical encounter with God and God's heavenly hosts. Slaves practiced moral responsibility in the everyday world, following the conversion experience, with an acute sense of being under the monitorship of God. It was being acutely sensitive to the fact that God saw all that they did and heard all of what they said. God kept a record of their moral conduct in the world.

Moral Empowerment: Doing and Being for Others

In contrast to *"hell's dark door,"* heaven is where the traveler can have dialogue with the tour guide (liberator), as well as with God. Satan uses the monological mode of communication. On the heavenly tour, the traveler can ask questions, as well as honestly express whatever doubts and fears she or he might have. The confused traveler might ask the question that Paul asked God on the Damascus Road: *"Lord, what will you have me to do?"* In response, the heavenly Liberator might be heard to instruct simply, *"Follow me."* Nowhere in the narratives does the witness-participator ask questions of the devil. This might very well reflect the fact that slaves knew that the devil, like the master, did not deem them qualified to be dialogical partners. The slave feels free to ask for clarification about anything that is confusing or alien to his or her experience, for example, *"Lord, how long do I have to lay here?"* and *"Lord, what is this?"* All such questions were indicative of the slave community's belief that to be in God's presence assured one of the freedom of inquiry. Awareness of this freedom made the slave a more effective moral agent in the world. It was a gift of God-consciousness that liberated the converted to be and do for others.

The slave's visionary account of his or her conversion has been viewed by scholars traditionally as being escapist in function and nature, the product of a childish imagination. Admittedly, there is the element of what scholars have preferred to call escapism, otherworldliness, in these stories. I have chosen to call it the element of radical dissociation. We are more capable of seeing the dialectical nature of the conversion story, perhaps, when that which has traditionally been understood as escapism is reassessed as radical dissociationalism. Radical dissociationalism requires that the convert has to be radically disengaged from the everyday world by the power of God in order to be commissioned for a radically new kind of moral engagement of it. It is the ethical imperative that grows out of this theory of radical dissociationalism that makes it dialectical in nature.

Historians of the slave sources have failed to address critically the following question: Why did slaves, if they were only interested in the other world, believe that they had been commissioned as God's moral agents to return to this immoral world? Has this question been avoided because of its profound theological implications? I would contend that the ethical imperative to be directly engaged, in the everyday world, is the climactic element of the conversion stories. It is the true sign, perhaps, of their authenticity. Had the slaves been merely indulging their childish imaginations, it would have made more sense for them to end their conversion stories with having been taken to heaven in the vision. This would have been understandable since there is a side in all of us that can be seduced by the "and they lived happily ever after" temptation.

Contrary to any such temptation, as real as it might have been, slaves claimed to have encountered the God who empowers the morally impotent of the world to be radically engaged in its moral transformation. This radical element, in my estimation, has been too long overlooked by the students of slave literature. The slave community identifies strongly with the theme of commissioned responsibility that is at the heart of Christian teachings. It was this element of the religion that white missionaries and preachers strongly accented as they taught slaves Christianity. They failed to see, however, that slaves would not be able to internalize this spiritual idea without being transformed by it. Also, they were unable to foresee, as well, the implications that this spiritual principle would have for slaves' response to the political and social reality of slavery. If the God of the conversion vision transformed them to be radically engaged as moral agents in the world, this meant that slaves had a new reason for being and doing in the world. We might say theoretically that the slave community's conversion experience language became its means of constructing a metaphysical understanding of the self that was grounded in its own social reality. Another look at the visionary language in the stories will illustrate this thesis.

In the vision, the heavenly liberator meets the helpless slave at *"hell's dark door"* and says, *"Behold yourself."* This directive implies that the victim of oppression was conditioned to see oneself only through the eyes of the master. The convert says that: *"I looked and I was all dressed up. I had a golden crown on my head and sandals on my feet and a long snow white robe covered my body."* All of this royal paraphernalia, of course, symbolized that the new convert had membership status in the family of God. The messenger explains for the convert "how," "where" and "the reason why" this new change took place: *"Behold, I have dressed you up at the doors of hell and you are ready for travelling."*[46] The power to see oneself independently of the oppressor was a true sign of the gift of spiritual liberation. Those who have seen themselves are now able to hear the heavenly messenger's *"follow me and fear not"* directive. When they are taken to heaven they are told by God who sits on the throne: *"Whomever my son sets free, is free indeed."*

The liberated is counseled in the vision to overcome fear, which is the source of enslavement: *"Trust me for one thing, trust me for all. I will take away all your fear."*[47] The liberated can trust the liberator *"not to put any more on him than he can stand."*[48] The God of the conversion experience assures the converted that God has the reins of life in God's hands; God cleans the convert of all iniquity and reminds him or her that: *"By grace are you saved and it is not of yourself but the gift of God. Weep not for you are a new child. Abide in me and you will never fear."*[49] Those of this experience trusted God to *"unstop their deaf ears, cut loose their stammering tongues and open their blinded eyes."*[50] God reassures the converted that God has been Creator, Redeemer and the Ancient Defender of his or her being:

I looked upon you in the dust of the earth and blessed you with an everlasting life. You are fixed and prefixed and brought at the lamb's sale and caught up in the election and ready for the building.[51]

God assures the converted eternal security against the *"plucking power of hell."* The critical elements of faith and trust will keep the subject: *"Believe and be of good cheer. You are my child and all hell is not able to pluck you out of my hand. I have loved you from the foundation of the world."*[52]

The ethical imperative demanded that the convert *be* an example of the new being: *"My little one, be not afraid"; "be strong"; "be faithful"; and "be ready."* The convert was to *be* God's *"workmanship and the creation of his hand."* In addition, the ethical imperative required that the converted become an active partner with God. This principle is asserted in God's response to the fearful complaint to the Lord of the one commissioned to reenter the world: *"If I did they would not believe what I say."* God's counterresponse signifies God's partnership with the newly commissioned: *"Go and I go with you. Open your mouth and I speak through you."* One was to go, and above all, *"tell the world what a dear Savior she or he had found."*[53] The command is *"Go and declare my name to the world and I will fill your heart with song."*[54] God is the one who tells the victim that *"I will be on your right and your left hand. I will be a refuge and a fortress."*[55]

The above principle is best illustrated in a story told by a former slave of South Carolina, who remembered the change in his mother's daily conduct following her conversion experience:

When I got to be a big boy my Ma got religion at the Camp meeting at El-Bethel. She shouted and sung fer three days, going all over de plantation and the neighboring ones, inviting her friends to come and see her baptized and shouting and praying for dem. She went around to all de people dat she had done wrong and begged der forgiveness. She sent for dem dat had wronged her, and told dem dat she was born again and a new woman, and dat she would forgive dem. She wanted everybody dat was not saved to go up wid her.[56]

Conversion gave the converted, according to this story, the moral energy to rise above the alienating psychological and social structures, caused by hatred of plantation life. It empowered the converted mother with a new sense of freedom that allowed her both to forgive her offenders and receive their forgiveness. Here we have a marvelous example of the way that converted slaves must have understood the biblical notion of the priesthood of believers.

Converts who were aggressive in their willingness to forgive and be forgiven made redemptive ethical conduct a living reality in the life of the human community. This was an authentic indication in the eyes of the slave community that true conversion had taken place in the total being of the claimant. True conversion was more than feelings of ecstasy and emotional catharsis. The converted mother was now free to be and do for others in God's name.

The converted mother in the story, also, is endowed with the gift for dialogical liberation with those who are enemies in human community. This gift gave some slaves, and understandably so, a sense of moral superiority over their cruel masters. Such is heard in the account of a former slave by the name of Charlie. Approximately thirty years following his escape, Charlie encountered his old master in the public square of an unnamed town. Charlie said that the following conversation took place between them:

> "Charlie, do you remember me lacerating your back?" I said, "Yes Mars." "Have you forgiven me?" he asked. I said, "Yes, I have forgiven you." There were a lot of people gathered around because we were a little distance apart and talking loud. ... He asked me the next question, "How can you forgive me, Charlie?" I said, "Mars when we whip dogs we do it because we own them. It is not because they done anything to be whipped for but we just do it because we can. That is why you whipped me. I used to serve you, work for you, almost nurse you and if anything had happened to you I would have fought for you. ... I used to drive you to church and peep through the door to see you all worship, but you ain't right yet, Master. I love you as though you never hit me a lick, for the God I serve is a God of love and I can't go to his kingdom with hate in my heart." He held out his hand to me and almost cried and said, "Charlie, come to see me and I will treat you nice. I am sorry for what I did." I said, "that's all right, Master, I done left the past behind me." I had felt the power of God and tasted His love and this had killed all the spirit of hate in my heart years before this happened. Whenever a man has been killed dead and made alive in Christ Jesus he no longer feels like he did when he was a servant of the devil. Sin kills dead but the spirit of God makes alive.[57]

A school of recent scholars, William Andrews being among them, have contended that such stories, often written by ghostwriters, were designed as political attacks against the religious hypocrisy of professing Christian slave masters. Their main objective, of course, was to demonstrate the slave's moral superiority in the face of the oppressor, as well as the barbaric nature of slavery itself. There might be an element of truth in such a claim. Our primary concern, however, has been to show that the slave community believed that a genuine conversion experience with God gave them the moral power to be bearers of God's forgiveness. We have in such idealism the making of the moral residue that anticipates the spirit of nonviolence that would not happen as a movement until approximately a century following slavery.

The objective of this discussion has been to show that the slave community reconstructed the Christian language to shape a new sense of the self that affirmed them as being sacred embodied selves in the sight of God. In an attempt to prove this thesis, we have made the case that the hermeneutical key for interpreting these stories is found in the community's structural method of narration. This language gave the individuals the needed radical dissociation from the oppressive structures of slavery. Individuals of the community, through the mode of dream consciousness, were allowed to see themselves transformed from an alternative perspective of timeless space. In short, they were shown themselves through the eyes of their newly discovered Creator, Redeemer, and Revealer. This made each converted slave a legitimate witness-participator of his or her newly changed self. This gift of radical dissociation from the temporal structures of oppression empowered slaves to become new agents of change in the lived world. It gave them a radically new sense of being for the other — even the oppressor — in God's behalf.

CHAPTER 4

The Spirituals: Community in Song

It was shown in the previous chapter that slaves, in their reconstruction of the conversion language, worked out a dialectical method of self-understanding about Jesus Christ and God. In doing so, they resolved the body and soul dilemma that masters imposed upon them. Slaves' resolution grew out of an existential need for a reconstructed conversion language reflective of both their personal and corporate experiences with God in the crucibles of slavery. This language gave the individual and group the critical interior distance from the oppressive structures of slavery. It gave converts the spiritual and social means for overcoming the oppressor's devaluation of their bodies and souls.

If personal salvation was the source of individual self-worth, communal singing among converted slaves gave them a sense of corporate self-worth. It forged them into a collective sense of being a new social body in God. Slaves undoubtedly valued this radical notion of subjectively being in Christ and God as a prophylaxis against the physical and psychological abuse perpetrated upon them by malevolent masters and overseers. They valued, as well, being identified as a member of God's social body in the world. Their new identity noted that God had radically disengaged the converted from the world so as to empower them to engage it prophetically and priestly. Conscious existence in God's social body gave converted slaves a prophetic and priestly sense of corporate responsibility in the sinful world. An acute communal consciousness of being in the master's world, but not of it, is what constituted a radical understanding of dialectical freedom in converted slaves. Each slave was reminded that it was only the power of God that could forge individuals into a prophetic and priestly social body without destroying their individuality.

Slaves were made to see that just as personal conversion was God's way of releasing the "concealed self" from its "old dead self," corporate conversion was God's power to forge community out of alienated selves. Many of the spiritual songs of the slave community are but lyricized affirmations and celebrations of this fact. The songs make evident the fact that converted individual slaves believed that God gave them the gift of liberation community. It was dialectical in the sense that they were made one in God while remaining individual persons of God.

The thesis of this chapter is that the converted slave community's lyricized conversion language reflects its ability to maintain creative tension between the individual and the community. Lyricized conversion songs must be seen as the community's pedagogical method of the celebrative affirmation of this fact. Songs made it possible to teach each other what it actually meant to have had one's soul anchored in the Lord. Lyricized conversion language gave slaves a radical sense of being free to dialogue among one another in the face of their slave masters' oppressive monological structure of communication. It afforded them, indirectly, a creative way to critique the oppressive nature of their masters' monologues. Lyricized conversion language put to song became the ritualistic means of forging a creative singing community. The singing act itself symbolized the socially objectified consciousness of the oppressed. This ritualistic way of creating community enabled slaves to overcome the problem, inherent in white Protestant evangelical rhetoric, of being an individual spiritual self of God versus that of being identified as prophetic and priestly social selves in the spirit of God. Lyricized conversion language mirrors how slaves overcame the social aspects of the body and soul problem. Slaves used primordial somatic symbols of the human body such as "hands," "feet," "eyes," to express their notion of the ideal community as God's social body. These somatic images allowed slaves to make the transition from being a mere individual self in God to being a body of social selves in God.

THREE PEDAGOGICAL TYPES

Our thesis will be illustrated by showing that three types of teaching methods are found in lyricized conversion language: the *communal* confessional and exhortation type; the *individual* confessional and exhortation type; and the *dialogic* confessional and exhortation type. All three of these types implicate the dialectic of individualism and community in slaves' faith claims about God. What did it mean to exist in a new I-we relation in Christ, and one another, when the conditions of institutional slavery were designed to foster an I-it relationship between master and slave? In reconstructing its language, slaves' greatest challenge was to find in Christianity the key for freeing themselves from alienation collectively and individually. Members of the community used conversion language for the following pedagogical purposes: to instruct the unconverted (in the community's own reconstructed language) about conversion; to receive and celebrate the neophyte's conversion testimony; and, to remind one another of their mutual duties ultimately to God, themselves in particular, and "everyman" in general. The lyricized language of slaves, reflects slaves' accumulative wisdom derived from their collective and individual sufferings. Also, it afforded them the constructive means of responding to each other from an I-we perspective rather than an I-it one. The individual slave converted in Jesus knew that his or her new birth of liberated "I" awareness was dependent, also, upon the contribution of the converted slave community. It had not taken place, by any means, in a vacuum. Critical examination of the exhortative and pedagogic themes in the spiritual song language is clearly indicative of the fact that the slave community understood this process.

The Communal Confessional Type

Contemporary readers and hearers, too often, tend to dismiss the song lyrics of the communal confessional type as having had only compensatory spiritual value, at best, for the slave community that created them. However, this lyricized conversion language commonly objectified two fundamental notions of freedom — as both a present and future reality — the converted community's messianic hope in the future and its realistic hope in the present. Scholarly investigation, such as is evident in the work of John Lovell,[1] has clearly substantiated this double meaning principle (i.e., spiritual and social) in the song language. Other studies have also taken seriously this principle operative in the spirituals.[2] Most have shown that slaves used the spirituals as both a code language for communicating with each other while on the plantation, and for organizing escapes from the plantation world to free territory in the North. Lovell's methodology was to study the spiritual song text of the slave community as a cultural phenomenon. This discussion follows Lovell's approach in that it focuses on the way in which the slave community created, through its song expressions, its own criteria for being individuals and community in Christ.

The Myth of Song Origin

Many slaves, because of whites' negative responses, readily came to see the latent power of their songs and their capacities to sing them. A folk tale, recorded by Langston Hughes, gives a mythic explanation of how this came to be. In summary, the story has it that the mythic hero of the slave community, High John De Conqueror, who walked among slaves on all of the plantations, happened to visit a particular plantation where they were being driven unbearably by a cruel master. Touched by their cries and groans, High John told the people *"What we need is a song."* Since it had to be a particular piece of singing, High John, who later came to be known as Brer Rabbit, concluded that they would have to go in search of the song. The slaves, however, were afraid to leave because of master. When they agreed to go on the condition that they had something to wear, John gave them the metaphysical challenge of finding what they needed inside of themselves. Then John summoned them to get out their musical instruments, which were inside where they got their clothes from, so they could play music on the way. A big black bird took them out straight across the deep blue sea. John took the party, among the many places, to hell where he married the Devil's daughter and whipped him for a popularity contest for the position of High Chief Devil. Although members of the party wanted to stay in hell, John reminded them they had come in search of *"a song that would whip Old Massa's earlaps down."*

John, after having led them in escaping out of hell, decided to visit heaven since they were in the neighborhood. After John and his party had had a great time in heaven, *"the Lord called them up before the great work-bench, and made them a tune and put it in their mouths."* Since *"the tune had no words,"* it *"could bend and shape in most any way you wanted to fit the words and feelings that you had."* After having quickly learned the tune, members of John's party were summoned to reenter the plantation world from which their vision had dissociated them. Trembling at the sound of the master's voice, John cautioned the members of his party:

> Don't pay what he says no mind. You know where you got something finer than this plantation and anything it's got on it, put away. An't that funny? Us got all that, and he don't know nothing about it. Don't tell nothing. Nobody don't have to know where we get our pleasure from. Come on. Pick up your hoes and let's go.[3]

In response to High John's assessment and directive regarding the situation, those of the party *"all begin to laugh and grabbed up their hoes."* On the way to work they *"broke out singing."* In the act of doing this the storyteller says: *"Their gift of song came back to their memories in pieces, and they sang about glittering new robes and harps and the work flew."*

Song Power and Community

Slaves quickly came to see that many whites were not so seduced by the aesthetic power of the tune that they ignored the lyricized messages. Justified fear provoked some whites to prevent slaves from singing spiritual songs in their presence once they sensed that the songs harbored subtle protest messages. Many came, as a matter of fact, immediately to sense subtle messages of collective rebellion in the singing rituals themselves. Whites detected that slaves shared a common consciousness of transformative power derived from the ritualistic act of singing that gave slaves a sense of transcending power over their masters' vetoing power. Masters who allowed slaves to create and sing their own songs always ran the risk of allowing them the right to be empowered artistically with a sense of uncontrollable spiritual autonomy. A corporate consciousness of togetherness in Jesus and the Spirit of God, always inherent with subversive possibilities, was what constituted this belief of liberated community. The personal reflections of an elderly former slave, Charity Bowery, are suggestive of how some whites feared slaves singing certain spiritual songs:

"They wouldn't let us sing that. They thought we were going to rise, because we sung 'better days are coming.' "[4] Another ex-slave explained:

> One time when they were singing, "Ride on King Jesus, No man can hinder Thee" the padderrollers told them to stop or they would show them whether they could be hindered or not.[5]

Another contributing factor to whites' suspicions of ritualistic singing acts, as well as the songs' content, was slaves' claim that spiritual songs had been given them by God. Olli Alho, a contemporary scholar of slavery, has noted that the "allusive language of the slave songs was not only experienced as a secret means of communication among slaves, but also the language by which God Himself could be approached."[6] In addition, Alho says that:

> Whatever meanings the slaves found in their songs as a result of their actual social conditions, those meanings could always be interpreted as planted into the songs by God Himself, as if they were his secret messages to the slaves, to be constantly interpreted and reinterpreted.[7]

These songs became the means, theologically and ethically, that slaves needed for creating and validating their own dialectical notion of the freedom of individualism and community. A former slave preacher from a God-fearing plantation in South Carolina made the following observation of the way in which this was done:

> Sometimes somebody would start humming an old hymn and then the next door neighbor would pick it up. In this way it finally get around to every house and the music started. Soon everybody would be together, and such singing![8]

Slaves were as desirous for freedom in this world as they were the world to come. Singers mutual exhortation of each other to *"Walk together children and don't you get weary for there is a great Camp Meeting in the Promised Land"* is a case in point of the double meaning possibilities of the language. The *"Promised Land"* could have been in reference both to an eschatological future and an immediate mundane future north of the slave territory.[9] It could have been the community's creative way of reading the biblical image of the ultimate future, as their white counterparts did in their journey westward, into the immediate future.[10] The spiritual songs are pregnant with such futuristic phrases as: *"We will soon be free"*; and *"how long 'Fore we done sufferin' here."*[11] They must not be heard as the singers' mere literary techniques for arousing emotions, but as their passionate longing for the actualization of freedom now.

I and We Consciousness Progress

Even when the songs are pregnant with the personal pronoun "I," it ought not be concluded that the singer's intention was purely subjective. One psychosocial reason, perhaps, for the slave's dominant "I" emphasis was undoubtedly for survival. The empirical givenness of social alienation in the slave community required possibly that each slave as an "I" live in creative tension with the hoped for normative "we" community that the slaves were becoming through a futuristic vision in Christ. Slaves intuitively sensed that were they too liberal in their use of the pronoun "we," they would have contributed to the master's suspicion of their subversive religious intent. It was slaves' individual and collective belief in Jesus Christ, their elder brother, that enabled them to keep this dialectical tension alive within themselves.

Converted slaves dared live out of a faith understanding that freedom in Christ required that they live between the "almost" and "not yet." This paradoxical faith posture empowered them to live in the creative tension of "being" and "becoming." The linear metaphors of "walking" and "running" in the songs indicate the modes of social action necessary for accomplishing the collective objective. Communal walkers as the social body in Christ were less likely to get weary than solo walkers. This notion of togetherness generated in converted slaves a sense of social strength. The act of communal walking itself was perceived as an organic symbolic gesture of freedom, suggestive of an open-ended future. The visionary possibility for movement itself symbolized freedom. Slaves realistically accepted the fact that corporate progress toward their vision of normative community, which was predicated upon faith in Christ, often came tediously slow. During such seasons of slow progress, slaves poetically admonished each other in terms of "inches," the lowest symbolic means of measuring their progress, rather than yards or miles: *"We'll inch and inch 'till we get home."*

It was the collective "inching" experience itself that forged a spirit of community in the hearts of the travelers. Another use of the poetic metaphors of "inching" progress was conveyed in the lyrical instructive: *"Keep a inchin' along like a po' inch worm, Massa Jesus is comin' bye an' bye."*[12] This construction reflects the community's consciousness that the salvation journey was one of two-way movement from believers to God and vice versa—believers are gradually moving *("inchin' along . . . ")* toward Christ while they are simultaneously expecting Christ to come for them at some unknown time in the future.

The vertical or ascending metaphor for denoting the progress of the travelers was that of *"climbing Jacob's ladder."* Climbers believed that their progress was to be measured in terms of "rounds." In a celebrative spirit of upward mobility they declared that *"every round goes higher and higher."* The fact that the scriptures do not credit Jacob with climbing the ladder in his vision is not the issue for the slave community. Remember they were not students of the Bible. It is the slave community's imaginary genius that must be appreciated here. They resolved that corporate effort was the only means of getting out of their alienated situation.

Future and present freedom in Christ are clearly celebrated in the following lyrical construction:

> O, let us all from bondage flee, . . .
> And let us all in Christ be free, . . .[13]

This is one of the few lyrical constructions where slaves explicitly celebrated social freedom as an existential experience in Christ. They must be credited with the wisdom of not being so foolhardy as to have done this, too often, given the punitive nature of institutional slavery. It stands to reason that this song might have been openly sung during the Civil War era.[14] The remainder of the lyrics suggests the social as well as the spiritual implications of this celebrated freedom:

> We need not always weep and moan, . . .
> And wear these slavery chains forelorn, . . .
> This world's a wilderness of woe, . . .
> O, let us all to Canaan go, . . .[15]

Believers are enroute to Canaan to celebrate fully the freedom that they are experiencing in part already, by virtue of their being in Christ. Those who heard the call to freedom in Christ and fled from bondage knew the difference between being free in Christ and living in the wilderness of slavery. They worked in great anticipation of going to Canaan since they were already relatively experiencing the true source of freedom in Christ.

The notion of freedom in Christ as a future reality empowered believers to anticipate a perfect future. In a word, it affirmed their right of free choice. Being free in Christ meant that they had chosen the Greater Other, God, over their lesser significant other, the master. This existential notion of community obviously emerged out of the sense of common struggle that individuals experienced collectively in Christ. It was this gift of freedom in Christ that helped the singers understand the temporality of their present hardships. The susceptibly faint-hearted were told to: *"Stand the storm it won't be long / We'll anchor by and by."* The exhortation to "stand" suggests that the travelers had a freedom of choice in Jesus that they were denied in the world of slavery. Free choice was acknowledged in the invitational summons to: *"Come and go to that land."* Doubters were warned by the exhortatory resolution: *"If you don't want to go don't hinder me."* Faint-hearted souls were encouraged by the promissory exhortation: *"We'll soon be free, . . . / When de Lord will call us home."* Claimants of such faith ran the risk of being humiliated by scoffers and cynics who would invariably ask them about their hoped for day: "When?" and "How long?" Seasoned believers mutually tutored each other against such cynicism by exchanging interrogator/respondent roles. The following line is an example of the friendly interrogator's question to the potential respondent: *"My brudder, how long, . . . / 'Fore we done suffer in' here?"* The respondent was expected to answer the friendly interrogator:

> It won't be long
> 'Fore the Lord will call us home.
> We'll walk in the miry road, . . .
> Where pleasure never dies.[16]

Courage was a necessary virtue for those who traveled the freedom path with Jesus. Those who had the courage to hope in the face of despair qualified for membership in the freedom "band." Cowards were deemed undesirables in the movement: *"We want no cowards in our band / We call for valiant-hearted men, / You shall gain the victory, you shall gain the day."*[17]

The Individual Confessional Type

This type illustrates the way lyricized conversion language required an individual's radical disengagement from the converted community. Radical disengagement was the precondition for qualifying the converted to prophetically engage the death-dealing world that their masters had created. It had to take place under the aegis of the transformative power of God's Spirit. Although "we consciousness" was pervasive in the converted slave community, it did not minimize the value that was placed on the right of individual self-assertion. The slave community at best, through lyricized conversion language, maintained creative tension between a notion of individual identity and that of communal identity as God's social body. Lyricized conversion language provided the individual with the constructive means of articulating personal experience to the community and vice versa. Testimony through song enhanced the opportunity for creative self-expression. It demanded the need for singers to listen as well as respond. Lyricized song language was generally structured in terms of song leaders and choral respondents. Individual self-expression was allowed under the rubric of "the song leader"; communal expression took place under the rubric of "choral respondent." Those who sought the conversion experience, commonly known as "seekers," were expected to take the leadership role in the singing ritual. This was designed to set the individual apart from the community in the rite of conversion, and to accent the personal aspect of the salvation quest. Every converted soul was expected to have gone individually through that part of the rite of conversion that the community lyricized as having been *"way down yonder by myself. And I couldn't hear nobody pray."*

The Seeker's Crisis

The confession of being a sinner is clearly made in the following lyrics: *"When I was a seeker, / I sought both night and day / I asked the Lord to help me, / An' / He show me de way."*[18] The same words were not used in every case when the song was sung. The singer might say: *"When I was a mourner just like you; / I mourn and mourn till I got through; . . . "*[19] Another might say that *"I fasted and prayed till I got through."*[20] It is the phrase "sinner just like you" that analogically allowed individuals to identify with each other's shared state of sinnerhood. Consciousness of shared sinfulness was an essential element that formed community among the converted.

The Seeker's Place of Transformation

Sharers in this conscious state of sinfulness were expected to experience radical disengagement in a place anonymously known as *"way down yonder."* It was a place that accented individual isolation: *"way down yonder by myself / And I couldn't hear nobody pray."* This "way down yonder" place was apart from the everyday world. It was where the individual was brought face to face with the fragility of his or her own being. Moreover, it was the place where the individual was brought face to face with God whose transformative power alone gave him or her the needed interior critical distance from the demonic social structures of the plantation world. This place that was *"way down yonder"* elicited a changed attitude from the individual in transition. No individual was able to go successfully through this *"way down yonder"* experience victoriously without being in partnership with Jesus, the Lord over all forms of loneliness and alienation. Partnership with Jesus required humility of every initiate: *"In the valley! / On my knees! / With my burden! / And my saviour!"* The initiate, of course, was not sheltered from the painful realities of alienation and loneliness involved in the rite of passage. Even partnership with Jesus did not preclude the inevitability of having to pass through the *"chilly water!"* of the Jordan. It was required by those desirous of *"crossing over into Canaan!"* The journey was completed when the seeker experienced having gone from loneliness and isolation, *"way down yonder by myself,"* to triumphant community symbolized in the doxological phrase: *"Troubles over! In the kingdom! With my Jesus!"* Now the transition has been made from radical disengagement from community to that of radical prophetic and priestly engagement in community.

The day of finding the Lord was always an unforgettable moment for all who had had such an experience. Language for expressing how it happened often varied among different individuals. One might say: *"One day when I was walking along, . . . / De element opened, an' de Love came down, . . . "* God's love to the individual was perceived as an unprecedented and mysterious gift. It was the spontaneousness of God's gift that prompted the singer to say that *"I never shall forget that day, . . . / When Jesus wash my sins away."*[21] Once having encountered Jesus, the "seeker" could say with the rest of *"the travelers along the heavenly way"* that *"I am on my journey home.*" Such resolution of faith was grounded in the belief that *"King Jesus died for every man,"*[22] Theologians such as Witvliet have been quick to point to this fact in the spiritual songs.[23] The transformed always found it necessary to compare their present status with the past one: *"Oh, when I was a sinner, / I liked my way so well; But when I come to find out, / I was on de road to hell."*[24] Modesty was not deemed a virtue when it came time to testify about the transformative power of Jesus. Every individual was quick to brag about the certainty of his or her salvation: *"I am anchored in Christ, Christ anchored in me, . . . / All de deb'ls in hell can't-a-pluck a me out; / and I wonder what Satan's grumbulin' about."* It was this consciousness of being inseparably bonded in Christ that gave every convert a sense of bragging rights. With this faith posture, every convert could celebrate Satan's captivity: *"He's bound in hell, an' he can't get out, / But he shall be loose an' hab his sway, / Yea at the great resurrection day."*

The Seeker, Satan and the Place

Just as the day of finding the Lord was unforgettable, every convert's previous encounters with Satan were remembered. Long rap scenarios were often given of Satan's persistent harassment tactics. The following lengthy lyricization is a case in point:

> I went down the hill to make a-one prayer, . . .
> And when I got dere, old Satan was dere, . . .
> Said, "Off from her you better be."
> An' what for to do, I did not know, . . .
> But I fell on my knees, I and cried, Oh,
> Lord, oh, yes,
> Now my Jesus bein' so good an' kind,
> Yea, to de withered, halt an' blind;
> my Jesus lowered his mercy down,
> and snatched me from dem doors ob hell,
> And took-a me in with him to dwell.
>
> I was in de church an' prayin' loud'
> An' on my knees to my Jesus bowed,
> Old Satan told me to my face,
> "I'll git you when you leave this place,"
> Oh brother dat scared me to my heart,
> I was 'fraid to walk when it was dark.
>
> I started home but I did pray,
> An' I met old Satan on the way;
> Old Satan -a made one grab at me,
> But he missed my soul and I went free.
> My sins went a-lumbering down to hell,

> An' my soul went a-leapin' up Zions hill;
> I tell ye what brethern, you better not laugh,
> Old Satan 'll run you down his path;
> If he runs you, as he run me,
> You'll be glad to fall upon your knee.[25]

Ecstatic joy in Jesus was considered a necessary part of the experience of every convert who had gone to the wilderness to be converted. Every transformed seeker was expected to return from the search praising God. Such phrases of praise as: *"I just come from the fountain Lord, . . . His name so sweet"; "I felt like shouting when I came out of the wilderness, . . . leaning on the Lord."* The seeker found grace and freedom at the salvation fountain that he could not find elsewhere.[26] Tenacity to hold on to Jesus in the face of the devil's threats was the mark of a genuine seeker. One's tenacious resolve might be as intense as Jacob's of the Old Testament: *"I will not let you go my Lord; . . . until you come and bless my soul."*[27]

The Seeker's Triumphant Joy

The knowledge of having triumphed over the devil was an experience of incomparable joy when the seeker remembered what Satan's attitude toward him or her was now since having been saved: *"Old Satan's mad and I am glad, He missed the soul he thought he had."*[28] Salvation took place for the convert despite Satan's deceitful advice: *"Old Satan told me not to pray, / He wants my soul at the judgment day."*[29] A story given by the collector of the spiritual song "I'm Troubled In Mind" illuminates how this notion of triumph in Jesus enabled slaves to engage the hostile world in a priestly manner:

> The person who furnished this song [Mrs. Brown of Nashville, formerly a slave] stated that she first heard it from her father when she was a child. After he had been whipped he always went and sat upon a certain log near his cabin, and with tears streaming down his cheeks sang this song with such pathos that few could listen without weeping from sympathy, and even his cruel oppressors were not wholly unmoved.[30]

This story might be read as a typical example of slaves relying upon religion as an opiate of the oppressed, or the reader might look for possibly deeper meaning in the narrative lines. If the latter does not happen the story merely reads as a blues lament. The hermeneutical clue for identifying the theme of hope is reflected in the following phrase of the old man's song: *"If Jesus don't help me I will surely die."* Hear the expressed affection for Jesus in the following lines:

1. Oh Jesus, my saviour on thee I'll depend,
   When troubles are near me, you'll be my friend.

2. When ladened with trouble and laden with grief,
   To Jesus in secret I'll go for relief.

3. In dark days of bondage to Jesus I prayed,
   to help me bear it, and he gave me his aid.[31]

Is the singer saying that without the constraining power of Jesus he, perhaps, would be tempted to take the matter of retribution in his own hands? It seems that he is more concerned about a death of the soul than that of the body. If this is the case, was Jesus but a delusion that kept him from facing reality? Or is Jesus being viewed, also, as a victim-victor along with the sufferer? Another way of asking the question is, what does it mean when the oppressed views Jesus as a suffering companion? What did this say about the slave's understanding of salvation certainty?

The Seeker's Certainty of Salvation Knowledge

The converted slave spoke with absolute certainty of having been transformed by God's power. Nowhere was this more pronounced than in the confessional line: *"I know the Lord's laid his hands on me."* This understanding of salvation knowledge must have been a critical factor in building self-confidence in those who had been regarded as being incapable of knowing much of anything. Salvation certainty meant that the convert knew something that was only refutable by God. Since it was God that made this knowledge possible, there were three things about Jesus that captured the slave's imagination: (1) Jesus preached the gospel to those of his class group. This is heard in the singer's claim: *"Did you ever see de like befo'... Jesus preachin' to de po'?"* (2) Jesus' message of salvation was a gift of joy to all who would hear it: *"Wasn't that a happy day, ... when Jesus wash my sins away."* (3) Jesus is a man of both word and deed: *"My Lord has done just what he said, ... He's heal de sick an' raised de dead."*[32] Such experiences with Jesus made the individual a confident witness of Jesus' transformative power: *"I'll tell you what de Lord done for me; / ... He tuk my feet from de miry clay."* The Lord gave him absolutely secure salvation status. Also, the Lord made the individual a consoler and entertainer of his enemies as the Lord did David: *"he sot me upon a solid rock; ... / An' gib me David's golden harp."*[33]

The certainty of salvation knowledge constituted freedom for which the slave expressed profound gratitude: *"Free at las' I thank God I am free at las'."* One of the marks of this freedom was in the gift of dialogue that the convert was assured to have with Jesus. This would be possible even in the lonely and alienating moment of death: *"Way down yonder in de grave yard walk, ... Me and Jesus gwinter meet an' talk."* Jesus gave the humble transcending power: *"On my knees when de light pass by, ... / Thought my soul would rise an fly."* Certainty of salvation knowledge meant that the individual could trust Jesus for the unknown future: *"Some o' dese mornin's bright and fair, . . . | Gwineter meet my Jesus in de middle of de air."*[34]

The converted individual found the nautical image of having had the *"soul anchored in the Lord"* very helpful. Being anchored in the Lord meant that: *"Befo' I'd stay in hell one day, . . . | I'd sing and pray myself away."* Such resolve certainly suggested a sense of absolute trust, as well as commitment to achieve the ultimate objective: *"gwinter to pray an' never stop, . . . | Until I reach that mountain top."*[35]

The certainty of salvation knowledge was based on where individual's confessed to having found Jesus in the first place. A classical example is seen in the lyrical phrase: *"I found Jesus over in Zion an' he's mine, . . . "*[36] The phrase "over in Zion" might suggest slaves' rebellion against the master's idea that Jesus was to be found in his church. Was the allusion to finding him *"way over in Zion"* slaves' way of radically disengaging the Jesus of their conversion experience from the evil structures of the slave world? It was *"over in Zion"* that the individual experienced the ritual of baptism and was filled with the "Holy Ghost." There the slave was converted and sanctified. This became each individual's source of soul contentment that was expressed in such a lyric as: *"I feel all right no condemnation in mah soul."* Discoverers felt justified in bragging just a bit about Jesus when they said: *"I got a key to the kingdom an' this uh worl' can't do me no harm."* Accessibility in the form of *"a key to the kingdom"* might have meant having communication rights with God. Those who were certain of that right could be assured when they went down in prayer that God would hear them. This was conditioned on them being in right relationship with God continuously: *"Oh, if you know you're living right, | serving God both night and day; | An' when you go down on your knees, | God will hear every word you say."*[37] Direct correlation was made between consistent right living and spiritual power. This was necessary for one to be able to say *"I am a every day witness faw my Lawd."*

Individuals' certainty of salvation knowledge in Jesus was perceived as an antidote against all adversaries in the human community, including the devil. Adverse criticism did not negate the certitude of one's salvation knowledge. Destructive critics were put on notice of this fact in the words: *"You may talk my name as much as you please, | And carry my name abroad, | But I really do believe I'm a child of God. | As I walk the heavenly road."*[38] Jesus was described as a buffer who stood between the individual and Satan: *"O Satan is a mighty busy ole man, | And roll rocks in my way; | But Jesus is my bosom friend, | and roll 'em out of de way."* It was for this reason that the slave could say that *"Jesus is my only friend."* His absolute friendship was valued because: *"Jesus make de blind see, | . . . de cripple walk, | . . . de deaf to hear."* It is no surprise that slaves were unconditionally trusting of Jesus. This unconditional openness to Jesus is heard in the invitational summons to: *"Walk in kind Jesus!"* Relationship with Jesus merited bragging about since he had proven that *"no man can hinder me."*[39] Helpless slaves rejoiced at the thought that Jesus was a very *"present help in the time of trouble; a fence all around the defenseless."* Jesus was the one who *"propped the weak up on every leaning side."*

Personal salvation knowledge made the convert an impulsive witness for Jesus in the world. It required radical prophetic engagement of the world for Jesus. Transformation in Jesus, often described as having been in the form of a personal touch, had to be proclaimed to the community. The transformed might have said: *"I don't feel like I used to feel / Since I touched the hem of his garment."* Being made whole meant that the individual did not *"mourn, walk, sing, or talk like he did before his transformation by Jesus."*[40] It was for this reason that the singer could exchange everything else for Jesus: *"You can have all of this world but give me Jesus."*

The Converts' Certainty of Jesus and the Phenomenon of Death

Converts could testify to at least two things that they could be certain about in their relationship with Jesus: that physical death could do no harm; since Jesus had taken the sting out of death. Despite the fact of the fear of death, slaves who had found Jesus were confident that he was Lord over death itself. The truly converted could joyfully say: *"I am not afraid to die."* Students of the spirituals are practically all in agreement that death in slave consciousness is associated with rewards and deliverances. Lovell has noted that this fact often softens the image considerably. Slaves used graphic personified images of death to characterize its negating activity in human community. One such metaphor was that of the cold stream: *"the river of Death is chilly and cold,"* but it chills only the body. The self's unchilled soul revels in the thought of death's limitation. Death's ability to only destroy the physical body, over which the master claimed ownership, was cause for much celebration. This being the case, it makes sense that slaves spoke of death as having *"cold icy hands."* Slaves must have consciously drawn a parallel between the coldness of death's touch and the coldness of the hands of auction block inspectors. Death was commonly spoken of in many uncomplimentary anthropomorphic terms, the behavior of all being analogous to the traders and stealers of slaves, as shown in the lyrics below:

> Oh Deat' he is a little man,
> And he goes from do' to do',
> He kill some souls and he wounded some,
> And he lef' some souls to pray.
> Death he ain't nothing but a robber, don't you see?
> Death came to my house, but he didn't stay long,
> I looked in de bed an' my mother [father, sister,
>   brother] was gone,
> Death he ain't nothin' but a robber, don't you see?

Characterized as behaving cruelly toward his prey, death, as were slave stealers, was famous for making house calls unannounced: *"Soon one mawnin' Death come creepin' in yo' room.''* It was the unpredictability of death's behavior that kept the slave on guard. While he crept for some, death might be mannerable enough to knock for others: *"Soon one mawnin' death come knockin' at yo' do'.''* Death was also characterized as a caller. All were warned to listen well since he called by name: *"Hush! Hush! There's some one callin' mah name.''* Death was known, too, to take advantage of the dark and steal prey:

> But death had fixed his shackles
> About his soul so tight
> Just before he got his bus'ness fixed,
> The train rolled in that night.[41]

Note that slaves make a fascinating parallel in the above lyrics between death's behavior and that of the nightriders of the plantations. Neither respected slaves' space or time.

Although this was death's reputation in the slave community, it was only the unconverted who were thought to fear death. Death intimidated sinners, the fear-ridden, as the following lyrics show: *"death went out to the sinner's house, / come and go with me. / Sinner cried out, I ain't ready to go, / I ain't got on my trav'lin' shoes.''* The sinner often begs death to spare over another year. Death has no mercy as the community knows toward sinners. In contrast, the anchored in the Lord saw death as an agent who mercifully disengaged them from their embodied existence in this world.

Converts, as opposed to the nonconverts, trusted Jesus as the protective force against death. They believed that Jesus had wrestled death into defeat as the following lyrics show:

> O didn't Jesus rule Death in His arms,
> Yes, rule Death in His arms,
> On the other side of Jordan,
> Ah! rule death in His arms.[42]

The image of Jesus having wrestled death to defeat must have suggested both his closeness to and triumph over it. Such knowledge as this took the fear out of death for each convert as the following confession notes: *"I am not afraid to die.''* The reason being that *"Jesus rides de milk white horse''* of victory that was in contrast to Satan who *"rides de iron gray.''*[43] The fact that Jesus rides "the milk white horse" (symbolic of death) symbolized his mastery over death. Jesus is the only one in this world, or, above it, qualified to go down to the grave with the converted soul. This is why the question *"who's going down to the grave with me?''* was heard by the community from the individual as being a pedantic technique for teaching younger slaves. The inquirer was quick to answer his own question: *"Jesus going down to the grave with me when I die.''* Jesus was trusted by the converted individual in every step of the dying process. It was Jesus who could be trusted in the most intimate act of the dying ritual to *"make up his* [the Believer's] *dying bed."* When all others (preacher, doctor, and the public in general) had given up on the individual, Jesus could be trusted to be with him in his dying hour. When some dreadful disease has reduced the sufferer to an unsightly spectacle for public gaze, the individual convert believes only Jesus can be trusted: *"When my face becomes a lookin' glass, . . . / When my room becomes a public hall, / Jesus is my ondly friend."* It was believed that no less was true for Jesus when it was time for the soul to make the most fearful part of its journey from earth to heaven. Each believer trusted Jesus to: *"meet me in de middle of de aiah, / So if my wings should fail me, / Meet me with another paiah."*

The Convert and Corporate Responsibility

Corporate responsibility is a dominant theme in the lyricized conversion language of the spiritual songs. Given this fact, two assumptions, at least, can be made about the converted slaves' notion of responsibility. First, they took seriously both the personal and collective aspects of the idea of responsibility. Second, they understood that freedom in Jesus meant responsibility. Being free in Jesus, as a matter of fact, meant that one had been freed for the neighbor in the body of Christ; and, freed for those outside of the body of Christ. Converted slaves understood experientially that experienced freedom in Christ demanded a Christlike disposition on the part of the recipient.

Responsibility to insiders. The exhortative words *"Let us cheer the weary traveler, Along the heavenly way"* clearly indicates the value priority given mutual responsibility in the converted community. These encouraging words summed up for believers the basic biblical intent of *"the strong bearing the infirmities of the weak."* Here we see the principle of the priesthood of believers operative in the community of the faithful. This sort of mutual caring for each other in Jesus must be seen as having formed the basic foundation of ethical values for the oppressed. Corporate care for each other in Jesus made the trust of each other possible among the oppressed. It made we-consciousness possible among those who had been victimized by social anomie. Partnership with Jesus in the salvation drama begot in the converted a "let us" spirit. Every convert was responsible for helping others just as Jesus had helped, as is illustrated in the following lyrical construction: *"I'll take my gospel trumpet, And I'll began to blow, / And if my Saviour helps me I'll blow where ever I go, An' brothers, Let us."*

Insurmountable adversity, along the road of travel, could only be overcome by those who shared in the cooperative strength of Christ. Beneficiaries of this strength, of course, were expected to be mutually responsible for each other. They told weaker brothers and sisters that: *"If you meet with crosses, An' trials on the way, / Just keep your trust in Jesus, / And don't forget to pray."*[44] Constant awareness of the brevity and the unpredictability of human existence served as a great inducement for the need to be cooperative as a social body in Jesus. Seasoned travelers would constantly remind the young and impatient ones of the need for patience: *"don't git weary, for the works mos' done."* They were told what they must do to counteract anxiety attacks: *"keep yo' lamp trimi'd an' a burnin' for de work's mos' done."* The older member, who was on the verge of ending his or her work, might be heard to leave the following message with younger members: *"I'm gwine down to de ribbuh ob Jordan,. . . . When my work is done."*[45]

They lived in anticipation of such celebrative events beyond the river of Jordan as *"setting at the welcome table"; "feasting on milk and honey";* and, *"marching with the tallest angel."* All of these activities would suggest that heaven was a place of freedom and celebration. It was not enough to view this life as being transitory. Those who traveled it together in Jesus characterized the fleeting transitoriness of their beings as analogous to: *"rollin' through this unfriendly worl'."* Disciplined spiritual cooperation was expected of all: *"O, brothers, . . . sisters won't you help me to pray;. . . ."*[46]

Responsibility to outsiders. In addition to the internal task of *"cheering the weary traveler along the heavenly way,"* believers were expected to critically engage those outside of *"the heavenly way."* They could do no other since it was believed that membership in the heavenly way was based on an egalitarian understanding of Jesus Christ. Although it was thought to be a narrow way to it, heaven itself was believed to be an all-inclusive community that traversed class, race, and nationality. Every outsider was told: *"there is room enough in the heaven for you."* Doubters were told why they ought not stay away: *"for the Lord [and the angels] say[s] there's room enough in heaven for you."*[47] The notion of free space in heaven obviously had great appeal to slaves. Sinners outside of the conversion community were told that there was *"plenty of good room in my father's kingdom."* It was room that allowed for the exercise of individual free choice. Sinners were told that they could: *"just choose your seat and sit down."*

Heaven as a place of free speech was another attraction that believers used to engage unbelievers. Informal conversation was even possible with God and Jesus. The precedent for this belief was based on the nature of the kind of conversation that took place between God and Jesus regarding such a serious matter as the salvation of sinners: *"The father looked at the son and smiled and the son did look at him/. . . . "* Shared mutual joy between father and son made it possible for believers to commune joyfully with both of them.

The source of this joy was in the awareness of the Father and Son having worked as partners for the sinner's salvation: *"the father saved my soul from hell and the son saved me from sin."* It was for this reason that the penitent sinner could live in anticipation of casual conversations with the son and formal conversations with the father in heaven: *"going to talk with the father and chatter with the son."*

Jesus' presence in heaven symbolized that it was free space there for everybody because he had died for "everyman." While it was presented to outsiders as a place of free space and free choice, the most attractive feature of heaven for believers was that it was the place where they expected to meet Jesus face to face. Jesus' love and friendship made going to heaven possible. Believers claimed that their relationship with Jesus gave all other commitments second place status. Jesus was celebrated as a crisis-proven friend. His record of loyalty was unquestionable even when one had been abandoned by such caretakers as preachers, doctors, and parents. The loneliest moment in life could not rob the believer of her or his personal conviction that: *"King Jesus is my only friend."* Every believer desired for every outsider to know that all shared equal access to Jesus. Community in Jesus was predicated on faith rather than race, class, or sex. When unbelievers asked who really qualified to be members of Christ's community, believers answered: *"all those who came by faith, To the dying Lamb."* When assured that they had been converted, outsiders would often come uttering the following song phrase: *"In the River Jordan, How I long to be baptized; . . . to the dying lamb."*[48] Faith in *"the dying lamb"* assured victorious travel *"along the heavenly way."*

Jesus was the source of spiritual egalitarianism for the converted slave community. He constituted, converts believed, the bedrock of spiritual and political freedom, giving all *"a right to the tree of life."* The following lyricized conversion language was undoubtedly used by the converted both to engage each other as well as the unconverted:

You got a right, I got a right, We all got a right, to the tree of life. Yes tree of life. O brother, o sister You got a right, I got a right, We got a right, We all got a right to the tree of life Yes tree of life.[49]

This understanding of "a right to the tree of life" must be seen as being foundational to the converts' view of salvation community. Nothing was more powerful in the consciousness of slaves than this notion that God had endowed them with "a right" that preceded all human forms of governments. This notion of primordial right gave believers an awareness of transcendence over death itself. It sustained their testimonial resolve in the face of death to say that: *"before I'll be a slave I'll be buried in my grave and go home to my Lord and be free."* Knowledge of this right was had only by those who could say that: *"The very time I thought I was los' De dungeon shuck an' de chain fell off."* It was this notion of primal transformation that gave converts the courage to tell all of their oppressors that: *"You may hinder me here, / But you cannot hinder me dere."* The joy of such knowledge was shared communally. Recipients were told to publicize it among the different biblical personalities such as: "Mary and Martha"; "John and Peter"; "doubting Thomas"; "Paul and Silas"; "All the Apostles"; and *"tell everybody, Yes Jesus is risen from the dead."* The *"and everybody"* phrase was an indicator of slaves' recognition that Jesus' gospel was intended for "everybody." The converted community assumed different moral postures for the purpose of making the gospel available to "everybody." First, we will examine some of the positive somatic images used by the community to convey its positive moral disposition. Second, we will examine several negative images that were used to convey moral disharmony in the community.

Positive Somatic Images of Behavior

The beggar image. No image manifests itself in lyricized conversion language as cogently as that of the beggar. Such phrases as *"sinner please"* denote the feeling of intense urgency that converts often felt welling up in themselves for the sinner's conversion. In regard to the time of salvation being at hand, sinners were begged to: *"please don't let the hares' pass / An' die an' lose yo' soul at las'."*[50] Could the hearer imagine a farmer not harvesting the crop at the harvest season? If not, how could she or he ignore having his or her soul saved? Begging took the form of an exhortative style of evangelical persuasion as is heard in the following lyrics: *"Get on board little children there is room for many a more."* Appeals to the right time and the right space is used to press upon the ambivalent sinner the need to make the right decision immediately. The plea is being made for sinners to become copartners with God, which was not allowed with the master, in God's destiny for them. It was the converted community's belief that God, the giver of freedom, was in search of every sinner through those who had become members of the begging community of faith. It was believed that God was in Christ as the begging savior. As begging savior, Jesus' recognition of the sinners' freedom of choice is heard in the following lyrical construction: (sinner) *"Somebody's knockin' at yo' do'."* Intense compassion for the sinner's salvation is heard in the converts' piercing call: *"Oh sinner why don't you answer?"* Here the outsider's capacity for hospitality toward the other—in this case the salvific Other—is being questioned. The singers warned that *"it knocks like Jesus"* as though to say *'you are not that insensitive are you sinner?"* Or, *"we could not imagine that you would knowingly refuse Jesus' request to come into your life."* All of this points to the fact that converts, while they recognized their freedom of choice, plead morally for sinners to change their ways. Different somatic images were invoked among believers to convey their moral good will for one another.

The hand image. A repetitive plea such as *"give me your hand"* runs through many of the spiritual songs. This image of hand-to-hand posture in Jesus was symbolic, undoubtedly, of shared strength among believers. It, also, was a call for mutual trust in Jesus. Hand-to-hand fellowship with each other in Jesus was predicated on believers' ability to be honest about their mutual intents. They must be able to say to each other *"All I want is the love of God."* Mutual trust among themselves, because they tend to internalize the oppressor's negative opinions about them, is always the most difficult obstacle for the oppressed to overcome. According to Du Bois' classical statement: *"they see themselves through the eyes of the other."*[51] Converts in Jesus made obligation to each other in Christ the number one priority. Self-deceivers were called the greatest threat to the fellowship of hand-to-hand cooperation. True believers disdained their hypocritical *"claim to seek God's face but will not seek it right, . . . / pray in the day but none at night."*[52]

Finally the image of hand-to-hand cooperation in Christ transcended the religious barrier of denominationalism. The ethics of communion in Christ took precedence over the white community's ethics of denominational competition. Slaves said to each other:

> It makes no difference what church you may belong to, / While travelin' through this barren lan', / But listen if you're workin' for Christ my Redeemer, / You're my brother so give me your han', / We may not belong to the same denomination, / While travelin' thru this barren lan', / But if you take me by the han' and lead me home to my Lord, / You're my brother so give me your han'.[53]

Communion in Christ presupposed that togetherness in Christ was more important than accenting divisive human barriers.

The head and knees images. Genuine Christian witness was symbolized by the dignified way that the individual honestly presented him- or herself to others. All were told to *"hold up your heads."* This expected upright posture, symbolizing self-dignity, was antithetical to slave masters' customary expectations that slaves must literally drop their heads in their presence. This phrase addresses the issue of human dignity. It is correlative to such other somatic images as those of "walking," "shouting," "standing," and "the holding of each other's hands." These somatic expressions were deemed most important for conveying those moral virtues that are foundational to community. What greater lesson in the virtue of perseverance than those in the lyrical phrase: *"stand the storm . . . we'll anchor bye and bye."*[54] Another popularized admonitory phrase used for teaching the same virtue was: *"keep your eyes on the prize and hold on."* The biblical hero who personified the virtue of perseverance and tenacity for the converted community was Jacob. He was known to the slaves as the fearless wrestler who dared struggle with his adversary of the darkness. The phrase *"hold on and don't let go"* became popular language that strong converts used to exhort the weaker ones among themselves. In the call-and-response idiom, the struggler resolved: *"I'll not let him go."* The community responded: *"De Lord will bless your soul."* The following lyrics give a scenario of the necessity for a hand-to-hand struggle:

> O, I hold my brudder wid a tremblin' hand;
> I would not let him go!
> I hold my sister wid a tremblin' hand;
> I would not let her go!

> O, Jacob hang from a tremblin' limb,
> He would not let him go!
> O, Jacob do hang from a tremblin' limb;
> De Lord will bless my soul.
> O wrestlin' Jacob, . . . [55]

The singers here must have seen themselves as contemporary Jacobs. In the biblical story, however, Jacob wrestles with an adversary of the darkness; in these song lyrics singers of the slave community were struggling with the reality of community. Their struggle to hold on to each other allowed them to preserve the angelic kinship among themselves. The positive resolve to hold on to each other was heard in the words: *"I will not let thee go!"* The reason being: *"He will not let me go!"* The primary objective of the strugglers was to maintain the bond at all cost. It became, in fact, a covenant-making ritual that constituted the very foundation of converted community consciousness amid the oppressed.

The lyric *"Let us break bread togedder on our knees"* is the community's collective summons of its members to the ritual of corporate worship. The virtue of humility is celebrated by the phrase *"on our knees,"* which symbolized the right spiritual posture necessary for sharing with God and each other. The "on our knees" phrase suggests, also, the notion of egalitarian status among the sharers of bread and wine. It was, too, the place from which both spiritual and social blessings could be shared together, symbolizing that all were bound by the law of interdependence.

The speaking and shouting images. Quality conversation, rather than excessive rhetoric, with Jesus was greatly emphasized by the converted singers. The song phrase: *"a little talk with Jesus would make things right"* clearly illustrates the point. Converts could base their assumption on the assurance that *"Jesus is our fr'en, 'He'll keep us to de en' / An' a little talk wid Jesus makes it right."*[56] Hope in God's miraculous power was another moral virtue that was taught and celebrated. One example of this was heard in the exhortation to *"wade in the water children God's gwinter trouble the water."* Moral inspiration was also drawn from faith visions of predecessors, as well as contemporaries, of the faith pilgrimage:

> See that host all dressed in white,
> De leader looks like de Israelite,
> See dat ban' all dressed in red,
> Looks like de ban' dat mose led,[57]

Contemporary students of slave spirituals always run the risk of misreading the original intention of the text. Such exhortative phrase as *"shout along children!"* might lead the hearer to see only an ecstatic group of slaves engaged in a primal mode of religious expression. Heard from the existential standpoint of the slave community, one sees the shout as a mode of expressive language. It can be seen as a direct physical mode of praising God and an indirect one of rebelling against the master. The phrase *"shout along"* is instructive of the fact that physical and spiritual cooperation with the other believers must be deemed as the primary ethical objective of the converted. It must be noted that converts did not make a distinction between the act of celebration and gospel labor. In the same song that admonished members to *"shout together,"* the Lord's command is given to: *"Oh! take your net and follow me / For I died for you upon the tree!"*[58] The act of shouting must be viewed as having had dramatic teaching value among slaves. It was commonly used as a means of acting out the story. The story told in the text of the song was mimicked in the bodily movements and gestures of the shouters.

Negative Somatic Image of Behavior

Sinners and hypocrites. Christian converts warned sinners of what their fate would be spiritually and physically, if they failed to follow Jesus. Flagrant disregard for God's normative plan of salvation through Jesus Christ was one of the chief characteristics of the genuine sinner as is shown in the following lyrical warning: *"mind my sister how you walk on the cross, your foot might slip and your soul be lost."* Walkers on the cross were thought to be gambling with their own eternal souls. Procrastination was another trait of sinners that was condemned as unfavorable moral conduct in the sight of God. The word in the community was: *"Tell that po' sinner he better get religion / For I know his time ain't long."*[59] Indifference was another detestable trait in the sinner as is heard in the subsequent personal appeal: *"Sinner do you love my Jesus?"* Doing the work of Godly love in the human community, rather than rhetoric, was deemed as the only proof that one loved Jesus. Subsequently, the question was asked that *"If you love Him why not serve Him?"* Lovers of Jesus were heard to testify boldly as to what they would do if they were in the position of the sinner: *"if I was a sinner, I tell you what I would do / I'd throw away my sinful ways an' work on the buildin' too."*[60] Common metaphors used for describing those out of sync with God's righteousness were: *"Dancer, gambler, liar, hypocrite, and backbiter."* Sinners were warned that: *"God's goin' to get you 'bout yo' low down ways."*[61] What *"low down ways"* does the singer have reference to here? Some of the acts that qualified one for membership in the *"low down ways"* society were: talking about his elder when he is trying to preach the word; talking about the neighbor when he is trying to praise the Lord; and, talking about his sister when she is on her knees a prayin'.[62] Those sinners who feared neither God nor man were warned that: *"you got to go to judgment to stand your trial."*

Converts warned sinners and hypocrites that their unchristian conduct would not deter them from doing their Christian duty of love. Emphatically they resolved: *"You may talk about me jes as much as you please, / You may spread my name abroad, But every lie that you tell on me just throws me higher in the heaven.''*[63] Converts were certain that sinners, regardless of their position in life could not escape the biblical truth that: *"You shall reap jes what you sow / On the mountain, in the valley."*[64] This truth alone reinforced the need for the sinner to repent and be born again. How could the sinner remain indifferent to the power of God that was made manifest in the natural order? Godly love for the sinner motivated the singer to warn him or her against the self-deceptive notion that escape from God was possible: *"Stop po' sinner don't you run, / Just let me tell you what the lightin' done. / Lightin' flashed and thunder roll, / made me think about my po soul."*[65] Repentance was the recommended panacea to the sinner's rebellion from God. The sinner was told that to *"give up your heart to God"* constituted genuine repentance. In relationship to the hypocrite, the sinner was seen as an outsider by converts. The hypocrite, however, pretended to be in the converted community. Converts, equally as condemning of the hypocrite, reminded them of the transparency of their double standard lives: *"You call yourself church member, / You hold your head so high, / You praise God with your glittering tongue, / And leave all the heart behind."*[66] Great value was placed upon honest speech.

The Dialogic Type

The dialogic nature of lyricized conversion language made it a great teaching resource in the slave community. Ritualistic techniques of "call-and-response" in the singing act constituted a form of dialogue. The call-and-response phenomenon worked structurally in the following way. The song leader called out the song to the group, and the group chorally responded to the lead call singer. The call-and-response dynamic of the singing act counteracted the monologic nature of slave masters' pedagogical techniques. All teaching techniques that are produced by oppressors for the oppressed presuppose a banking philosophy of education.[67] Themes of lament and celebration are basic to the call-and-response structure in the lyricized language construction.

Our inquiry will be limited to the celebrative type of call-and-response discourse. Casual students of the spiritual song genre might hastily conclude that the "I" motif in the songs precludes any emergence of a dialogic mode of pedagogy. Failure to read the song texts for their deeper meaning would understandably lead to such shallow perception. James Cone has rightly observed that one cannot account for the "I" emphasis in the African-American spirituals by saying that it is merely the influence of white Protestantism and revivalism of the nineteenth century. While his defense of the African-American uniqueness of the songs' content has merit, Cone tends to glide over the more basic issue of how the community construed its own notion of "I" consciousness apart from direct white influence. He says that the existential "I" in African-American religion did not have as its content the religious individualism and guilt of white religion or refer to personal conversion in those terms. Neither was it simply an African-American duplication of the Protestant idea of the priesthood of all believers. Cone thinks that it was the following:

> the affirmation of self in a situation where the decision to be was thrust upon the slave. . . . The "I," then who cries out in the spirituals is a particular black self affirming both his being and his community, for the two are inseparable. Thus the struggle to be both a person and a member of community was the major focus of black religion. The slave knew that an essential part of this struggle was to maintain his affirmation even — and especially — when alone and separated from his community and its support. He knew that alone he was accountable to God, because somewhere in the depths of the soul's search for meaning, he met the divine. The revelation from that encounter made it plain to him that the divine and human are bound up together. When a black slave suffered God suffered.[68]

Cone's analysis does not delineate the role of the dialogic mode of pedagogy that slaves used to maintain the creative tension between the redeemed "I" and the redeemed community. His definition of African-American individualism borders on being an explanation that is grounded in a mystical understanding of the self and God. It does not account for how slaves reconstructed their own pedagogical method for counteracting the false body-soul dichotomy inherent in the oppressor's instructions (see chapter three). The premise here is that the spirituals (and often the blues) constituted a dialogic language that emerged out of a call-and-response communication structure. This dialogic took place between the songsters (leaders and respondents) themselves in the act of singing the songs. John Work noted in his study of the spirituals that:

> The leader is a most important factor in the singing of spirituals. It is he who sets the pitch and the tempo, it is he who sings the verses. The leader sometimes must sing his refrain through several times before his group will join him. He must have at his disposal many verses for each song.
>
> Many churches have spirituals which are led exclusively by special singers. Thus, within a church a spiritual may be designated as "Brother Jones' song," or "Sister Mary's song." Such a song may have been composed, or merely introduced into the church singing by the song leader. The "ownership" of such a song carried with it the indisputable ability to sing it effectively. In this manner traditions of singing grew around certain spirituals. It was not unusual that a song ceased to be sung in a church after a famous leader of it had died.[69]

In the act of singing the spiritual song, the leader summons brothers and sisters to participate. This often became the lead singer's means of making a personal statement about the state of his or her soul to other brothers and sisters. The same song became respondents' means of affirming the lead singer's right to bear witness through that song. Choral respondents, in the singing ritual, were understood to be affirming the validity of the lead singer's personal salvation testimony about God, and celebrating and sharing the lead singer's joyful convictions of both the existential and promissory dimensions of God's gift of salvation. The faith community was experiencing God's salvation while simultaneously living in anticipation of its perfect realization.

Scholars of the spirituals have debated extensively the question of the possible method that the singers employed to compose the spiritual songs. It practically boils down to the question of whether they were the spontaneous outburst and expression of the group, or, chiefly the work of individual talented makers. James Weldon Johnson doubted whether either theory was exclusively correct. His presupposition was that the spirituals were true folk songs and originally intended only for group singing. He wrote:

Some of them may be the spontaneous creation of the group, but my opinion is that the far greater part of them is the work of talented individuals influenced by the pressure and reaction of the group. The responses, however, may be more largely the work of the group in action; it is likely that they simply burst forth.[70]

Johnson illustrated his thesis by citing his childhood remembrance of "Ma" White who was a song leader in the church of his youth. A recognized leader of spiritual singing in the church, Johnson recalled that "Ma White" understood and took seriously the functional duties of her singing duty in the life of the church. He delineates what he remembered some of the psychosocial duties were: *"to 'sing-down' a long-winded or uninteresting speaker at love feast or experience meetings, and even to cut short a prayer of undue length by raising a song."*[71]

The contention of this discussion is that the lyricized conversion type of spiritual song, which has both theological and ethical implications, was used for instructional purposes by converted slaves. These songs became the pedagogical means of dialogical communication among the converted in Jesus Christ. It was by so doing that the converted slaves became God's social body. The following analysis examines some of the possible ways in which this might have taken place.

Pedagogic Resources

It is very apparent that the slave community used the spiritual songs pedagogically as a means for teaching the young slaves the conversion rhetoric, warning "the rank sinner" about the ways of God, and familiarizing each other to God's ethical expectations for their lives. A song such as "We are Climbing Jacob's Ladder" might have very well been used both to teach the young unconverted the normative duties of Christian faith, as well as to warn the complacent in the faith of what God required of them. The chorus says that *"every round goes higher and higher, soldier of the cross."* The verse *"Do you think I'll make a soldier?"* has a catechetical structure and tone. In lyricized conversion language the question is both asked and answered by the inquirer as well as the respondent. The question might function to elicit an affirmative response from the hearer. That affirmation is heard in the following: *"Yes I think I'll make a soldier, soldier of the cross."* In the singing act, leaders and respondents share each others' common questions and answers. In the subsequent question: *"Sinner do you love my Jesus?"* a plea is heard. The answer, of course, is: *"Yes I do love Jesus."* What sinner would publicly state a dislike for Jesus? The community notes, however, that the claim to love Jesus is inadequate without demonstrated sacrificial service on the part of the claimant. Every confessor is warned: *"If you love him why not serve him?"*

A classical demonstration of the spiritual as a pedagogical resource for teaching faith values to young slaves can be seen in the "Farewell Mother" spiritual. Allegedly it was originally used as a parting ritual by mothers and their children when they were sold away from each other to different masters. It shows how mother and children communicated their sense of moral obligation to each other in the face of forced separation. The lyrical construction of the "Farewell Mother" song reflects both the despair and the hope of the victims of such existential situations. It became the communicative means for mother and children conversing with each other in the face of despair. They find in the value presuppositions of the text the means for transcending the master's violation of their humanity. Each stanza of the song conveys a dramatic scene that takes place between the mother and her children as they await the inevitable moment of being sold from each other. The anxiety of being sold by the master the next day provokes the children to inquire of their mother: *"is Massa gwine to sell us tomorrow?"* The mother, who is anxiously affected by their inevitable moment of forced separation, prescribes prayer as an antidote for her children's insecurity in the face of the irreversible moment of fate: *"Yes, yes, O watch and pray."* Interestingly enough, the children express serious concern about the efficacy of prayer in alien slave territory where, according to rumors, the treatment of slaves was more brutal: *"But will prayer be adequate if he gwine to sell us down in Georgia?"* The confident mother does not lose faith in the power of prayer: *"Yes, yes, yes! O watch and pray!"* On the morning of the sale, separation vows are made between mother and children:

Children:	Farewell, mother, I must lebe you
Mother:	Yes, yes, yes! O watch and pray!
Children:	Mother, don't grieve arter me
Mother:	No, no, no. O watch and pray![72]

Note that mother and children find a creative way to remain spiritually bonded to each other in the face of their master's inhumane actions. They vow to maintain a spiritual relationship with each other that cannot be severed by the master's brutal decision. In other words, mother and children would not allow the master's actions to exhaust their veto rights. Physical separation would only strengthen their spiritual resolve to stay together. Given the danger of physically resisting the master, the mother instructs her children in the wisdom of spiritual cooperation. She will not allow herself or her children to despair in the face of the master's act of human degradation. Slaves lived out the paradox of the religious philosophical principle of both consent and hope. Paul Ricoeur says that this paradox manifests itself when we have "consent[ed] as much as possible, but hope[d] to be delivered of the terrible at the end of time to enjoy the new body and a new nature granted to freedom."[73] Slaves' commitment to the spiritual ideal of family reunion in heaven is grounded in an ultimate hope in God. While they have no power to alter the master's course of decisive action, mother and children refuse to participate fully in his evil scheme against them by promising, in the spirit of God, to remain in communion with each other. They make it clear in their testimony that the master does not have ultimate separation powers:

Children:	Mother, I'll meet you in heaven.
Mother:	Yes, my child! O watch and pray![74]

The notion of heaven here must be viewed as a metaphor that has the operative power in the consciousness of mother and children to create participation in a level of reality that is not fully realizable. It opens up thoughts and allows movements between normally closed domains via the use of powerful symbolic forms.[75]

Another example of the pedagogic value of lyricized conversion language can be seen in what I call the seeker-answerer structure. The words *"If you want to see Jesus You better go in the wilderness"* illustrates this point. Converts of Jesus Christ taught the unconverted what was necessary to have an authentic conversion experience in the liberating Christ. Exposure to the oral instruction of the catechism, taught by white religious leaders, obviously shaped the dialogical style and content of this pedagogic process in the song texts. Those unconverted who were desirous of knowing Jesus were to assume the status of "the seeker." The converted expected "the seeker" to ask about the wilderness Jesus: *"An' if I find Him how'll I know / 'round any other man?"* The question suggested slaves' need to be clear about the criteria necessary for distinguishing Jesus from other men. Every seeker was told what the marks of identification were for making this critical distinction: *"He has salvation awn His brow / He has a wounded han'-wounded han'."* The point being paradoxically that in the wilderness Jesus bears the signs of having once been a suffering victim in the world and now has become triumphant Lord over it. The place of the wilderness itself denoted, undoubtedly in the consciousness of slaves, that this Jesus was not to be domesticated by the owners of the plantation churches. An old slave was quoted when invited to go to a Sunday school: "I don't want any of your book-religion. I got my religion from God in the wilderness."[76] Identifying criteria of this wilderness Jesus, heard in the phrase *"Salvation awn His brow / . . . has a wounded han',"* were not to be taken lightly by the seeker. First, because no other mortal person had the distinction of wearing this sign. *"Salvation awn his brow"* signified that Jesus was victor over the meanness of this hostile world; *"wounded han'"* signified that he was victimized by its cruelty. That was the price Jesus paid for the openness with which he priestly and prophetically engaged the world. Paradoxically, the signs of *"Salvation awn his brow / . . . and a wounded han' "* suggested possibly that slaves could, all too well, appreciate the fact that Jesus was an embodied enigma of both strength and weakness. His salvation glory was not to be had without suffering mistreatment at the hands of the hostile world.

Converts' Jesus and Celebration

The pedagogic power of lyricized conversion language can be seen at its climactic best following conversion experiences of brothers and sisters. Wilderness seekers, who found this Jesus with *"salvation awn His brow / . . . and a wounded han',"* were enamored with an authentic testimony. Gathered converts awaited their return from the wilderness. They became both the community of affirmation and celebration. Inquiry about the seeker's wilderness experience, of course, was deemed a prerequisite of the community's affirmation. The basic question of the inquiry was: *"tell me how did you feel when you come out of the wilderness?"* As was expected, the newly converted would answer: *"I felt like running, . . . felt like shouting when I come out of the wilderness leaning on the Lord."* Such testimony often set off the following celebrative responses of "shouting, running and praying" among the community of hearers. Demonstrative activities of this nature became the community's way of sharing the joyful salvation moment with the newly saved. Shared ecstasy was just one phase of the new convert's testimony from the wilderness. The convert was expected to do more than repeat familiar lines about the conversion experience phenomenon. It was necessary to be tested in detail by those already converted. The new convert's capacity to love inclusively was the true test, in the eyes of the converted, of whether or not one had really been transformed by the wilderness Jesus. Every returner from the wilderness who claimed to have been converted was asked the pointed question: *"Did you love everybody when you come out of the wilderness leaning on the Lord?"* It was a question of critical theological and ethical implications about the community's understanding of conversion. Jesus' wilderness transformation required that the transformed produce the fruits of love in their everyday encounters. Old converts were concerned to know from the recent ones from the wilderness: *"Did you love everybody when you come out the wilderness leaning on the Lord?"* Converts would monitor new converts' behavior to see if their verbal claim was consistent with their conduct. Seasoned and neophyte converts mutually sensitized each other to their moral duties by the constant internal critiques delineated in these words: *"You better mind how you walk, you better know where you walking to / you got to give in account at the judgment you better mind."* The same principle applied to talking: *"You better know what you are talking about."* It was no different about praying: *"You better know who you are praying to."* Theirs was the concern to maintain true consistency between word and deed. Those who were oblivious to such warnings were reminded of the impending Day of Judgment upon their lives. John Lovell's comments on how this idea worked in the consciousness of slaves is instructive:

> If on the last day he had to be judged on the wholesomeness of his personality, he was willing at once to make the necessary changes. He did not intend to be found wanting. He did not intend to use his powerful friends and associates for matters he knew himself to be personally responsible for; such as the purity and righteousness of his own heart, such as his courage and fortitude, such as his personal toughness and faith. When he sang of these demands of Judgment Day, as he did so mainly to prepare himself against those demands. He knew that charges of such great magnitude did not come all at once.[77]

Works of love were proof of having been transformed by Jesus *"in the wilderness."* Those transformed by this Jesus had resolved: *"You may have all this world but give me Jesus."* Being celebrated, among the many things, was the convert's right to choose Jesus in the first place. It does not mean, however, that the convert has resigned from the world as it sounds in the lyrical construction: *"you may have this world but give me Jesus."* Instead, the phrase *"give me Jesus"* must be heard as the convert's resolution to radically engage the world. Jesus radically engaged it through his prophetic life, priestly death, and glorious resurrection. It was for this reason that brothers and sisters were confident in Jesus' ability to change both personal and interpersonal situations.[78] Those who experienced emotional disturbances were told that: *"A little talk with Jesus makes things right."* Known as a friendly partner with whom dialogue was always possible, Jesus was portrayed as a genuine friend. Converts could even trust Jesus to be conversant with them on an informal basis when they got to heaven: *"when I get to heaven I am going to talk with the father and chatter with the Son."* The convert is confident that Jesus will understand his or her world of origin: *"Gwin tell him [Jesus] about the world that I came from."*

The right of free speech assured by the conversion experience gave converts a sense of radical disengagement from the plantation world of inhibited speech. If the plantation world denied them of it, heaven was that envisioned place of assured free speech. Converts envisioned heaven as that one place they could file indictments against all earthly adversaries as the following lines indicate: *"I am gwin' to tell God how you treated me one of these days."* This notion of the gift of free speech was initially given in the rite of passage at the conversion experience. It was the consequences of having experienced what the converts termed being "struck dead" by the power of God. This was a metaphorical expression for having been radically disengaged from the world by the power of God. Commonly experiencers associated having their "jaws locked by God" as being one of the characteristic traits of this experience. This left the old self in a state of speechlessness. The gift of new speech, symbolized by unlocked jaws, was the sign of having been truly changed by God. Slaves poetically said that: *"The Lord unlocked my jaws and cut loose my stammering tongue."*

Converts' intense urge to share the joy of their salvation was considered a primary sign of having been truly converted. Salvation joy drove the newly saved to engage others in the experiential knowledge of God's saving power. Transformation by the Spirit of God in the wilderness required that the transformed become radically engaged in the life of the community. The gift of salvation joy could only be truly enjoyed by those who shared it. It was for this reason that the converted was often heard to say that *"I said I was not going to tell anybody but I just couldn't keep it to myself what the good Lord's done for me."* Harriet Tubman's description of her initial escape from the slave territory of the South affirms the principle of the need to share liberation joy. The self-styled Moses of her people, Tubman characterized her crossing into the Promised Land of free territory as being analogous to the rite of passage in the conversion experience. Note the attention that she gives in the descriptive portrayal to her own embodied self, and her relation to the natural order:

I looked at my hands to see if I was the same person now I was free. There was such glory ober everything, the sun come like gold trou de trees, and ober de field, and I felt I was in heaven.[79]

Tubman's euphoria, derived from being in the land of free territory, soon dissipated at the thought that her brothers and sisters were still slaves. Having crossed into free territory alone meant that she was not completely free without a community with which to share her newly found freedom:

> I had crossed de line of which I had so long been dreaming. I was free; but dere was no one to welcome me to the land of freedom, I was a stranger in a strange land, and my home after all was down in the old cabin quarter, wid' de ole folks, and my brudders and sisters.[80]

How could she be free when she had no embodied community with whom to share? Haunted by this question, Tubman resolved that she would, risking her newly acquired freedom, return immediately to the old plantation and help liberate those she had left behind.

> But to dis solemn resolution I came; I was free, and dey should be free also; I would make a home for dem in de North, and de Lord helping me, I would bring them all dere. Oh, how I prayed den, lying all alone on de cold ground, "Oh, dear Lord," I said, I haint got no friend but you. Come to my, help, Lord, for I'm in trouble.[81]

The phrase in Tubman's account *"I was free; but dere was no one to welcome me to this land of freedom, I was a stranger in a strange land,"* commands our attention in several ways. First, it suggests that the Tubmans of the slave community believed that real freedom was only realizable when the newly freed were able to share their freedom with brothers and sisters still in bondage. There is no place here for the notion of individual existential freedom that flourished in European philosophy during the nineteenth century. Also, Tubman's notion of communal freedom militates against the modern American notion of secular individualism.

The notions of freedom and responsibility manifest themselves in converts' lyricized conversion language about the crucifixion and resurrection of Jesus. In such lyrics pedagogy was perfected to an art. The following question demonstrates our claim: *"Were you there when they crucified my Lord?"* It was the sort of question that caused the hearers to do a lot of probing of their souls. Also, it could be designated the primary theological and ethical question formulated by the slave community. Each member was called upon privately to critique where she or he was existentially in relationship to Jesus' sacrificial death. The call was being made in this inquiry for the hearers, who would feel sorry for themselves, to consider what happened to Jesus. John Lovell has noted that slaves used both the pronoun "you" and the possessive pronoun "my." He thinks that their implicit intent "was to engage everybody regarding this question."[82] Herein is a bill of indictment that is delivered against all human persons, whether guilty by the sin of omission or commission. Lovell says further that the singer is asking:

> If you were there, what were you doing? How in the world could you have let it happen? Were you there when the blood came twinkling down? Surely, you could not have stood there watching and done nothing. To think of your neglect, "O ooooo oh, sometimes it causes me to tremble, tremble, were you there when they crucified my Lord?"[83]

Explicit in the lyrics is a message of warning. Lovell's commentary again is helpful when he writes:

> Every great wrong . . . is committed under the eyes of frightful or uncaring people. For the wrongs of humankind the finger points at us all. We are all guilty. We are not so much because of what we do as what we allow to happen. And without a doubt the slave singer was including the slavery of the human flesh in the bill of the indictment.[84]

The objective of the indictment is ultimately to create hope rather than despair among the guilty. The singer asks the question on which every hearer can hang his or her faith: *"Were you there when he rose up from the dead?"* This question echoes the note of triumph, signifying that God has demonstrated once and for all that no human act of cruelty in this world can separate trembling confessors from God's love (Rom. 8:35–39). Converts believed that they were victorious participants in God's great salvific drama of suffering and redemption.

It was the community's unequivocal resolve that God had made each of its members responsible witnesses to those both outside and inside of the social body of God. The understanding of this responsibility was expressed in the lyrics: *"The Lord made me a watchman upon the city wall."* The metaphorical phrase "the city wall" signifies the boundary between the converted and the unconverted. Watchers have a duty, despite the risk involved, to engage all who are within and without: *"Go tell it on the mountain, / over the hills and every where that Jesus Christ is born."*[85] This gospel mandate necessitated that they be helpers of those of such status as: *"the po' and needy, in the lan' . . .; / the widows and orphans in the lan' . . . / the hypocrite members in the lan' . . . / the long tongue liars in the lan' . . . "*

Hospitality was the genuine trait of the watcher of God. It was the primary theme of the slave community's prayers, songs, testimonies, and sermons. The following words by a preacher of the slave community is a case in point:

Brothers! This being true we ought to love one another; we ought to be careful how we entertain strangers. If your neighbor mistreats you do good for evil.[86]

Believers were told to practice such a Christian disposition toward others so as to place themselves in good standing with the moral governor of the universe on the Day of.Judgment. They expected that on that day God would judge them by the "what you have done to the least of these my little ones" principle that is found in the New Testament. It was the community's hope in the inevitability of this expected day that kept all of its members morally alert. Preachers of the slave community constantly warned all within the fellowship of the "heavenly way" that it would be a day when God would demand moral accountability: *"For away by and by our God that sees all we do and hears all we say will come and woes unto him that has offended one of these little ones."*[87]

We have shown in this chapter that slaves developed what I have termed the lyricized conversion language in response to the need for community. This community became the symbol of God's social body in the world. It had both a priestly and prophetic mission that manifested itself in the way that believers responded both to each other and to their masters. As the social body of God, slaves were able to overcome an oppressive notion of individualism that the slave system itself perpetuated. Conversion was not understood in the slave community as an isolated individual experience with God. Instead, the convert in the social body of God lived in creative tension between "I" and "we" awareness. Spiritual songs of the slave community became the primordial language for keeping this creative dialectic alive.

The objective in chapter five will be to show that the body and mind problem becomes the analogue for what we have termed the body and soul problem to this point of the discussion. Ex-slave autobiographies and trickster stories (Brer Rabbit) are the primary sources that manifest the body and mind problem. These sources clearly symbolize what I have termed in the beginning of this discussion the religio-moral language of the slave community. In contrast to the slave conversion testimonies and songs which were construed from the language of Christian conversion, the religio-moral language of the slave community does not always affirm Christian principles. The content of these literary genre types tend to reflect more of a holistic understanding of religion than the literary genre types of the conversion stories and spiritual songs.

In these literary genre types, slaves are drawing less upon the Christian language of white plantation missionaries and preachers. They, however, are still being confronted with the same racist problem involving their anthropological natures. Instead of there being a question about the relationship between the slave's body and soul, the basic question has to do with the relationship between the slave's body and mind. These literary sources reflect the slave community's creative response to the white community's false dichotomy of slaves' minds and bodies.

CHAPTER 5

Ex-Slaves Tell Their Stories

*Autobiography became a very public way of declaring oneself free,
of redefining freedom and assigning it to oneself in defiance of one's
bonds to the past, or to the social, political and sometimes even the
moral exigencies of the present.*

—William Andrews[1]

Autobiographies of ex-slaves such as those of Frederick Douglass and
Jarena Lee constitute excellent sources for understanding how former
slaves, via this literary genre, dealt with the phenomenon of the body and
mind duality.[2] Autobiographical narratives became the ex-slave's literary
means of presenting an image of autonomy that countered the stereotypical
image of the servile slave fostered by the master.

An identity crisis was created for the escaped slaves, who found it necessary to dissociate themselves physically from the extended slave family of
the plantation. Narrators often allude to this phenomenon as the "fugitive
period" that characterized the time from the slave's initial escape to that
of being securely received in a community in the North. It was a time when
the slave was caught in a betwixt-and-between state of identity consciousness: the slave's body was in the free territory and his or her mind was
back on the plantation with the extended slave family. This fugitive status,
being betwixt-and-between, became the source of great internal conflict.
While freed from chains and shackles, physical escape from slavery merely
intensified the freed slaves' desire to work with all of their minds and bodies
to free other slaves.

THE RIGHT TO TELL THEIR OWN STORIES

Some abolitionists believed that slaves could use the literary means of
autobiography to demonstrate that they were made in the image of God.
In the pretentious name of objective reporting, abolitionists required that

ex-slaves only value themselves as bodiless minds. White sponsors were more interested in sponsoring the stories of those who had been observers, rather than experiencers, of slavery.

These abolitionists were very interested in the slaves' memories of slavery, but they expressed little or no interest in what the slave remembered having suffered personally. Bereft of economic means and literary skills, ex-slaves were left with little option but to compromise with the dictates of the white abolitionists and narrate the experiences of their escape from slavery in a style that placated the literary sensibilities of their white, liberal readers. These literary godparents were careful to require that ex-slaves portray themselves as bodiless minds. This meant that abolitionists were guilty of showcasing the ex-slave's mind as a sacred value, while totally disregarding the sacredness of the body. They devalued the slave's body on the premise that white readers were only interested in whether the ex-slave could think. A published narrative of what the slave *felt* would merely reinforce the idea that she or he was no more than a feeling animal. This paternalism of northern white liberals was another confusing factor for the escaped slave. For these reasons ex-slaves had to struggle for the right to become the formal literary creators of their own stories.[3] The determined ex-slaves had the burdensome challenge of proving that they were a combination of feeling bodies and reflective minds.

Many missionaries and preachers of the plantation South conveniently assigned spiritual value only to the slave's soul, not the body. Their objective was to reduce slaves to mere emotionalized religious robots who were of no threat to the social order of the plantation world. Such an idea, when internalized by the slaves, required that they think only of themselves in relationship to their masters and God. The ex-slave was expected to reduce his or her identity to the ontological dictum: *"Master knows that I am a Christian therefore I am."* It was another way of saying that *"Master knows that I feel God therefore I am."* Ironically slaves' capacity to "feel God" had very little value for them in the social world of the plantation. No correlation was drawn between spiritual feelings thought to be the attribute of the soul, and physical feelings associated with the capacity of the body.

The ex-slave of the abolitionist community in the North, on the contrary, was ever having to convince abolitionist supporters that *"I feel therefore I am."* It was important to show that this form of self-affirmation was as necessary as saying *"White abolitionists say that I can think therefore I am."* It was the whole scheme of southern slavery and northern abolitionism to deny slaves or ex-slaves the right of independent self-affirmation. Even in the presence of liberal northern whites, the slave still had to struggle to be recognized as a socially embodied self. The slave who would be fully liberated dared say: *"I-am-my-body."*

William Andrews' critical literary assessment of ex-slave autobiographies clearly shows how abolitionist sponsors' editorial hand often shaped the style of ex-slave's story—if not always content. Whites of the North, who thought that the mind was the "measure of the man," believed that their editorial hand was necessary to make ex-slaves' stories acceptable to white readers. Demonstrated rational ability was judged as a sure sign of "civilized man." Given a common assumption about the liberating power of education, slave owners and abolitionists mutually agreed that literacy was the greatest enemy of institutional slavery. It was for this reason that the ex-slave's autobiography became such a symbolic statement about his or her basic human capacity: that those of African extraction were capable of being "civilized" according to the white man's standards of civilization.

An ex-slave's name on his or her own autobiography was of primary importance. It was an unequivocal indication that he or she had made the rite of passage from a socialized "slave status" to a "literate citizenship status." It was the sign that the ex-slave had made the rite of passage from the world of the illiterate to that of the literate; from being a simple child of nature to having been maker or comaker of him or herself into the literary image of the western world. It was the route from depersonalization, typified in the slave experience, to that of personalization. It was the means of becoming a westernized metaphysical self. It was the direct contrast of the illiterate slaves only being able to boast of the angel in heaven having signed their names. Writing one's autobiography meant that the slave had become the signer of his or her own name on the literary roll of western civilization.

Despite their role in the shaping of their own stories, ex-slaves had to struggle no less to keep from becoming a "set of objective facts" in the minds of white readers. Whether she or he was the transcriber or scribe of it, every ex-slave narrator was invariably affected by the value judgments of powerful white publishers and editors upon his or her story. Such judgments were often so weighty in the earlier years of publications that William Andrews has concluded "that whites required that the ex-slave autobiographer alienate him or herself from his or her own past." In such a case, the intent was to have the narrating ex-slave report his or her experience from the perspective of an observer rather than that of an embodied experiencer. This means that white sponsors of ex-slave autobiographies had already presumed that the slave's story could not be authentic if it had not been told from an objective point of view. If it was perceived to be told otherwise, the story was characterized as being subjective in nature and therefore to be viewed with suspicion. That is to say that white sponsors perceived what they termed the "objectively told story" to be from the slave's head as opposed to the "subjectively told" one that was based on the feelings of the narrator. Ex-slave narrators were expected to suppress the feeling side of themselves. This left them faced, on the one hand, with the dilemma of having to tell their stories for the primary purpose of placating the literary sensibilities of white sponsors. It compelled them, on the other hand, to tell the heartfelt story of their true experience of slavery. In the words of William Andrews, the ex-slave narrator was in a "no-win choice between two alienating alternatives."[4] Andrews concludes that ex-slaves "instead of conforming to the rules of the literary game or refusing to play, they [ex-slaves] set about changing the rules by which the game was played even as they played along with it."[5] The reader might quickly note that I have located the body and soul issue in what Andrews has identified as the problem of objectivity and subjectivity in the narrator's story for whites.

It was presumed that white readers were more interested in the mental anguish ex-slaves had experienced than they were in any physical torture slaves had suffered during slavery. One reason for this might have been that it would have been much easier for whites of the North to deal with the ex-slave as a literary idea than an embodied social fact. Undoubtedly, few whites were willing to take the embodied slave "as their text," as Douglass said that Garrison, the abolitionist, did.[6] The ex-slave's autobiography must be read with the fact in mind that there is partnership between text and interpreter. That is to say that the ex-slave as literary text was expressed only through the other partner, the interpreter, who in this case was the white reader.[7] In this way, the ex-slave was narrating him or herself into being a permanent fixture in the literary imagination of white Americans — including southern readers who disclaimed the writer's authenticity. Literate southerners invariably felt obligated to read the autobiographies, if for no other reason than to refute the charges that ex-slaves made against the institution of slavery. It was for this reason that these narrations of ex-slaves took on a life of their own — by virtue of their detachment from both the author, writer, and reader. In the autobiography ex-slaves raised themselves publicly into "a sphere of meaning in which everyone who can read has an equal share."[8]

The ex-slave's autobiographical text stood as an intermediate literary buffer between the white reading audience of the North and the narrators themselves. Many whites, undoubtedly, came to see these texts as a way of dealing with the victimized from a safe distance; a less threatening way of dealing with the alien other. Slave stories in autobiographical form often gave whites a cerebral experience of slavery without their having to be directly involved with an embodied African-American ex-slave. White readers could satisfactorily utilize the autobiographical text of the ex-slave to prove that the ex-slave was an aberration, rather than the norm, of the slave population. The theoretical work of Paul Ricoeur is helpful at this point for understanding how the relationship works between the text and the reader in general. Ricoeur notes that the reader, in appropriating the text, discovers in it "a proposed world which I could inhabit and wherein I could project one of my own most possibilities." Revealed in the act of appropriation is "an enlarged self" that the text has "potentialized" for the reader. In the process of making the text his own, the text makes the reader its own by "metamorphosing" the ego of the reader and revealing "new capacities for knowing himself." The reader's appropriating capacity is "broadened in his capacity to project himself by receiving a new mode of being from the text itself." Finally, metamorphoses are possible since "appropriation thus occasions a dispossession of the ego and a discovery of the new self that emerges from the understanding of the text."[9] Ricoeur's theory is valuable for looking at some of white readers' formal responses to ex-slave autobiographies.

WHITE READERS' RESPONSES

A more complete understanding of how white readers interpreted ex-slaves' autobiographies can be gained through an examination of reviews. Particular attention will be paid here to the reviewers' use of two different metaphorical phrases in their reviews: "an honest face text," and "a mirror of the slave's mind."

An anonymous reviewer said of Gustavus Vassa's autobiography:

> The novel has an honest face; and we have conceived an honest opin-
> ion of the man, from the artless manner in which he has detailed the
> variety of vicissitudes which has fallen his lot.[10]

For whites of this persuasion, the ex-slave's autobiography was a literary reflection of the truthful nature of its creator. "I can not believe it; it cannot be true" was a common response of many white readers to any book published carrying the name of an ex-slave. It was the challenge of abolitionists to prove that the ex-slave's book "wore an honest face."

Debate over the authenticity of the ex-slave's autobiography understandably arose between abolitionists and southern slave masters. Many southerners claimed that the ex-slave's autobiography was merely a concocted story created to fuel the propagandist mind of the abolitionists. Countering such claims, northerners often wrote testimonial letters, generally published in the front of the books, vowing for the ex-slave writer's character. Aware of the ideological warfare that ex-slaves were often caught in, William Andrews concluded that slaves at this period had no option but to try and play the ends against the middle for the survival of the victims in the middle. Southerners referred to some slave authors as writers of "ridiculous falsehoods." Other Southerners denounced these stories as the "mischievous invention of some fanatical abolitionist."[11]

Equally as interesting was the fact that many slaves interpreted Southerners' disclaimers as proof that their stories were true. Frederick Douglass wrote, in this regard, to one white doubter of the South that "I will insert your article with my reply as an appendix to the [second] edition [of my narrative] now in progress."[12] All positive attempts by abolitionists to prove that ex-slave authors were honest did not remove the atmosphere of suspicion that surrounded their publications.

The narrative functioned for the white reader as "a mirror of the slave's mind." In the words of another anonymous writer:

It is a mirror, it is of the very best plate glass in which objects appear so clear and "natural" that the beholder has perpetually mistaken it for an open window without any glass at all.[13]

The narrative "as a mirror" metaphorically suggested the reader's perception of a correlation between the writer and the story written. It was commonly presumed that the ex-slave's autobiography was an objective reflection of his or her mind. This can be seen in one writer's assessment of the function of the ex-slave's autobiography:

to introduce the reader, as it were, to a view of the cotton fields, and exhibit, not to his imagination, but to his very eyes, the mode of life to which the slaves on the southern plantations must conform, has been the primary objective of the compiler.[14]

This anonymous evaluator noted that a second objective of the story was

to make the citizens of the United States acquainted with each other, and give a faithful portrait of the manners, usages, and customs of southern people so far as those manners, usages and common customs have fallen under the observation of the common Negro slave, imbued by nature with a tolerable portion of intellectual capacity.[15]

Another aspect of the ex-slave narrative that gave it a "mirror of the mind" status was what the anonymous reviewer called "its nonpartisan nature." It was said of such a book that it "broaches no theory in regards to slavery, nor proposes any mode of time of emancipation." The ex-slave writer whose autobiography lived up to the mirror metaphor was expected to write without manipulating the emotions of the reader. No ex-slave writer wanted to be condemned by a white reader for being an "over-enthusiastic brain."

Clearly, white readers expected ex-slave writers to be what they termed objective in the accounts of their slave experiences. The credible autobiographer was expected, by white readers, to give a spectator's view, as opposed to a subjective one, of slavery. It was to be an objectification of the slave's mind rather than his or her embodied experience. In the words of William Andrews, "abolitionists were more interested in the slave having been 'an eye-witness' than an 'I' witness of slavery." Although this was the case, some abolitionists believed that the ex-slave's narrative was a signal proof that God had endowed even the African American both with a "soul and mind." It was for this reason that some saw nothing to prevent those who had been slaves from becoming "Christians or philosophers." Others wondered how African-American slaves were able, under the withering conditions of slavery, to write poetry. These acts of writing poetry and autobiography were all proofs that "blacks of the south," in comparison with "their fathers when brought from the shores of Africa, had ceased to be savages." The claim was that exposure to "the white man's civilization" had developed in those of African descent a higher level of affections and moral sensibility.

The whole ideological objective of slave masters was to prove that African-American slaves were literately inferior to their white counterparts. Such a view is heard in one white reader's review of Douglass' autobiography:

> He does not belong to the class, always small, of those who bring to light great principles, or who originate new methods of carrying them out. He has, however, the vividness of sensibility and of thought which we are accustomed to associate with a Southern climate.[16]

The fact is that abolitionists had no less of an agenda themselves that sometimes reflected itself in the writings of ex-slave writers. Andrews concludes that,

> Autobiography became a very public way of declaring oneself free, of redefining freedom and assigning it to oneself in defiance of one's bonds to the past, or to the social, political and sometimes even the moral exigencies of the present.[17]

AUTOBIOGRAPHY AND SELF-AUTONOMY: TWO DOMINANT THEMES

Ex-slaves, through the writing of their own autobiographies, were able to overcome the distorted mind and body dichotomy imposed upon them by white abolitionists. They constructed their own stories so as to present themselves as embodied minds. In those autobiographies where ex-slaves exercised some voice of significance at least two dominant themes manifest themselves: autobiography as symbolic of the embodied self; autobiography as symbolic of womanist consciousness.

"I Think and Feel, Therefore I Am"

Ex-slaves used the genre of autobiography to express themselves as both "feeling" and "thinking" selves. They used it to impress upon the literary minds of white America that they were embodied selves. In so doing, ex-slaves transcended the false dichotomy that northern abolitionists had made between their minds and their bodies. For an appreciation of this phenomenon, it is necessary to understand ex-slaves' perception of the community for which they were writing. At least two factors would dictate that ex-slaves were not writing directly for brothers and sisters in slavery: the majority of slaves were illiterate, and the slave owner would have considered such a literature inflammatory rhetoric in the hands of any literate slave. However, ex-slaves did assume the scriber's role of being intercessors, and interpreters for those illiterate slaves still in bondage.

Autobiography became the formal means, as opposed to the second-order language of the converted slave community, of ex-slaves' communicating their experiences in the first-order language of the oppressor (note a formal distinction between first-order language and second-order language).[18] The primary objective of the autobiography was to convince white readers that ex-slaves' minds plus their bodies equal themselves. The ex-slave's autobiography symbolized to the white community that all slaves had the potential to be self-determining moral agents.

In addition, the autobiography symbolized a formal means for ex-slaves to express themselves honestly as "feeling" selves to white readers. Honesty, rather than dishonesty, became the norm for communicating with the white reading audience. Published autobiography symbolically suggested that ex-slaves had reached a level of self-autonomy that defied all stereotypes of the servile slave. As writers of their own autobiographies, ex-slaves became self-autonomous moral beings capable of creating their own self-images. This says, in fact, that ex-slaves used the first-order language of their oppressors to bear public witness to their own genuine thoughts and feelings about slavery and their enslavers. It was tantamount to saying that "I can think my feelings in the oppressor's first-order language, therefore I am."

Ex-slaves who had acquired the literary skills to write their autobiographies in first-order language of the oppressor were analogous to Prometheus, of Greek mythology, who stole fire from the Gods. Mastery of the literacy skills of reading and writing held for ex-slaves the secret of their white oppressors' power. Their desire to know this secret undoubtedly became the primary criterion that separated the "contented slave" from the "restless slave." Slaves who had learned the art of reading and writing were more likely to run away.

Numerous accounts would indicate that many slaves understood, although they could not verbally articulate it, that there was some sort of magical power in their masters' acts of reading and writing. Such conclusions were often reached as a result of slaves watching their masters read the Bible to them. Reading and writing understandably became a greater allurement to the imagination of slaves when masters forbade them to learn to do so. One slave recalls having had an almost fairy tale kind of experience when he first saw his master read from a book: "I was . . . surprised . . . when I saw the book talk to my master, for I thought that it did, I observed him look upon it, and move his lips." The slave was in for a rude awakening when he tried in secret to do with the book what he saw his master do in the open. Accordingly, this painful moment of disillusionment drove the slave to the point of self-hatred. Subsequently, he said "that I thought that everybody and everything despised me because I was black." Secret acquisition of literary skills, for the master, amounted to slaves eating the forbidden fruit of the Garden of Eden. Denying slaves literacy was to deny them the civil means of acquiring for themselves either sacred or secular knowledge. Curious slaves such as Frederick Douglass saw that the mastery of the oppressor's literacy techniques was a means of self-empowerment.[19] Illiterate slaves had no choice but to stand in awe of the literate oppressor who always stood as the superior creator of culture. The oppressor used his position of cultural dominance to justify biological and intellectual domination over slaves.

Stealing from the oppressors the techniques of reading and writing, slaves discovered the necessary method for demystifying the aura and power that often surrounded the master's persona. What was even more radical, of course, was the fact that as slaves clandestinely acquired skills of literacy they discovered themselves as being both the creator and the created. That is to say that writers were able to project themselves in the written text.

Autobiographical texts became the means of ex-slaves' objectifying themselves into the public consciousness of the white society—even that of slave owners. Literary power in the hands of an ex-slave signified that the author was able to create him- or herself into the image of a self-autonomous agent. Autobiographical texts clearly became a reflection of the slave's respective journey to self-autonomy. Readers of the autobiography must always submit to the predefined rules of the storyteller. As writer of his or her own story the ex-slave was in charge of justifying his or her right to be and do unapologetically in behalf of him or herself.[20] When ex-slaves wrote their own stories it could be said that they were philosophically "restructur[ing] their own consciousness" as well as "creat[ing] new interior distance within the psyche."[21] Ritualistic acts of writing allowed the slave, as writer, to separate oneself as knower from the external environment of slavery, as well as from oneself.[22]

Autobiographical text freed ex-slaves to extenuate themselves as embodied minds upon the world of the oppressor. It afforded them the rational means for countering the white writers' stereotypes of them as mindless bodies or bodiless minds. Textual evidence indicates that ex-slaves, in the main, wrote their stories with the understanding that their bodies were the ultimate instruments of all their external knowledge.[23] This notion was illustrated in the words of Austin Steward, an ex-slave, who wrote in the preface of his book that he "sends out this history," his *Twenty-Two Years a Slave and Forty Years a Freeman*, "presenting as it were [my] own body, with the marks and scars of the tender mercies of the driver upon it."[24] Steward does not view his body as the property of the slave master. He, instead, understands it as his instrumental self that made possible all of his external knowledge about slavery. In the world of slavery, Steward was only supposed to think and feel through his master. He was not allowed to say: "I think and feel therefore I am." Ex-slaves attended the world of slavery from their bodies, making their dream of freedom functional by both incorporating freedom in their bodies and by extending their bodies to include it—so that they came to dwell eventually in the land of freedom.[25] It was for this reason that Harriet Tubman could use somatic imagery in characterizing her first experience after having crossed over into the free territory of the North: "I looked at my hands and they looked new; I looked at my feet and they did too."[26] What happens here is that Tubman explains her experience in the first-order language of the African-American slave community to the white community.

Countering the "Mammy" and "Jezebel" Stereotypes

Autobiography as a symbolic womanist statement[27] reflects a unique type of radical African-American female response to the problem of literacy and spirituality. It documents the creative response of women to the false duality of mind and body. As writers and dictators of their own stories, ex-slave women constructed positive images of themselves as embodied minds who had been sanctified in Jesus, God, and the Holy Spirit. Their strength to survive absurd assaults upon their personhood was often derived from this belief.

The Strong Woman Myth

Systemic slavery was certainly a test of African-American women's strength of body and mind. Females' bodies in slavery were valued for their utility purposes of procreation and work just as males' bodies were. On the slave market, slave women's bodies were highly valued for their childbearing capacities. Mythic lore about race and sex emerged during slavery that still haunts the American society. Slave women were viewed contrastingly in two stereotypical ways: "Jezebel" and "mammy." The mammy myth conjured up the image of the African-American slave "woman of inordinate strength, with an ability for tolerating an unusual amount of misery and heavy, distasteful work." It was assumed that this woman varied in both physical and emotional makeup from her white counterparts in that she did not have: "the same fears, weaknesses, and insecurities as other women, but believes herself to be and is, in fact, stronger emotionally than most men." Michele Wallace, a contemporary writer, concludes that this power was a primordial strength derived from the mother of all creation itself. In Wallace's words the African-American woman is paradoxically:

Less of a woman in that she is "feminine" and helpless, she is really more of a woman in that she is the embodiment of Mother Earth, the quintessential mother with infinite sexual, life-giving, and nurturing reserves. In other words she is a superwoman.[28]

It is a fact that,

> One of the most prevalent images of the black woman in Ante-bellum
> America was of a person governed almost entirely by her libido, a
> Jezebel character was in every way the counterimage of the mid-
> nineteenth-century ideal of the Victorian lady.[29]

In a comparative assessment of those characteristics that distinguished
the "mammy" from the "Jezebel" stereotype, Deborah Gray concludes that,
on the one hand, there was the woman obsessed with matters of flesh, and
on the other, was the asexual woman. One was carnal, the other maternal.
One was at heart a slut, and the other was deeply religious.[30] Mammy was
completely dedicated to the white family. She served also as a friend and
advisor. She was, in short, a surrogate mistress and mother.[31] Mammy
reflected two traditions perceived as positive by Southerners—that of the
idealized slave and that of the idealized woman.[32]

The Sanctification Myth

Autobiographical genre became many ex-slave women's medium for constructing a positive self-image that countered the self-negating influences
of "Jezebel" and "mammy" images. The acquisition of reading and writing
skills gave some ex-slave women accessibility to the oppressor's world of
literacy. It afforded them the means for constructing themselves in their
own image. Their publications gave them a public medium for self-expla-
nation as well as self-description.

Sanctification is the term, in their autobiographical writings, that symbolized the radical way in which these women perceived themselves ontologically and ethically. It must be understood as a term that had both
theological and ethical implications for its users. For analytical purposes
we will refer to these women as the subjects of the "sanctified" myth. The
degree of these women's commitment must be seen in their willingness to
place the Lordship of Jesus Christ above the authority of their masters.
Sanctified women perceived themselves as having been called by God, Jesus
Christ, and the Holy Spirit to do the work of heaven in a sin-cursed world.
Ex-slave women such as Zilpha Elaw daringly waded back into slave territory for the purpose of preaching the liberating gospel of Jesus Christ to
slaves.

What did these women mean by the term "sanctified"? A gleaning of
their writings suggests that they meant by it the "second blessing" of the
conversion process. The "first blessing" was understood to be the initial
phase of the conversion experience itself. According to their narrations,
these women were never satisfied until they were convinced by a sign from
heaven that they had received from God the "second blessing." It was
believed that the "second blessing" made them holistic servants for doing
God's work. "Sanctification" strengthened a fragile body to do the will of

God. It made the dialectical existence of being Christ's strong mind in a fragile female body possible. William Andrews notes that the concepts of "justification, or forgiveness of sins, and the ethical regeneration of sanctification" are given primary concern in the autobiographies of ex-slave women. About these three concepts Andrews says:

> First, repentance as a result of the conviction of one's sinfulness; second, justification from the guilt of sin by Christ's atonement and forgiveness; third, sanctification or a "new birth," free from the power of sin by the virtues of the indwelling power of the Holy Spirit.[33]

Andrews reminds us that in the first event of the process the converted has a role to play. In the last two stages of the process the converted is absolutely at the disposition of God's mercy. The hard question, however, was: What was the advantage of having been "sanctified" in a society that was cursed by the evils of slavery and sexism? Andrews contends that it gave the sanctified "the sense of being in total harmony with the will of God, of being perfectly pure in intention and action insofar as his or her acts were determined by individual intention."[34] An inner peace was believed to be the fruit of this gift of sanctification. The sanctified could enjoy the peace of having been liberated by God from sin.

The intense manner in which these women identified with God in thought, word, and deed manifests itself in their metaphorical allusions to intimate relationships with Jesus. Amanda Smith, an evangelist in the A.M.E. Church spoke of having been married to Jesus Christ: "I am married to Jesus / For more than one year, / I am married to Jesus for during the war."[35] Women of Smith's disposition were not by any means subscribing to the notion of celibacy that is adhered to by the Catholic church. Instead they were proud spiritual bigamists. One slave woman was heard to say: "I have been married two times, once wid Jesus an' once wid a man whut God put heah to marry."[36] This metaphorical description of what it meant to be twice-married unequivocally reflected the priority that these women gave Jesus in their lives. It gave them the power of transcendence over the self-negating "Jezebel" and "mammy" images. Marital status with Jesus assured these women of an intimate companion who could heal their fragile diseased bodies that often prohibited them from being good spouses. Jesus was, also, the regulator of their troubled minds. No mortal man, earthly husband or master, would keep this kind of woman from doing Jesus' work. She trusted Jesus to empower her weak body and regulate her confused mind. Nothing was more troubling to the minds of the women of this type than the thought that they had broken the vows of their relationship with Jesus Christ. They lived with the intense awareness of God's presence as the normative directive for their daily behavior. Zilpha Elaw credits the awareness of the judging presence of God and Christ, during

the writing of her autobiography, as having been the critical factor in moti-
vating her to write the truth:

> I write as before God and Christ and declare, as I shall give an account
> to my Judge at the great day, that everything that I have written in
> this little book, has been written with conscientious veracity and scru-
> pulous adherence to the truth.[37]

Sanctified women believed that Jesus secured them emotionally with a
constant companionship. He provided them with his secure arms of love
and protection. It was for this reason that they even requested to die in his
arms. They believed, as well, that Jesus called them to preach the gospel
in a society that was in opposition to female preachers.[38] But to be married
to Jesus meant literally that these women submit their fragile bodies to
Jesus' will. Infirmity of the physical body, which some women interpreted
to mean that they were not in perfect harmony with the will of God, is a
repetitive theme in the autobiographies of these ex-slave women. To have
been healed physically by the power of God was generally interpreted by
these women as a sign of the genuineness of their faith. It was often cited
as living proof that they had received God's "second blessing." Women who
believed that this had happened to them refused to be pushed around by
men physically stronger than themselves. Their indomitable steel-willed
minds compensated for their lack of body strength. That God could bring
strength out of her weak body was spoken of by Zilpha Elaw as a humanly
irresolvable riddle:

> Divine goodness raised me and honoured me as an angel of God; yet
> my bodily presence continued weak; the passions, frailties and imper-
> fections of humanity abounded in my own consciousness; the union
> of such meanness and honour rendered me a riddle to myself.[39]

It was believed that the consciousness of such an "irresolvable riddle"
kept such women, as Elaw, in humble disposition as "servants of the
cross."[40] Servant of the cross status required that the sanctified woman
exchange her right of self-autonomy for the gift of a strong mind (will) that
assured her of victory in Jesus:

> Whatever of sorrow or difficult I met with in the paths of the Lord,
> I was able to sustain, and cheerfully to bear the cross after my loving
> Lord and Master; but the privilege of self-direction the Lord did not
> permit so ignorant and incompetent servant as I was to exercise.[41]

Female servants of the cross considered themselves "the poor and
weak instrumentality in the gospel of Jesus."[42]

Prayerful intercourse with Jesus was the communicative way that these women resolved difficult matters. Elaw confesses that it was a hermeneutical, although mystical, means of having obscure scripture passages illuminated:

we ascertain and enter into the mind of God; therein beholding as in a mirror, the glory of Jesus, we become increasingly assimilated to the same image, from one degree of glory to another, as by the Spirit of the Lord.[43]

Contemporary readers might quickly conclude that these female autobiographers were merely concerned about the matters of the soul. Such conclusion is definitely an unfair assessment of their stories. It fails to take into consideration the fact that these "sisters of the soul" lived with the challenge that God's call of them to preach the gospel included the self as body and soul. Therefore, they presented themselves even in foreign countries as God's messengers. When called upon to address their social superiors the sanctified female was motivated by the belief that she was called by God. Zilpha Elaw remembered being made to feel inadequate when called upon to address an audience in England. She confessed to being overwhelmed by what she termed

my ignorance, my sex, my color and my inability to minister the gospel in a country so polished and enlightened, so furnished with Bibles, so blessed with ministers, and so studded with temples.[44]

Elaw said that her doubt was countered by the voice of God which said: "say not I cannot speak; for thy shalt go to all to whom I send thee, and what I command thee, thou shalt speak."[45] Amanda Smith makes a direct correlation between the piety and faith of slaves and the coming of freedom.[46] God's providential way of freeing slaves, Amanda Smith believed, was always mysterious:

In some way or other
the Lord will provide;
It may not be my way,
it may not be thy way,
And yet in his own way,
The Lord will provide.[47]

Sanctified women, although simplistic in their declarations about God's actions, were profound in their understanding of the self's struggle between good and evil. This is portrayed in their narrations of the reflexive struggle between the self as the potential agent of the Lord and the self as the potential servant of the devil. The mind was viewed as a stage where God and the devil vied for the soul of the individual. The narrator believes that the devil, through his signifying strategy, causes her to be a victim of her own self-doubt. She understood that it was Satan's objective to "produce a cloud of self-doubt" over her. This is clearly demonstrated in Amanda Smith's recollection of an event that took place in her mind on Tuesday, the seventeenth day of March, 1856. Smith remembers that she was sitting in the kitchen by the ironing table, thinking it all over. It was then that the devil seemed to say: "You have prayed to be converted." The dialogue went as follows:

> "You have prayed to be converted."
> I said, "Yes."
> "You have been sincere."
> "Yes."
> "You have been in earnest."
> "Yes."
> "You have read your Bible, and you really want to be converted."
> "Yes, Lord, Thou knowest it: Thou knowest my heart, I really want to be converted."
> Then Satan said, "Well, if God were going to convert you He would have done it long ago: He does his work quick, and with all your sincerity God has not converted you."
> "Yes, that is so."
> "You might as well give up, then," said he, "it is no use, He won't hear you."[48]

While being tempted by the devil's logic, Smith hears a counter voice saying: "Pray once more." As she prepares to do what this voice tells her, the devil says: "Don't you do it." Smith courageously tells the devil: "Yes I will." She discovers the key to her new being in the "Yes I will" self-resolution that opens her up to God's transforming power of salvation. This is heard in the account of what happened to her once she resolved to obey God: "and I felt it [the transforming power of God] from the crown of my head clear through me." It was in the moment that Smith exercised the freedom of her will that she intensely desired God's gift of salvation immediately. This is illustrated in her response to the voice: " 'I will,' and I got on my feet and said, I will pray once more, and if there is any such thing as salvation, I am determined to have it this afternoon or die."[49] The knowledge of salvation certainty does not free Amanda from the taunts of the devil's cynical voice at every turn of events in her life. The devil attacks Smith's claim of salvation certainty by asking who could bear witness to her claim? Momentarily confused by the question, Smith recalled how she had heard other slaves brag to the devil about the "witness of the Spirit." It was a resolve to do likewise that gave Smith a sense of being seasonally freed from the devil's torment. Awareness of the "witness of the Spirit" gave "sanctified" women the power to counter the devil's claim upon their lives.

If the Spirit was their witness, Jesus was understood to be sanctified women's defense "amid all the storms of temptations and trial that they had to pass through." This conviction anchored them at the time of the storm. Jesus liberated them, according to Smith, and other women of this type, from the fear even of white people. This happened despite Satan's shrewd attempt to make them fearful. They used warrior language to speak of Jesus as "a mighty captain, . . . who never lost a battle." This was their way of celebrating the fact that Jesus had empowered them to overcome all the seeds of fear and doubt that the devil sought to plant in their minds. Smith narrates several incidents of the devil's efforts to make her doubt. One incident occurred when worshiping at a white camp meeting service. The devil told her: "Look, look at the white people, mind, they [white people] will put you out."[50] Smith says that at the moment she sought to place her hand over her mouth the Spirit of God left her. Then Satan chided her for having reneged on her promise to God that "she would confess the presence of God's Spirit upon her anywhere." Smith acknowledged that she had always had a conscious fear of white people primarily because they were white and she was black. It was Jesus' revelatory voice and the witness of the Holy Spirit that assured Smith of the authenticity of Paul's words that: "There is neither Jew nor Greek, there is neither bond nor free, there is neither male nor female, for ye are all one in Christ" (Gal. 3:28).[51] Smith says that, while she had never understood that text before, Holy Spirit made it clear to her. Seeing white people through this scriptural frame of reference, Smith said of her changed perception of them that: "now they looked so small. The great mountain had now become a mole-hill."

In another incident Satan provokes in Amanda a "man-fearing" and a "woman-fearing spirit" regarding her position as a female minister who believed in the doctrine of sanctification. In answer to her request to God to make it clear to her, God directs her to the biblical passage that says: "Perfect love casteth out all fear. He that feareth has not been made perfect in love."[52] Amanda dealt with the temptation to be white by saying that

as the Lord lives, I would rather be black and fully saved than to be white and not saved; I was bad enough black as I am, and I would have been ten times worse had I been white.[53]

Smith said that she preferred being black if for no other reason than to share the great honor of the richness of Africa's historic civilization.[54]

Autobiography as a womanist statement accents the value of the slave woman being a "sanctified" exhorter in Jesus Christ. These women, to say the least, employed unconventional language in the narrative constructions of their escapes from slavery.

STYLES OF AUTOBIOGRAPHICAL NARRATION

I identify two styles of autobiographical narration: conventional and unconventional. Conventional narration reflects the will and mind of white editors, ghostwriters, and publishers. In unconventional narration, the writer accents the way in which personal choice is exercised in the plantation escape. The unconventional narrator describes him- or herself as a codeterminer with God in the escape episode. Contemporary scholars of African-American literature are of the opinion that very few of unconventional type narrators' autobiographies were actually published. The lack of economic means, literary skills, and racism all dictated the degree to which ex-slaves might exercise self-autonomy when encountering white people.

Unconventional

I begin this section with a discussion of the unconventional style illustrated by the autobiographical narrative of Frederick Douglass. Douglass has been held up as the classical example of a slave who sought a marginal degree of self-autonomy in the face of abolitionists' paternalism. The style and content of Douglass' novel suggested that he was greatly influenced by the rhetoric of northern abolitionists. He employed rhetoric from the Bible, the Declaration of Independence, and the U.S. Constitution in his attempt to justify even his violent actions to become a free man. Such rhetoric armed Douglass with more inclusive philosophical categories for engaging the opponents of slavery.

An examination of Frederick Douglass' narration of his conversion experience with that of his violent encounter with Covey, the slavebreaker, is a case in point. Douglass only scantly uses the slave community's traditional conversion language to explain his conversion experience. For him the convert is not violently attacked by God in the conversion experience episode. Conversion, instead, was an experience of having the mind radically transformed by the Spirit of God. Douglass does not mention having felt any change in his somatic self. The God of Douglass' conversion experience enlightens the mind, transforms the heart, and converts the soul of the sin-conscious all in a quiet way. This is the God of traditional evangelical Christianity. Narrating what his disposition was before he became self-conscious of his own sinful state, Douglass wrote: "I was a wretch and had no means of making myself otherwise." Douglass stated the initial stage of his identity crisis tersely: "for weeks I was a broken hearted mourner traveling through doubts and fears."[55] In the next statement Douglass comes closer to approximating the slave community's traditional conversion language:

I finally found my burden lighted, and my heart relieved. I loved all mankind, slaveholders not excepted, though I abhorred slavery more than ever. I saw the world in a new light and my great concern was to have everybody converted.[56]

The phrase "I loved everybody" captures the ethical axiom of the slave community's traditional way of talking about the conversion experience. Douglass' use of such metaphorical phrases as "new light" and "great concern" reflects the extent to which he understood conversion as both spiritual and social enlightenment.

An examination of Douglass' violent confrontation with Covey, the slave breaker, will allow us to compare and contrast, if need be, the metaphors that the former used. Douglass implies that God is the Great Ideal Observer in his reconstruction of Covey's attack upon him. Contrary to the God of the slave community, the Great Ideal Observer has no direct personal contact with the human self or the created order. The point of connectivity between creator and humanity is that the latter is made with the capacity to self-determine their existence. For this reason this God has no need to "strike" the soul or the body of the person. Douglass concludes that, given the fact that he was made in the image of this God, God had empowered even slaves with the intelligence to defend themselves against their would-be annihilators. Douglass, the slave, concluded that his act of self-defense against Covey's assault upon his somatic self signified that he was made in the image of the Governor of the moral universe.

It was Douglass' conversion experience, coupled with other episodes, that created an acute self-awareness in him about his being and social status in the world. This is manifested in the way in which Douglass shares his discontented mind with Uncle Lawson, an elderly slave, who was his secret spiritual mentor on the plantation. During shared secret sessions with Uncle Lawson, Douglass questions the relationship between his newly enlightened mind (the consequence of his conversion) and the seemingly eternal character of institutional slavery. This is heard in Douglass' query of Uncle Lawson's charge that "God had a great work for him." Douglass' counterresponse to the old man was: "How can these things be? and what can I do?" To these radical questions the old slave countered with the traditional answer of the victimized: "Trust in the Lord." It is to this reply that Douglass dares think the critical question that defies the logic of the plantation masters' false doctrine of anthropology. He thought "I am a slave, and a slave for life, how can I do anything?"[57] This was a question that one who had accepted social status as having been eternally fixed as a slave was not supposed to think or ask. That Douglass dared ask the question meant that he was evolving into being more than a slave. Uncle Lawson's answer was: "Trust God in faith and he will give you liberty."

Douglass' inevitable violent confrontation with Covey, the slave breaker, reminded him afresh that he was perceived as mere property of the master, that is, a body minus a soul. Slavery had rendered Douglass what he termed "a living embodiment of mental and physical wretchedness."[58] Douglass likens the positive feelings derived from his valiant efforts of self-defense against Covey's brutal aggression to a conversion experience. The three phases of the conversion experience (see chapter three) are evident in Douglass' account of the episode. First, Douglass experiences great anxiety as a result of abusive treatment at the hands of Covey. That provokes him to question his own identity as well as the existence of God, (which was not part of traditional conversion language). For Douglass to question God was certainly an unconventional response for a slave—at least we have no documented accounts to the contrary. All of Douglass' conversations with Lawson and Sanday, his confidants on the plantation, did not abate his desire for immediate freedom. Contrasting his condition of slavery with that of the mobile freedom of the ship upon the waters of the Chesapeake Bay, Douglass, the believer, laments, "O, God, save me! Let me be free!"[59] In the next breath, Douglass, the doubter, asks: "Is there any God? Why am I? Why am I a slave?" As though he gets a critical distance from his own soliloquizing, Douglass resolves that it would be better to risk physical death than remain a slave for life. Douglass was atypical in the sense that he claimed to have suffered mentally and physically under the yoke of slavery. Such claim was counter to the slave master's stereotypical assertion that slaves, Douglass included, were merely soulless bodies or bodiless souls. Douglass says that slavery had "rendered me the living embodiment of mental and physical wretchedness."

Second, Douglass' experiences his greatest nadir of the soul following his first flogging at the hands of Covey. Having been physically brutalized, Douglass portrays himself to the reader in the gory imagery of a suffering servant: "From the crown of my head to the sole of my feet, there were marks of blood. My hair was all clotted with dust and blood, and the back of my shirt was all clotted with the same."[60] Moreover Douglass says: "Briars and thorns had scarred and torn my legs and feet." Even though in this deplorable state, Douglass' appearance before his master did not win "the interposition of his authority and power." The master refused on the grounds that Douglass had probably done something wrong to provoke the beating from Covey. Haunted by sleepless nights and weary days, the wounded Douglass remembered wondering aloud to himself if "I had a friend on earth or in heaven." Douglass could not possibly understand what he or his parents could have done to bring about such personal suffering. Contrary to the traditional conversion stories that portray the subject suffering from bouts of self-condemnation, Douglass condemns institutional slavery for his plight of victimization. While hiding from Covey, Douglass thinks to himself: "Life in itself had almost become burdensome to me." In this temporary place of refuge, Douglass concluded that he must face Covey or remain in the woods of the plantation and starve. After being fed by Sanday, Douglass resolved that he must face his nemesis. Traditional conversion language of the slave community would have called this the "old hell's dark door" aspect of the experience of the self's odyssey. For more than two hours Douglass struggled successfully to defend himself as an embodied self against Covey's physical and psychological attacks.

Third, Douglass rejoices over the fact that he used an "undignified" method, that is, physical violence, to attain his liberated sense of manhood: "I was a changed being after that fight. I was nothing before—I was a man now." Cleverly, Douglass celebrates the power of inner self-transformation derived from his inevitable moment of violent resistance. Douglass uses the selected metaphors from the slave community's traditional conversion language to convey his euphoric attitude following the violent encounter: "It was a resurrection from the dark and pestiferous tomb of slavery, to the heaven of comparative freedom."[61] Having overcome the fear of death itself, Douglass resolved that it was the spirit of defiance that made him "a freeman in fact, though I still remained a slave in form."[62] Douglass joyfully realized that he, in his act of defiance, had brought body and soul together within himself, thereby creating his own space upon the earth: "When a slave cannot be flogged, he is more than half free. He has a domain as broad as his own manly heart to defend, and he is really a power on the earth."[63] Self-defense of the body for Douglass was inevitable for becoming free in body and soul. As Douglass said: "Hereditary bondmen, know ye not who would be free, themselves must strike the blow?"[64]

When called upon by abolitionists to answer the question of how he felt following his escape from slavery, Douglass used none of the slave community's traditional conversion language, that is, that language that does not make any explicit reference to God as having been his liberator in his defeat of Covey. He, instead, characterized his experience in unconventional terms:

A new world has opened up to me. If life is more than breath, and the "quick round of blood," I lived more in one day than in a year of my slave life. It was a time of joys and excitement which words can but tamely describe. . . . "I felt as one might feel upon escape from a den of hungry lions."[65]

The only mention Douglass makes about God pertains to his doubts about God having been on his side:

I had at times asked myself the question, may not my condition after all be God's work and ordered for a wise purpose, and if so, was not submission my duty?[66]

Conventional

Use of conventional conversion language is very evident in most published ex-slave autobiographies. It presents God as the author of the Creation as well as God having been the author of one's salvation. God also is portrayed as working in partnership with the narrator in his or her quest for freedom. Narratives that made use of the conventional conversion language were very determined to counter the prevailing myth of the "contented slave." Users of the conventional conversion language, as well as the nonusers, were usually committed to showing that slavery constituted mental anguish for those who dared be critically self-conscious.[67] All slaves who had plotted and successfully executed their escapes were considered violators of their master's ethical code of conduct. They had broken the stereotype of what was considered the "loyal" slave. Douglass correctly observed that the success of institutional slavery was contingent upon the ability of slaveholders to reduce slaves to thoughtless entities. The reflective Douglass said: "To make a contented slave, you must make a thoughtless one. He must be able to detect no inconsistencies in slavery."[68] Such a slave would know no law higher than the master's will.

Careful study of a selected number of ex-slave narratives reveals two basic themes that tended to have preoccupied the consciousness of conventional type narrators. First is that faith in the self was the prerequisite to accomplishing a successful escape from slavery. And second, the slave loyal to the plantation community was without an equal among slave peers.

Faith, Self, and Escape

Basic concepts that are found in all conventional narrators' autobiographies are faith, self, and escape—reflecting the conviction that faith in oneself is necessary for a successful escape from slavery. Converted slaves reasoned that having faith in God equaled having faith in themselves since it was believed that God worked through them. God, in the conversion act, worked in the fearful slave to bring forth a courageous self. This sort of language, when used by the narrator, raised the plausibility level of the ex-slave's story for the abolitionist readers. The slave who could testify to God's demonstrative salvation power in his or her life was looked upon even by abolitionists as being trustworthy. Thus, the published autobiographies often served as symbolic indicators that the writer's life was a testimony to the fact that slaves had the capacity to realize what appeared to be visibly impossible.

Faith was believed to have been a basic structure that organized the narrator's story. Reason alone, for the narrator, could not have adequately explained how the ex-slave had overcome the barriers of both nature and human adversaries in order to find his or her way North. It was the faith that God gave the convert during his or her conversion experience that turned what could have been a disaster into a triumphant journey. Ex-slaves who completed the escape were ever reminded that many of their brothers and sisters, for different reasons, died not having received the promise. Some were caught by slave catchers and taken back to the South; others became sick while enroute and were left to die on the wayside. This is what might be referred to in the narratives as "autobiographical faith."

I mean by autobiographical faith the self's awareness that God is both its genesis, middle, and its ending. That is to say that the self can only exist and come to being within God's parameters.[69]

The notion of autobiographical faith makes it clear why most narrators marked their conversion experiences as the pivotal point for becoming a free social self. This spiritual freedom that came with conversion was valued as being foundational of all political freedom.[70] Slaves of the conventional conversion language interpreted all political and natural phenomena as being the consequences of God acting in both spheres of existence.

A narrator might use a political metaphor to characterize one's conversion experience. One such conventional metaphorical phrase regularly used to describe this experience was "my dungeon having shook and my chains having fallen off." Most fugitives from the world of the plantation believed that God, the author and finisher of their new spiritual beings, gave them the mental aptness to escape. James Watkins, in the narration of his experience of slavery, draws a direct correlation between his conversion experience and his escape. He attributed the hearing of the gospel from a preacher at a camp meeting, which he had attended without his master's permission, for being the crucial turning point in his awareness of salvation in Jesus Christ. It was the hearing of the preacher's message that Watkins says drove him to the point of "wrestling with God for the space of three or four hours." Here Watkins "poured out [his] soul to the Almighty in [his] weak and ignorant way, beseeching Him mightily to pardon his sins." Watkins recalled that the consequence of his petition was that of a radical self-transformation: "My heart was so filled with the love of God that the fear of the whip, or even of death, was entirely taken away from me."[71]

The radicalness of Watkins' transformation was displayed in his demonstrated courage in the face of his master's readiness to physically punish him for attending the revival service. The other approach of Watkins' master was to humiliate him psychologically by reminding him that he had "no soul." The master's demoralizing rhetoric did not undermine Watkins' new confessional resolve that had grown out of his conversion experience: "I told him that my soul was happy, and although he might punish my body he could not harm my soul." This radical sense of new being had merely increased Watkins' discontentment with being a slave of his master. He wrote: "I never gave up the idea of one day trying to obtain my freedom. The notion considerably increased with me after my conversion."[72] Contrary to the traditional conversion paradigm of slaves, where God was perceived as the planner and the implementor of freedom, ex-slaves were expected to initiate and execute their own escapes from slavery. Watkins did not understand his case to be an exception to that rule. He had to resist physically the foes of nature and humanity in his escape route from the plantation of the South to Hartford, Connecticut. Watkins characterized God as his providential guide from bondage to freedom.

According to conventional narrators, God revealed God's self in the signs of nature, as well as other persons, for the illiterate slave who sought to escape. Many slaves, in the words of Gustavus Vassa, were "accustomed to look at the hand of God in the minutest occurrence, and to learn from it a lesson of morality and religion." Slaves such as Nat Turner depended upon God to inform them through signs of the natural order. It was by reading these natural signs that such slaves took their cue for rebelling against or running away from the master. Turner, who was reputed to have led the most heralded rebellion, claimed that he was given an apocalyptic sign from God while plowing in the field. Narrators, also, reported that it was customary for them to consult the voodoo doctor before making their escape from slavery. It was popular for many fugitive slaves to travel with the rabbit foot around their necks, or in their pockets as a good-luck charm.

Godly intoxication was deemed as the greatest antidote against fear by those slaves who escaped successfully from the plantation. Harriet Tubman's biographer seemingly captured this aspect of her life when she wrote graphically of Tubman's God consciousness:

> Her whole soul was filled with awe of the mysterious Unseen Presence, which thrilled her with such depths of emotions, that all care and fear vanished. Then she seemed to speak with her Maker "as a man talketh with his friend"; her child-like petitions had direct answers, and beautiful visions lifted her up above all her doubts and anxiety into serene trust and faith.[73]

It is safe to say that converted slaves who escaped the plantations used the conversion experience language to communicate with their new abolitionist friends. This language won many new friends for them in the cold environs of the North.

Loyalty and Community

Slave owners, when describing a slave's character, commonly used the term "loyalty." Slaves were typified according to their character in three ways: the servile cooperation type; the covert passive aggression type, and the open rebellion type.[74] Conversion to Jesus Christ often empowered the slave to accommodate all three types of behavior in their daily conduct. The master's ideal intent was that Christianity would transform the slave into a loyal subject of a servile temperament. At the baptism ceremony the master expected the slave to answer satisfactorily such questions as: "Do you feel as if you loved your master better than you ever did before, and as if you could do more work and do it better?" Another primary question to be answered was: "Do you feel willing to bear correction when it is given to you like a good and faithful servant, without fretting, murmuring or running away as has heretofore been your practice?"[75] If the slave could answer positively to all of these questions, the master might pronounce him a "good boy" and approve him as a candidate for baptism.

What about duty to God and what the slave called his or her "brothers and sisters"? This becomes the genuine test of whether or not the slave has experienced real conversion to the master's definition of Christianity or the Christ of the slave community. It was a question that would determine which social body the slave would identify with. Loyalty to Jesus' social body, comprised of believers in Jesus, required that slaves be responsible both for the bodies and souls of each other. Slaves' collective existential visionary understanding of Jesus gave them a radically new sense of what it meant to be an embodied community amid structures that fostered alienation. All of the negative imputations of slave theology was not able to negate slaves from sharing love for each other in Jesus' name and spirit. The name and spirit of Jesus converted slaves to the assurance of a positive community amid life-negating forces. Herein existed the margin of choice that slaves could rejoice in knowing that they possessed. It allowed them the needed strength to place loyalty to Jesus above self-interest. There was no discipleship in Jesus, subsequently, without the element of self-risk being involved.

Loyalty to Jesus versus self-interest. Slaves internalized the notion that salvation in Jesus meant that the convert had been empowered by Jesus, God, and the Holy Spirit for a new mission. It meant that they had been empowered to withstand the assaults of the devil upon their physical bodies and minds. Before we condemn it as being merely another classical example of Karl Marx's notion of "religion being no more than an opiate of the people," we need to look more closely at the phenomenon of slave religion. What most Marxist analysts of slave sources have concluded generally is that the slave's very confession that she and he had been converted by Jesus, according to the slave community's criteria, was an act of spiritual rebellion itself. For slaves to say that they had chosen Jesus as their Lord and master was in actuality to say that they had set themselves in opposition to the ethos of slavery. Being converted by God meant that God had freed the slave's latent self to rebel against all forms of oppression. This is what is heard in the testimony of slaves who had the courage to passively resist their master even at the cost of being physically beaten.

Nothing is more powerful in the slaves' narratives than their testimonies of how conversion to Jesus empowered them to withstand the master's whip upon their backs. Rather than a deterrent to their faith, physical persecution apparently became its principal motivator. Identification with Jesus as God's embodied sufferer gave slaves the courage to sacrifice their own bodies for Jesus' gift of freedom. It often lit a passionate fire in their souls that drove them to take a daring posture of courage. Neither the driver's lashes upon their backs, nor salt and pepper rubbed into their wounds could keep them from their resolve to follow Jesus. Numerous stories tell of slaves who valued loyalty to Jesus above all human authority. This was the case even when masters offered some slaves an opportunity for less punishment if they would change their commitment to Christ. There were rare cases in which some slaves were known to be so faithful in their commitment to Jesus that they actually persuaded their masters to become Christians.[76] Such slaves obviously were able to gain certain moral victories over their masters as they persevered in their faithfulness to the cause of Christ. Each moral victory must have helped them to see themselves as being "the least of God's little ones." This sense of moral empowerment could have very well been used to shame some Christian masters in the same way that blacks used it during the civil rights movement of the fifties and sixties to embarrass southern white Christians.

Appeals to their masters' consciences through love and forgiveness became the most powerful method that many slaves used to relate to them. Some of the more striking cases of forgiveness and the appeal to masters' consciences are found in letters written by ex-slaves.[77] Some slaves seemingly saw it as a great moral strength to be able to demonstrate that Christ had given them the power both to forgive and love them. No example of this is any more powerful than the statement in the letter that Bibb wrote from Canada to his master back in Kentucky: "If you should ever chance to be traveling this way, and will call upon me, I will use you better than you did me while I was a slave." Bibb would have his master to know that he does not have any malice against him for the mistreatment of him while he was his slave. He attributes his behavior to the fact that he was a victim of the country. Bibb tells the master "I can freely forgive you."[78]

Loyalty to immediate family. Bibb, a former slave, likened separation from his own immediate family on the plantation as having been analogous to "tearing off the limbs of my body."[79] Conflict between becoming free and leaving one's family in bondage was a painful reality for every sensitive slave.[80] James Pennington, ex-slave, writes pointedly of one of "the two great difficulties" that stood in the way of his flight:

> I had a father and mother whom I dearly loved — I had also six sisters and four brothers on my plantation. The question was, shall I hide my purpose from them? Moreover, how will my flight affect them when I am gone? Will they not be suspected? Will not the whole family be sold off as a disaffected family, as is the case when one of its family flies?[81]

Such realities as we have just cited clearly indicate that becoming a fugitive from the plantation called often for making very painful psychological adjustments. It was not as easy as one saying I will run away from the master and slavery. There was a real sense in which the fugitive's decision to flee the plantation meant that she and he would have to sever all familial ties temporarily.

Many slaves were aware that slave masters were great violators of the biblical injunction that said: "What God has joined together let no man put asunder." Daily, slaves witnessed the painful experience of masters breaking up relationships between parents and their children and husbands and wives all for the purpose of economic profit. This did not, however, prevent many slaves from expressing their feelings of familial loyalty. These feelings were expressed in two ways in ex-slaves' narratives: first, the degree to which fugitive and ex-slaves were willing to risk their newly acquired status of freedom for the freedom of their family members; second, the intensely passionate desire that slaves expressed to contribute to the freedom of all slaves. Many ex-slaves made note of how difficult it was for them to enjoy their own freedom knowing that others were yet in slavery.

Some slaves, such as William Brown, refused to marry because they were fearful that the emotional ties to wife and children would make it more difficult to escape.[82] Despite this fact many slaves were not satisfied with being what some referred to themselves as "self-redeemers," but the redeemer of others who were yet in slavery. Persons such as Harriet Tubman did it by going by night back into the slave territory on numerous occasions to bring brothers and sisters out via the Underground Railroad. Women such as Elaw did it by penetrating the slave territory as an evangelist of the gospel of Jesus Christ. Still others did it by working, among antislavery groups of the North as embodied witnesses, often bearing the scars upon their backs, of the evils of slavery. No slave was more graphic than William Brown in his passionate desire to be an authentic witness for the need of the freeing of all slaves. He graphically wrote in his autobiography:

> If it were not for the stripes upon my back which were made while I was a slave, I would in my will leave my skin as a legacy to the government, desiring that it might be taken off and made into parchment, and then bind the constitution of glorious, happy, and free America. Let the skin of an American slave bind the charter of American liberty![83]

Brown's words might be interpreted as a kind of satire against the way white Americans had defined liberty. Brown makes the point that, despite his self-sacrifice to the ideals of liberty, he has been its victim.

Here again slaves were deeply influenced by the fragmented teachings of Christianity that were given by whites. Conversion in Jesus meant that familial relationships came to be grounded on the supposition of being born again in Jesus Christ. Sisters and brothers became those who dared do the will of the Jesus Christ who came that all might have a right to the tree of life.

This chapter has shown that the ex-slave's autobiographical genre is another constructive type of response to the masters' false doctrine of anthropology. Autobiography uniquely veers from what we have referred to in the previous chapters as the conventional conversion language of the slave community. This type response reflects the journey of the slave's mind as she and he moved from slave to ex-slave status. Here, we see the making of what I would call the secular version of the African-American mind. It is the making of the ideally literate African-American citizen. Ex-slaves tell their stories in a more secular language than does the traditionally converted slave. They tend to credit much of their success to the use of their own intelligence rather than the direct intervention of the providential hand of God. Ex-slaves are striving to become the ideal citizens of America rather the ideal Christians of the kingdom of heaven.

Chapter six will show that the trickster-story genre of the Brer Rabbit stories was the slave community's other creative type response to the false doctrine of anthropology. Brer Rabbit symbolized the slave community's constructive personified response to the problem. According to the community's accounts, it seems that elderly slave men took great delight in telling these Brer Rabbit stories. In the elderly male slave we have the symbol of the fragile body and the deceptively strong mind. The community's genius operative here seemingly is that male slaves, by projecting their minds through the fragile body of Brer Rabbit, presented a facade of harmlessness to the rulers of the plantation world. The Brer Rabbit stories make up what I have termed above the religio-moral language of the slave community.

CHAPTER 6

Brer Rabbit Stories

Weak Body and Strong Mind

Nothing is more powerful than when adults tell children's stories for more than entertainment purposes. This is what slaves did during slavery with their fictitious hero that they affectionately called "Brer Rabbit." While they entertained themselves with them, slaves, also, educated each other to the realities of human nature with the Brer Rabbit stories. This probably explains why no fictitious character in the folklore of slaves compared, for them, with Brer Rabbit. He was the paradox of both weakness and strength. The Brer Rabbit stories, also, show the creative way that the slave community responded to the oppressor's failure to address them as human beings created in the image of God. The stories reflect the genius of the oppressed community to create its own symbols in defiance of the perverted logic of the oppressor. Brer Rabbit paradoxically symbolized the combination of a fragile body and a deceptively strong mind. It was the fragility of Brer Rabbit's small body that gave him such a deceptive appearance in the eyes of the slave community. Slaves knew that his adversaries rightly wondered how such a tough mind could be embodied in such a little fragile body.

FACTS AND FICTION

Brer Rabbit and the Male Slave

It was because "Brer Rabbit" paradoxically symbolized both the weakness of body and the strength of mind that slaves vicariously identified with him. Male slaves learned quickly the wisdom of masking their mental prowess behind the believed innocent mask of Brer Rabbit. They took delight, before their masters, in minimizing their physical strength. Documented folk sources all seem to indicate that storytelling about Brer Rabbit's capers was a typical pastime of elderly slave men. This paradoxical symbol of being a weak body and strong mind symbolized the way that these elderly men portrayed themselves to the imposing authority figures of the plantation. In the same vein, slave masters saw elderly slave men as the personification of docility. They believed that the aging process, having rendered them no longer a physical threat, had cured elderly slaves of all desires of rebellion. Masters commonly, for this reason, related to many elderly slave men as one would a trusted house pet. These male slaves (e.g., Uncle Remus) were considered safe around white women and their children. They were affectionately loved for their buffoonery and their often uncanny art of storytelling. Behind the mask of Brer Rabbit, old slaves of the plantation often demonstrated their intellectual prowess in a way that was not fully comprehended by those whites who heard and laughed at them.

The ingenious act of telling animal stories involving the protagonist Brer Rabbit became a ritual, employed by elderly slave men, for the self-preservation of young male slaves. Had male slaves confronted their masters as the actual living embodiment of the spirit of High John de Conqueror the consequences would have been that of violent confrontation. It stands to reason that the animal tales of elderly slave men had profound meanings for the slave community. The storytellers and the stories themselves created a needed buffer between powerful white males of the plantations and enchained black males. Brer Rabbit symbolized the mediator, in a system that disallowed male slaves the right of free speech. It was Rabbit's genius for applying humor to potentially dangerous encounters with superiors that prevented inevitable bloodshed. Violently inclined male slaves readily came to see the wisdom of Brer Rabbit. Slaves, male and female, knew that powerful white men were less threatened by a deceptively strong mind in a weak body.

High John and Brer Rabbit: The Making of a Myth

Many scholars of African-American culture, from Melville Herskovits to Sterling Stuckey, have posited the idea that the Brer Rabbit myth for slaves had its antecedents in the Anansi myth of West Africa. Anansi was the spider trickster about whom slaves wove tales.[1] The explanation for the need for this weak body and strong mind paradox, personified in Brer Rabbit, slaves mythically traced back to having been brought by ships from Africa. Evidence of this fact is seen in an account of a folktale, recorded by Zora Neale Hurston, about High John de Conqueror. Slaves attributed High John de Conqueror with being the *"source and soul"* of laughter and song; they called him *"our hope-bringer."* Slaves believed that High John, who it was said came from Africa *"walking on the waves of sand,"* was really a supernatural spiritual force that became flesh. Slaves said of him: *"First off, he was a whisper, a will to hope, a wish to find something worthy of laughter and song."*[2] In their description of his transition from the world of the supernatural to that of a person of the natural state, slaves implied that High John became embodied in the flesh: *"Then the whisper put on flesh."* As a consequence, *"the black folks had an irresistible impulse to laugh,"* because *"High John de Conquer was a man in full, and had come to live on the plantations, and all of the slave folks knew him in the flesh."* High John's gift of laughter empowered slaves to endure their burdens in the heat of the day *"when the work was hardest, and the lot most cruel."*[3] Slave masters were oblivious to the fact that High John was among slaves giving out laughter daily to them.

The transition from being a supernatural force to that of being a natural person did not take place until slaves arrived in America. All during the Middle Passage *"High John de Conquer was walking the very winds that filled the sails of the ship,"* while *"black bodies huddled down there"* in the hull of the ship. It was said that High John *"followed over them like the albatross."*

Slaves' rationale for why white people were unable to discern the presence of High John among the members of their community must be considered insightful for our discussion. The first explanation given was that: *"Slaves were secretive around white people about who High John was. They refused to tell them who he was."* The second was that *"If the white people, heard some scraps, they could not understand because they had nothing like that to hear things with."* Third, white people *"were not looking for any hope in those days, and it was not much of a strain for them to find something to laugh over. Old John would have been out of place for them."*[4] The subsequent statement clearly illustrates slaves' rationale for construing the paradox of the weak body and the strong mind as a way of protecting themselves from the master's wrath:

> Old Massa met our hope-bringer all right, but when Old Massa met him, he was not going by his right name. He was traveling, and touristing around on the plantations as the laugh-provoking Brer Rabbit. So Old Massa and Old Miss and their young ones laugh with and at Brer Rabbit and wished him well. And all the time, there was High John de Conquer playing his tricks of making a way out of no-way. Hitting a straight lick with a crooked stick. Winning the jack pot with no other stake but a laugh. Fighting a mighty battle without outside-showing force, and winning his war from within. Really winning in a permanent way, for he was winning with the soul of the black man whole and free. So he could use it afterwards. For what shall it profit a man if he gain the whole world and lose his soul? You would have nothing but a cruel, vengeful, grasping monster come to power.[5]

All of the different traditional folk accounts about what High John looked like, physically, clearly illustrate why slaves believed there was a need to create for themselves the paradoxical symbol of physical weakness and deceptive mental strength. There was no established picture of the physical appearance of High John de Conqueror. According to the story-teller, there were varied opinions: *"To some, he was a big physical-looking man like John Henry. To others, he was a little hammered-down, low-built man like the devil's doll baby."*[6] Different accounts of the physical appearance of High John de Conqueror undoubtedly explain why slaves accented and celebrated Brer Rabbit's mental strength. In the words of the former slave, Simon Brown, Brer Rabbit was adored for his intelligence rather than ferocious strength: *"Brer Rabbit can't fight like a wild cat or climb a tree. But he's got big eyes that can see to the front and the sides and behind without turning his head. He's got long legs and a heap of sense! To the slave, he's like a brother!"*[7] The community's belief that its members were of the same intellectual fraternity with Brer Rabbit gave them a potent weapon of self-defense. It gave them a creative way of surviving in the midst of inhumane conditions. An analysis of several different versions of the Brer Rabbit stories from both the white and slave communities stand to illuminate our thesis.

BRER RABBIT: A WHITE MAN'S VERSION

White men and women of the plantation South had a deep pyschological need for both the mythic figures known as Uncle Remus and Brer Rabbit. This is clearly seen in Chandler Harris' voluminous collection of Brer Rabbit stories as told by Uncle Remus. Joel Chandler Harris (1848–1908) was a son of Georgia. A journalist, novelist, and short-story writer, Harris was primarily known for his formal literary creation of the fictitious character known as Uncle Remus. Harris claims that he heard these stories told by an old slave while coming up in the master's house of the plantation. It was for several decades that Harris ran his version of Uncle Remus and the Brer Rabbit stories in the *Atlanta Constitution* where he worked as a writer. Harris obviously redacts these stories for the white readership of his newspaper.

Harris' Uncle Remus portrays the legendary hero Brer Rabbit as having "creature sense." Remus' remarks about Brer Rabbit's intelligence are made in response to the little white boy's observation that his father says *"that the animals have got sure enough sense."*[8] Remus tells the little white boy that while the animals do not have *"law sense"* and *"business sense,"* they have "creature sense." Uncle Remus continues in his observation to make a distinction between animal size and sense:

> The littler the creatures are, the more sense they got, because they have to have it. You hear folks say that Brer Rabbit is full of tricks. It is just the name they give it. What folks call tricks is creature sense. If old Brer Lion had as much sense as Brer Rabbit, what the name

of goodness would the rest of the creatures do? There would not be none of them left by this time.[9]

It is not accidental that Uncle Remus, in the conversation with the little white boy, explicitly compares himself physically and implicitly mentally with Brer Rabbit. Uncle Remus, correcting the little boy's opinion that Brer Lion does not have much sense, notes that *"he had some but he ain't got as much as Brer Rabbit."*[10] It is at this point that Harris has his old slave storyteller make a subtle statement that the little white boy will obviously not understand until he is a man:

"Them what got strength ain't got much sense. You take niggers — they are lots stronger than what white folks is. I am not so strong myself," remarked the old man, with a sly touch of vanity that was lost on the little boy, "but the common run of the niggers is lots stronger than white folks. Yet I have done took notice of the times that what white folks call sense do not turn out to be sense every day and Sunday too. I ain't never seen the patter-roller what can keep up with me. He may go hoss-back, he may go foot-back, it do not make no difernce to me. They never have caught me yet, and when they do I will let you know."[11]

Harris, who is the white creator of this slave folk hero, has Uncle Remus compare himself with Brer Rabbit:

That is the way it is with Brer Rabbit. The few times that he has been outdone he mighty willing for to let them talk about it, if it will do them any good. Those that have outdone him have the right to brag and he makes no deniance of it.[12]

The inevitable question that readers of Harris' stories are faced with is: Why has Harris a need for a mythic character such as Uncle Remus? Before answering this question the point ought be made that African-American scholars have found Harris' stereotypical image of "the old darky" story-teller very offensive and degrading to African Americans as a whole. Harris creates for the reader the image of an impotent old male slave, plantation handyman, who yarns what appears to be childish stories during his leisure time for the plantation owner's male children. It is my contention here that African-American scholars have been too quick to dismiss Harris' stereotypical image of Uncle Remus before trying to understand critically his suppositions. Beyond the race stereotype, the critical student detects a radically subtle process of pedagogy at work in the mind of the old slave storyteller.

We noted above that Harris has Uncle Remus portray himself as being physically weak but in the mold of Brer Rabbit mentally strong. Remus truly personifies what I call a creative counterresponse to the oppressor's false mind and body dichotomy. Note that Harris has Uncle Remus define himself so as not to appear as a violent threat to his white reading audience. Harris, also, has Remus make note of the fact that those young male slaves who are physically strong are nonthreatening to white people because they are mentally weaker. Harris' view, as voiced by Uncle Remus, rightly reinforces the stereotype that his white readers believed already. Such description of Uncle Remus presents him as a benignly qualified storyteller on the plantation. What Harris knows, and subtly demonstrates, is that Uncle Remus' age and fragile physical appearance won him the privileged position of being the storyteller of the plantation owner's male children.

It is my contention that Harris, by virtue of the fact that he places the old slave in the role of storyteller, creates a role for Uncle Remus to be the shaper of the consciousness of the next generation's plantation owner. Theoretically the storyteller, according to Socrates, indulges in two kinds of discourse, *"the true and the untrue."* Socrates reminds his students that the one in a society who tells stories to the children is the one who leaves the greatest impression upon them. They are in the position to shape the soul and character of children. It was for this reason that Socrates asks:

> Shall we then carelessly allow children to hear any kind of stories composed by anybody, and to take in their souls beliefs which are for the most part contrary to those we think they should hold in maturity?[13]

What Harris makes clear in the *Nights with Uncle Remus* on the plantation is that Uncle Remus was an uncensored storyteller primarily because he was deemed harmless. The other point is that Uncle Remus constructs for these little white boys a hero figure, in Brer Rabbit, who is antithetical to the heroic values of the plantation masters. Socrates' definition of "the bad story" was the one that "gives a bad image of the god and heroes, like a painter drawing a bad picture, unlike the model he is wanting to portray."[14] The lesson that Uncle Remus teaches has been learned all too well by Harris who himself was a son of "Brer Lion."

"Sense Do Not Stand for Goodness"

Harris makes Uncle Remus less of a threat to the white community by having him define *"creature sense"* for the little white boy as being of neutral value: *"sense do not stand for goodness."*[15] The creatures of Uncle Remus' world live by the first law of nature—the survival of the fittest. Remus says that *"they do not know nothing at all about that that is good and that that is not good. They do not know right from wrong."*[16] There are no moral boundaries in the world of the creatures. This is Remus' way of counteracting the criticism that the little boy's mother has made about the animal stories.

She observed that his stories are in conflict with the moral lessons of the Bible that the little boy learned in his Sunday school class at church. Keenly aware of this fact, Uncle Remus proceeds to tell the boy why he is telling him these stories in the first place. He says that: *"I am telling them on account of the way the creatures do."* It is at this point that Remus implicates the moral lesson that the stories have for critiquing the oppressor's behavior toward the oppressed. Uncle Remus asked the little boy: *"How the name of goodness can folks go on and steal and tell fibs like the creatures do, and not get hurt?"*[17] Uncle Remus makes the point that he does not like stories about folk because *"folks can not play tricks, never get even with the neighbors, without hurting somebodies feelings, or breaking some law, or going against what the preachers says."*[18] It is for this reason that Uncle Remus says that he *"does not enjoy telling his stories to grown white folks."*[19] It seems that the point being made here is that in the mythic realm of creatures there is no sacred space or time. Uncle Remus protects himself, against the little boy misrepresenting his words to his parents, by explaining that his stories originate from the realm of dream consciousness.

"They Will All Come Slippin' In"

One of the fascinating things about Harris' Uncle Remus is the source of his stories. Harris makes it clear that Remus' stories about animals and their behavior originate from the subconscious mind. These imaginary animals surface on rainy and wintry days in the mind of the old slave when it is impossible to do hard jobs on the plantation. Harris notes that it was on such days that Remus would find himself dozing into the twilight zone of sleep. It was at this moment when Brer Rabbit and the other creatures entered his conscious mind. Harris has Uncle Remus say that:

> It is at this moment that Brer Rabbit sticks his head in the crack of the door and see my eye partly shot, and then he'll beckon back at the other creatures, and then they will all come slipping in on tip toes, and they will set there and run over the old times with one another, and crack jokes same at they use to.[20]

The idea being conveyed is that there was a mythic moment when animals and human beings conversed with each other freely. Uncle Remus says that these animals *"created a regular Jubilee; a regular time of freedom."* What is unique about what Uncle Remus experiences is the creatures' activity in the dream. Remus says that they *"take up his cooking utensils, the trivet, and the griddle, and the frying pan, and play tunes"* of some mythic past. When the little boy wants to know *"if they play like a band,"* Uncle Remus responds:

> They come just like I told you honey. When I shut my eyes and doze, and they come and play, but when I open my eyes they are not there.

Now and then that is the shape of matters, what does I do? I just shut my eyes and hold them shut, and let them come in and play them old time tunes until long after bedtime done come and gone.[21]

It is not surprising that Harris called the collection of these stories *Nights with Uncle Remus*. Uncle Remus' imaginary animal creatures come out of his subconscious mind. They come from that part of the mind that is easiest evoked by a child's innocent questions.

"This Is All the Far the Tale Goes"

Harris recorded the stories so as to show that they come to Uncle Remus' memory best when the little boy raised innocent questions with him about the daily events of life. The reader gets the impression that what are simple childlike questions in the mouth of the little boy require complex answers from Uncle Remus. These answers are often so complex that Uncle Remus can only answer them by appealing to the myth-making realm of the mind. The little boy asked Uncle Remus, after the latter had initiated him into the imaginary animal world: *"Did not Brer Fox never catch the Rabbit?"*[22] It was this question that provoked Uncle Remus to tell "The Wonderful Tar-Baby" story where Brer Fox is credited with having caught Brer Rabbit. The little boy is concerned at the end of the story to know: *"Did Brer Fox Eat Brer Rabbit?"* Uncle Remus gives a coy response to such question by telling the little boy *"That is all the far the tale goes, he might have and then he might not have."*[23]

Contrary to what might be seen in the stories when slaves told them for their own entertainment, Harris portrays the storyteller, Uncle Remus, as being the embodiment of subtlety. This is understandable since Harris' main objective undoubtedly was to share these stories with white literate audiences of the North and South. Consequently Harris' Uncle Remus has a pedagogical task to help whites understand his mythic world of animal behavior; the world of his dark mind. For Harris, Uncle Remus is a craftsman at telling stories that were loaded with biting subtlety. It was the challenge of the little white boy to understand the secrets of Uncle Remus' complex mind. This was no less the burdensome challenge of every plantation master. If they fail to understand this phenomenon, the little boy and the master would be unable to make any sense out of Uncle Remus' tales about Brer Rabbit. But what was more important was that their failure to make sense of Uncle Remus' childlike tales meant that masters were not as powerful over slaves as they might have deceived themselves to believe. According to Harris' portrait, the little boy was in a better position than his father, primarily because of his innocence, to share the mysteries of the old man's mind. Harris has the little boy, regarding the Brer Fox and Brer Rabbit story, ask Uncle Remus:

"Did Brer Rabbit have to go clean away when he got loose from the Tar-Baby?" The boy's question merely evoked in Uncle Remus the enthusiasm needed for telling the story. The old slave therefore countered: "What he going away for?" Then Uncle Remus tells the boy a sobering word: "You do not know anything about Brer Rabbit at all."[24]

In the next breath of the narration, Uncle Remus mentioned "Miss Meadows" at whose name the boy inquired: *"Who is Miss Meadows?"* It is in response to this question that Harris' Uncle Remus reflects the embodiment of subtlety in his answer: *"Do not ask me, honey. She was in the tale, I give it like it was given to me."* The point here is that it is not the duty of the storyteller to explain the tale when it is being told to white folks; that is left to the hearer. The hearer who pushes his inquiry too far will be told by Uncle Remus: *"That what is in the tale I can tell you; that what is not you have to figure out for yourself."*[25]

On another occasion, when vexed by the boy's effort to catch him in a contradiction, Uncle Remus' angered response portrayed him as the living embodiment of hermeneutical subtlety:

> Is I the tale are is the tale me? Tell me that! If I am not the tale and the tale ain't me, then how come you want to take and rake me over the coals for?[26]

The point that Harris would have Uncle Remus make to the little white boy was that the story has a life and character of its own when being told by the storyteller. Uncle Remus reminded the little boy that the white hearer of the story had no right to tell the slave, the one who embodies it, how to tell it. This was why when the little boy commented *"That was the end of Brer Wolf"* that Uncle Remus said *"That is what the tale say. Old Remus one nigger and the tale, it is another nigger."*[27] Remus' point here is that if he and the story that he was telling were not synonymous it really made no difference whether Brer Wolf was dead or alive.[28]

Another significant point Harris makes in his construction of Uncle Remus and the Brer Rabbit stories was that the storyteller was not to be rushed. Remus controls the tempo at which he told the story by comparing himself to *"a broke-down plow-mule."* Refusing to be dictated to by another, Remus took *"the broke-down plow-mule"* metaphor full circle when he told the little boy: *"I'll go along if you let me take my time, but if you push me, I'll stop right in the middle of the row."*[29] Storytelling was that communicative art of the oppressed that the oppressor had no control over. Uncle Remus makes it clear that the story that he tells is not the property of the oppressor. Remus said that: *"The tale come down from my great-granddaddy's great-granddaddy: it come on down to my daddy, and just as he give it to me, just that away I done give it to you."*[30]

Just as subjective time was necessary for storytelling, Harris' Uncle Remus tells the little boy that the recognition of objective time was just as important for the white hearer to believe it. When the boy asked *"Can't you tell the story unless you can find out about the time?"* The old slave countered: *"Tooby sure I can, honey, but you would believe it much quicker if you knew what time it happened."*[31] Even with this Uncle Remus recognized in the face of his rival African-American storyteller, Daddy Jack, that *"Folks tell tales differently."*[32]

It is the contention here that slaves had a different pedagogical and entertainment objective in mind when they told the Brer Rabbit stories among themselves for themselves.

BRER RABBIT: BLACK PERSPECTIVES

Contrary to the above analysis of the white perspective, Brer Rabbit, rather than the storyteller, becomes the living embodiment of subtlety. First, I will draw upon William Faulkner's remembered version of the Brer Rabbit stories as told to him by a former slave named Simon Brown. Second, we will examine blacks' portrait of Brer Rabbit found in Edward C. L. Adams' *Nigger to Nigger* animal stories.

Brer Rabbit as Told by Simon Brown

William Faulkner (1897–1962), a black American author and a student of folklore, published a recollected version of the Brer Rabbit stories he heard as a youth growing up on his widowed mother's farm in Society Hill, South Carolina. In the introduction to the book, *The Days When Animals Talked*, Faulkner recalls, as a ten-year-old boy, being richly entertained by a former slave named Simon Brown, who then lived as a tenant-farmer on the family farm. In his adult years, Faulkner came to see that Simon Brown was more than an artful storyteller and a great entertainer of children like himself with these animal stories. He saw that

> the stories were not just children's entertainment, but were deeply significant allegories created by tortured, subjugated people to sustain and encourage themselves in a hostile world.[33]

Faulkner saw a direct correlation between the scars upon Simon Brown's back, caused by a whipping he received as a slave, and the Brer Rabbit stories.[34] Brown took great pride in the fact that he never allowed himself to be whipped after that one incident. Faulkner recalled that Brown could be heard to say repeatedly: *"I was a mighty man in those days."* Brown taught Faulkner that slaves, out of the crucibles of their common suffering, were caretakers for each other during seasons of grief and sickness. It was

Brown's position that slaves' greatest sense of triumph came in knowing that *"no man could own their souls or keep them from loving one another."*[35] Simon Brown, in his conversations with the young Faulkner, stressed the value of the slave using his head for self-preservation on the plantation.[36] The last resort was for one to openly stand up against a white authority figure.

In contrast to Harris' intention, discussed in the previous section, to share the stories with white audiences, Faulkner's account of Simon Brown provides insight into how these animal stories functioned pedagogically among the slaves to create a subtle moral protest community. These stories became the slave community's means of making its own way in the world. Storytellers and hearers of the Brer Rabbit stories understood them to be communal protest statements against white exploitation.

Faulkner remembers that it was the uproar caused by the activities of the Ku Klux Klan and the Night Riders in the South Carolina of his boyhood that provoked him to seek Simon Brown's opinion about the moral protest nature of the Brer Rabbit stories. Brown responded by telling of Brer Rabbit's "Called Protest Meeting." Brown prefaced his story with the observation that "people like the animals of the woods live, too, by the first law of nature rather than the law of God." The events of the time reminded Simon Brown of the time when Brer Rabbit and the smaller creatures *"called a big meeting to complain to the Lord about long-tails and short-tails."*

Long tails, in this case, symbolized the possessors of an abundance of political power; short tails symbolized those who lacked it. The presupposition of Simon Brown's story was that: *"at the time of Creation, when the Lord made all the beasts and things, that he didn't give any of them tails."*[37] All of these insect-pestered animals asked the Lord for tails and the Lord granted their request. Among the short tails there surfaced great dissatisfaction, however, over the fact that their tails were of inadequate length to defend them against the pesky insects. Brer Rabbit called a meeting of all short-tail creatures to discuss their problems. Simon Brown said that *"Brer Elephant, Brer Deer, Brer Billy Goat, Brer Groundhog, Brer Wild Hog, and others all met in Brer Rabbit's front yard, and there they decided to call a convention in the Big House."*[38] It was Brer Rabbit's opinion that they could register their complaint to the Good Lord about the inadequacy of their short tails. All agreed with Brer Rabbit that it was a matter of injustice that they were given short tails by the Creator.

Long-tail animals such as Brer Tiger and Brer Lion were upset when they heard of the plans of the short-tail creatures. Brer Lion raised the political question that imaged the fear of all of the long-tail animals: *"Who knows what might happen to us?"* He went on to note that:

We're in a favorable situation and very comfortable. If the Lord hears from those short-tail varmints, He might decide to chop off pieces of our long tails and give them to other creatures and that would never do.[39]

Brer Tiger, in agreement with Brer Lion's assessment, proposed that the long-tail creatures organize and break up the planned convention of the short-tail creatures. It was a matter of *"keeping the short-tail creatures in their place."* At the twelve o'clock Saturday meeting at the Big House there was hardly standing room for the short-tail creatures. Brer Rabbit stepped forth up to the platform to sit in the ruling chair. Beating him to it, Brer Lion grabbed up the gavel, and hit on the table, bam! And then he called the meeting to order. He made everybody sit down, including Brer Rabbit who protested that this is our meeting—the short-tail creatures. Brer Lion refused to recognize Brer Rabbit on the grounds that he was the moderator and whatever he said was law. He decreed that only the long-tail creatures would be able to vote in the meeting. All of Brer Rabbit's protest was to no avail since *"might had overruled right."* Brer Lion ordered Brer Tiger and Brer Panther to clear all of the short-tail creatures from the Big House. Brer Rabbit and the short-tail creatures met in the front yard of the Big House to plan the strategy for their next course of action. In the yard of the Big House Brer Rabbit said:

There isn't any justice in the land. The big long tail creatures are the most and they run over us who are the least. They don't want us to even tell our troubles to the Lord. But this time they have gone too far, for no creature can stop another creature from talking to the Good Lord. We'll just keep on working and praying for him to deliver us from our misery, and one day, by and by, He will answer our prayer, and that's for sure.[40]

Simon Brown's story has many fascinating aspects. First, we note that the variable of skin color is never mentioned in the story. This undoubtedly suggests that slave storytellers, even among themselves, left some things to the imagination of their hearers. It was not safe even among other slaves to make everything explicitly clear. Color was obviously viewed as being a natural given by God in this situation.

Second, the long-tail and short-tail descriptive language here symbolized the imbalance of political power that absolutely favored whites of the South. It symbolized the natural injustice of slavery. This issue was most dramatic for former slaves during the Reconstruction and the post-Reconstruction era of the South. Brown's version of the story obviously has its origin in the great political transition that took place in the South when African Americans were forced out of political offices by white mobs. At stake here in the story about the "long-tail and short-tail" animals is the issue of whether African Americans have natural political rights. What the "short-tail" animals found out was that the very place where laws were legislated became for them the symbol of unfairness.

Third, the symbolism of the "Big House" has political ramifications for understanding how African Americans lost political power following the Reconstruction period. The "Big House" of the state symbolized the same kind of political hegemony that the "Big House" of the plantation did. It is a cultural symbol rather than a political one. While African Americans during slavery had no political voice in the "Big House" of the plantation, those during the period of Reconstruction had a political voice only temporarily. Just as slaves were not allowed to meet on the plantation without the master's permission, African Americans were forbidden to caucus at the "Big House" of the state for political purposes. Brer Rabbit and his cohorts had to learn that it was not the objective of those who built the "Big House" of either the state or the plantation to do what was fair. The "Big House" of the state, like that of the plantation, was built on the law of the survival of the fittest.

Fourth, the story delineates the way that African Americans learned to use religious power for the accomplishment of political power. This is one of the few stories where Brer Rabbit is credited with leading his people in a prayer protest against social evil. Narrators have commonly portrayed Brer Rabbit as being the personification of vanity and self-centeredness. Even here, of course, Simon Brown's Brer Rabbit was not addicted to a pie-in-the-sky version of religion. Brer Rabbit suggested that prayer be used as the means, not the substitute, for accomplishing political power. His words merit our attention: *"We'll just go on working and praying for him to deliver us from our misery, and one day, bye and bye, He will answer our prayer, and that's for sure."* Brer Rabbit, according to Simon Brown, understands himself to be a copartner with God in the liberation process. God liberates those who "work and pray." Ironically, in most of the stories that were recorded by Harris, Brer Rabbit symbolized one who saved himself by learning to work his mind cleverly and quickly. Simon Brown presents a version of Brer Rabbit who understands that he is saved both by his "works" and faith in God. What we might have here, in this difference of perspective in the telling of the story, is that when slaves told the Brer Rabbit stories mainly for each other they recognized that even the trickster had a streak of piety in him.

Brer Rabbit as Told by Congaree River Blacks

In the 1920's Edward C. L. Adams, a white physician from the area around the Congaree River of South Carolina, made a remarkable record of African-American life. Adams called one collection of stories from African Americans of this part of South Carolina *Nigger to Nigger*.[41] A number of the Brer Rabbit stories appear in this particular collection. The portrait of Brer Rabbit in these stories is of a paradoxical nature. On the one hand

Adams' community characterizes Brer Rabbit as being "vain," "low down," and "without a conscience." He is disliked by the members of the community for being what they termed "stuck-up." Given his self-conceited nature, Brer Rabbit of Adams' account mainly uses all of his talents and power for himself. He lived to entertain the women and play the fiddle. It was said that without his fiddle, with which slaves associated magical powers, Brer Rabbit would not exist. Such a portrait of Brer Rabbit, undoubtedly, was a literary technique that the black community, since slavery, had used to critique its own members as well as whites of the power structure. There were obviously individual slaves on the plantations who were merely concerned about their own welfare. Individuals of this type used their talents and influences to promote themselves in the eyes of the master. Ironically the community, however, was attracted to Brer Rabbit for his entertainment genius. Although lacking moral scruples, Brer Rabbit was such a charismatic entertainer that he could transform a graveyard setting into a party. It was Brer Rabbit's conjuring powers that enabled him to bring the living community and the spirit world together for celebration. He was acknowledged by the slave community as a supernaturally gifted entertainer.

One of Adams' characters tells of having *"seen a rabbit setting on top of the grave playin' a fiddle, for God's sakes."* By virtue of Rabbit's charisma as a supernaturally gifted entertainer, he was able to create community among all of the animals of the field. Adams' character proceeds to say:

"All kind er little beast been runnin' 'round, dancin' an' callin' numbers. An' dere was wood rats an' squirrels cuttin' capers wid dey fancy self, an' diff'ent kind er birds an' owl. Even dem ole owl was sachayin' round-look like dey was enjoyin' dey self." In the midst of such a festive Brer Rabbit was seen exalting himself: "An' dat ole rabbit was puttin' on more airs dan a poor buckra wid a jug of liquor an' a new suit er clothes on."[42]

It was when Brer Rabbit used his conjuring power to unite the world of the living and that of the dead that Adams' character reports in the end:

While I been watch all dese strange guines on, I see de snow on de grave crack an' rise up. An grave open an' I see Simon rise up out of er dat grave. I see him an' he look jest as natu'al as he done 'fore dey bury him. An' he look satisfy, an' he look like he taken a great interest in Bur Rabbit an' de little beast an' birds. And he set down on de top er he grave, an' carry on a long compersation wid all dem animals. An' dem owl look like dey never was guh git through. You know dem ole owl—de ole folks always is say dey is dead folks. But dat ain' all. Atter dey done worked dey self out wid compersation, I see Bur

Rabbit take he fiddle an' put it under he chin an' start to playin'. An'
I watch, I see Bur Rabbit step back on de grave an' Simon were gone.[43]

On the other hand, the other image presented of Brer Rabbit was that
he occasionally used his trickster powers to warn the other animals of
impending danger. This truth was illustrated in the story of "The Dance of
the Little Animals." The party takes place in the graveyard on Christmas
night under the luminous moon-lighted sky. Brer Rabbit was seen standing
on both of his hind legs playing his fiddle: *"he th'owed dat fiddle up under
his arm an' started playin' reels."* It was believed that Brer Rabbit had unusual power over all of the small animals: *"An' it look like he call all kind er
animals to him — all kind er little animals. An' dey all went to dancin."*
One of the great mysteries that even the storyteller had a difficult time
understanding is that Brer Rabbit hangs around graveyards although he
seems to love life. During the graveyard gathering, Brer Rabbit warned all
of the animals who had come to his party to flee in the nick of time from
Brer Fox. Although they knew that he was not "a Christian," the community
reveled in the idea that *"Brer Rabbit is got a heap er sense an' er heap er
scheme, an' er he love to sport around an' enjoy he self."*[44] Blacks, since the
days of slavery seemingly, took great pride in the idea that Brer Rabbit was
a free spirit who defied conventional logic. This was the case despite the
fact that Brer Rabbit lived purely by the law of self-preservation.[45]

SELF-PRESERVATIONIST AND ETHICAL REALISM

Existential, as opposed to eschatological, liberation is the common theme
that runs through the slave community's accounts of the Brer Rabbit stories.
While Jesus is generally perceived as the symbol of eschatological hope in
the spirituals and conversion stories, Brer Rabbit is projected as the symbol
of existential hope in most of the trickster stories. One of my major con-
tentions in this section is that even converted slaves saw the major ethical
advantage in embracing these antithetical symbols. Slaves learned in the
crucibles of their own suffering the importance of living creatively on what
I will term "the ethical boundary" between moral idealism and realism.
If Jesus was the embodiment of moral idealism, Brer Rabbit personified
ethical realism for the slave community. In so doing, Brer Rabbit defied all
moral rules of conventional behavior. In the mind of the slave community,
Brer Rabbit's maverick behavior generally always defied the predictability
of the oppressors' logic. Brer Rabbit's behavior could not be explained fully
by such moral categories as right and wrong, or good and evil. This was
due mainly to the fact that he delighted in living on the very moral boundaries where oppressors had drawn lines of demarcation between good and
evil, right and wrong. Brer Rabbit, as a matter of fact, specialized in confusing the oppressors' demarcated boundaries that the oppressor had estab-

lished as being absolutely definitive of what constituted good and evil, right and wrong. It was for this reason that slaves saw Brer Rabbit as being morally ambiguous. Such a notion of Brer Rabbit, on the part of the community, gave him somewhat of a semigod status among mortals. Interestingly however, slaves did not think of Brer Rabbit as always being immortal. They could even accept the fact that Brer Rabbit could get killed. Because he could neither be defined as moral, amoral, or immoral, Brer Rabbit could assume the posture of one who daringly played the boundary lines of what was defined as right and wrong, good and evil over against each other. In doing this, Brer Rabbit cleverly reflected slaves' common sense conclusion that the truth about right and wrong, good and evil was not arrived at simplistically; it was not reducible to an either-or phenomenon. Such reasoning directly contradicted masters' objective of reducing the moral life of slaves to a simplified either-or phenomenon. It was masters' simplistic reasoning of either-or moral reductionism that led them to equate slaves' obedience to them with satisfying God's moral imperative. Slaves learned for themselves in the moral school of trial and error that genuine obedience to God, as a converted Christian, required a subtle, if not always a blatant act of disobedience of the master.

Brer Rabbit came to symbolize for slaves the both-and, rather than the either-or, paradox of morality. He illustrated, by his daring anti-Christian behavior, that human beings always experience the moral life as a complex phenomenon of both good and bad, and right and wrong. Assuming an ambiguous moral posture, Brer Rabbit symbolized in his acts of defiance slaves' critical awareness of the woeful inadequacies of oppressors' definitions of moral, amoral, and immoral. He helped even Christian slaves to see that the pious language about "love" and "forgiveness" that masters assigned to the servile Jesus was inadequate and misconstrued textually. Brer Rabbit symbolically helped slaves understand that masters' sermonic and catechetical lessons of servile Christian virtues were intended to render slaves powerless. The rabbit symbol was designed to prevent slaves from dealing honestly with their own legitimate feelings of raging anger, which they were required to repress daily. Consequently, Brer Rabbit symbolized in his persona the moral complexities of life that slaves lived with daily. Amoral is an inadequate category for characterizing the slave community's perception of Brer Rabbit since they acknowledged that he knew right from wrong. This fact was often demonstrated in some of the stories that the community told about his acts of benevolence. In some of their stories, community members portray him as a kind of Christ figure.

In the Brer Rabbit symbol, converted slaves were now able to hold in creative tension "the natural law" of self-preservation and "the spiritual law" of self-denial. Brer Rabbit and Jesus came to epitomize in the consciousness of the slave community antithetical moral symbols that allowed its members to forge their own parameters of ethical decision making. These contrasting symbols gave slaves a dialectical way of understanding what it means to live in creative tension with the demands of the flesh and those of the spirit. By holding these two symbols, Brer Rabbit and Jesus, in creative tension of each other, slaves were able to counter the destructive impact of institutional slavery upon their lives. In so doing, they were able to counter the oppressor's false doctrine of anthropology—body or soul, mind or body. Just as they valued the Christian doctrine of self-denial, symbolized in Jesus' life and death, slaves found the counter doctrine of self-preservation, symbolized in Brer Rabbit, of equal value. Given such an assumption, it might be safe to say that the morally mature slave, in the eyes of the slave community, was the one who knew how to live creatively on "the ethical boundary" between the principle of self-denial and that of self-preservation. The morally mature slave credited God as being the giver of such wisdom.

God, Creation, and Brer Rabbit

The slave community believed that God gave Brer Rabbit exceptional mental ability in the world of larger predators. While it was for his self-preservation, God was quick to remind Brer Rabbit that this special gift of intelligence was to be used prudently. Brer Rabbit's genius, in the judgment of the slave community, was his ability to combine knowledge and wisdom for his own self-preservation. The knowledgeable, but unwise, slave was always a candidate for self-destruction. Clear warning was given to every young slave by the community in the story: "Brer Rabbit Seeks Wisdom." Tradition has it that one day Brer Rabbit went to God in quest of wisdom. God reminded Brer Rabbit that every person, himself included, already has a *"little wisdom"* evidenced, in Rabbit's case, by the fact that he had sense enough to come to God for it. The adventurous Brer Rabbit, who would not be deterred, makes a rational case to God as to why he *"wants much wisdom."* God promises to honor Brer Rabbit's request on the condition that he accomplishes the following impossible feats: *"First, bring me the scales of the great ocean fish. Second, bring me milk from the wild cow. Third bring me two teeth from the mouth of a living crocodile."*[46]

Despite the fact that any one of the three cited challenges required that he place himself in great physical danger, Brer Rabbit arrogantly told God (saying that *"it was nothing"*) that he would accomplish all three feats. In each case Brer Rabbit got what he needed by talking the stronger creatures into following his game plan, baiting them into believing that it was in their better interest. With all three assignments accomplished, Brer Rabbit went back and told God how he had done such tour de force. In each case Brer Rabbit talked those animals who were physically superior to himself into doing foolish things that led to their own self-destruction and to Brer Rabbit's success. Brer Rabbit exploited Brer Crocodile's greed, Sister Cow's stupidity, and Brer Ocean Fish's gullibility all to his advantage. God's response to Brer Rabbit's perfect feat might very well suggest that the slave community understood that it was not to play the fool with the gift of Godly wisdom. The story's narrator has God respond:

> You have done three impossible things. It required great wisdom to do what you have done. You already have what you came to get from me. I can add nothing to the cleverness in your head. But take care, Rabbit! Cleverness like this can kill you.[47]

There were varied accounts, obviously, in the slave community about how Brer Rabbit came to be endowed with his rare gift of extra sense. One such an example is the account of Brer Rabbit "Catching the Snake and the Yellow Jackets." This story has Brer Rabbit going to the Conjure Man in quest of extra sense. Here Brer Rabbit is given the challenge of having to catch the snake and the yellow jackets. The story ends with the implication that the slave community possibly saw Brer Rabbit as a type of Conjure Man himself. This is heard in "The Conjure Man's words" of admiration for Brer Rabbit's ability to accomplish what seemed to have been the impossible feat:

> Buh Rabbit, you is suddenly the smartest of all of the animals, and your sense shall get more and more every day. More than that I am going to put white spot on your forehead, so everybody can see you have the best sense in you head.[48]

In the mind of the slave community, Brer Rabbit's superior genius was, also, in knowing when to use his knowledge. This was reflected in the fact that Brer Rabbit never does the *"same trick twice"* when in a survival contest with creatures of superior physical strength and speed such as Brer Fox. The capacity for versatility is Brer Rabbit's strength. This truth is vibrantly heard in the storyteller's account of Brer Rabbit tricking Brer Fox into crossing Brer Bear. The moral lesson to be learned from Brer Bear putting a whipping on Brer Fox is that: *"it don't do you no good to learn the right trick at the wrong time."* The storyteller goes on to observe: *"Trouble with Buh Fox, if he had done that trick on Wednesday instead of Thursday he'd made good on it. Time is one element you ca't fool around with."*[49] In this statement Brer Rabbit is credited with knowing how to be both versatile and spontaneous.

A classical story that the community used to illustrate the danger of being arbitrary was in the "Brer Rabbit and the Tar Baby" account. Brer Rabbit displays a lack of prudence in his encounter with the Tar Baby when it becomes his ultimate aim to make him talk. In this futile attempt, Brer Rabbit falls right into the trap that Brer Fox cleverly has set for him. Those stories that allowed Brer Rabbit to be destroyed by the stronger and faster animal seemed to have been designed for the purpose of teaching slave children that divine wisdom used selfishly was self-destructive. Such a moral lesson was evidently intended to be taught by the "Brer Rabbit" and the "Brer Tarrapin" story. The clever minded individual could very well become a candidate for self-destruction by using his or her personal knowledge in total disregard of the collective knowledge and wisdom of the community. This fact is clearly accented in "The Well" story where the narrator concludes by wisely telling the listening audience that the moral of the story is that:

> No matter how sharp you are, you got to keep on the good side of people, else your smart ways goin' to get you in difficulty. There's a lot to bein' sharp and maybe you can use it against one critter at a time and come off good, but when it comes to bein' sharp against the whole community at once, it don't pay off.[50]

First, every individual is warned not to play God with the gift of knowledge. A second lesson being taught is that the knowledge and wisdom of the whole community equals a power greater than that of the so-called smartest individual.

WORK, PLAY, AND GOD

The Ethic of Playful Versatility

Plantation masters put forth a theological claim that God had preordained slaves to work for their masters. Their doctrine of the servile Jesus was also designed to legitimate the role of the bond servant. Thus in the mind of the slave, Brer Rabbit became the unconventional symbol for countering the ethic of servile labor. If this Jesus demanded that they arbitrarily be committed to this ethic, Brer Rabbit offered a philosophy that fused work and play. It amounted to what I term "the ethic of playful versatility" through which the negative impact of the depersonalized nature of the plantation's work structures was reduced. This philosophy enabled the slave as worker to play the oppressor's definition of the good servile work ethic over against the slave community's philosophy of work as human survival. In so doing, the *playful worker* creates what might be characterized as the "ethical gap," created when the conventional boundary between right and wrong is intentionally confused or reversed by the oppressed. While the intentional actions causing confusion look like moral chaos to the oppressor, the oppressed see it merely as being the creative inversion or reversal of oppressive ethical logic. It is only in creating the ethical gap that the oppressed are able to get the attention of the oppressor, which is prerequisite for moral discourse. This ethical gap requires the oppressor to become a partner with the oppressed in the redefinition of ethical norms and values.

We have shown descriptively that slaves told their own stories of Brer Rabbit to counter, psychologically, the depersonalizing structures of slavery. Had slaves not been able to accomplish this feat they would have been destroyed by the drudgery of work itself. Instead Brer Rabbit, their fantasized hero, enabled them to create a psychological distance between the oppressive duty of work itself and themselves as workers. Philosophically Brer Rabbit's genius as a *playful worker* symbolized the distinction that slaves needed to make between the worker as functionary and the intrinsic value of the being of the worker. In the eyes of the slave master, the worker was considered to be worth no more than the product of his or her labor. That is to say he or she was valued as only a means to an end. Informed by the Brer Rabbit philosophy, the worker is valued for the capacity to critically assign intrinsic value to the work project. It, subsequently, is the worker who makes work meaningful because of his or her capacity to juxtapose work against play and vice versa. That is to say that work itself is recognized as having value only because human beings have been made with the capacity to name and define the activity. In order to keep forced labor from being no more than an activity of structured depersonalization, slaves needed Brer Rabbit to juxtapose play against work and vice versa. In the act of juxtaposition slaves came to see that both work and play as creative projects are dialectical in nature. They saw that the *playful worker* and the *working player* were dialectical sides of the same coin.

Brer Rabbit, as a matter of fact, symbolized for slaves the very personification of "the ethic of playful versatility." This was the case despite the fact that slave masters stereotyped Rabbit and his venerators as being lazy, cunning, conscienceless, and chaotic. Even with such a negative evaluation, masters were unable to break the bonds of psychological fixation that slaves had for Brer Rabbit and vice versa. Slaves venerated the very character traits that masters detested in Brer Rabbit. What masters often failed to understand, however, was that slaves identified with Brer Rabbit as a protest symbol to counter the psychological exploitations of slavery. This common psychological method of affirming self-dignity permeates the Brer Rabbit stories. The stories clearly dramatize the community's understanding of the false dichotomy that slave masters created between concepts of "right" and "might," "power" and "justice." Clearly, the slaves intuitively understood the value of what scholars commonly call situation ethics. They recognized that the immoral structures of slavery made it expedient for Brer Rabbit, at times for his own self-preservation, to lie, steal, and kill. What is apparent, of course, is the fact that no stories portray Brer Rabbit as a *willful* liar, thief, or murderer. For this reason, it might be argued that all of this is indicative of the fact that the community never lost its sensitivity to what was right and wrong at a higher moral level. We might say that this is the mark that distinguishes the slave community's appropriation of trickster stories from other ethnic groups.[51]

The community's protest against the master's definition of the work ethic is dramatized in the story about "Brer Wolf's Magic Gate." Here Brer Rabbit refuses Brer Wolf's invitation to jointly plant a garden with him on the premise that *"the sun's too hot, and the grounds too hard."* Brer Rabbit affirms the master's stereotype of the slave being a lazy liar. The subtle fact is, which was known by the community, that Brer Rabbit knows that Brer Wolf's hidden plan is to exploit his labor by taking the best of the produce for himself. Brer Rabbit will not be cajoled into cooperating in such a project, even when Brer Wolf tells him that he will plant his favorite foods such as collard greens, cabbages, turnips, and carrots. Brer Rabbit responded that *"I don't like those things I eat wild clover leafs myself."* Brer Wolf planted his garden and fenced it in so as to keep Brer Rabbit out. Affirming Brer Wolf's suspicion, Brer Rabbit came to raid his garden while he was sleeping at night only to find that the gate of the garden was locked with a combination lock. Persistent, Brer Rabbit resolved that he would hide near the gate until Brer Wolf came and learned the magic code for opening it. When he had written the code down in his little black notebook, Brer Rabbit waited until the next night to enter Brer Wolf's garden. Surprisingly Brer Rabbit on the following evening, because the bright moon was covered by a dark cloud, was not able to get the proper code from his notebook. Trusting his memory Brer Rabbit gave the wrong code causing the gate to make a shutting sound that awoke Brer Wolf from his sleep. When Brer Wolf got to the garden the cloud disappeared from the face of the moon and there stood Brer Rabbit, in the moonlight, with a basketful of vegetables from Brer Wolf's garden. Brer Rabbit hid trembling under the collard stalks, listening to Brer Wolf revel in the fact that he had caught him by the hind leg. Brer Rabbit laughed at Brer Wolf and called him crazy. Brer Wolf, puzzled by Brer Rabbit's response, wanted to know why Brer Rabbit had called him crazy. Brer Rabbit told him that he had said what he did because Brer Wolf had the collard stalk rather than his hind leg. Brer Rabbit asked Brer Wolf *"why don't you turn the collard stalk a loose and grab my leg?"* Brer Wolf's response and Brer Rabbit's reaction became the liberating truth that the slave community was able to celebrate:

Old Brer Wolf gasped in surprise. Then he turned Brer Rabbit's leg loose and grabbed the collard stalk. And Brer Rabbit ran out of the garden and down the road lickety-split and Brer Wolf never did catch him.[52]

What is the point being made in this story that illustrates the ethic of playful versatility? Primarily, it is that Brer Rabbit, when in the grasp of his predators, knows how to respond creatively. This is demonstrated by Brer Rabbit's ability to laugh, rather than cry. Laughing frees him to think creatively. In so doing, he provokes his predator to rethink the definiteness of his action. Brer Rabbit's capacity to respond creatively gives him the foresight to invert the logic of discourse in his exchange with Brer Wolf in an adverse situation. It was Brer Rabbit's "playful versatility" that caused Brer Wolf to doubt his own actions. He makes Brer Fox question whether he really has his leg or the collard stalk by telling Fox that he *"must be crazy."* It is Brer Rabbit's charge of Brer Wolf *"being crazy"* that makes the latter question the saneness of his own action. In so doing, Brer Wolf had to let go of Brer Rabbit's leg, which Brer Rabbit told him was the collard stalk. The slave community must have clearly heard the ethic of playful versatility operative in this story. Its members must have concluded that Brer Rabbit created his own existential freedom the moment he could seduce his oppressor to think an unconventional thought. Brer Rabbit's genius, unlike his arbitrary predators such as Brer Wolf, is that he can see the logical formation of an idea from more than one side, for example, from the bottom up as well as from the top down; from inside out and from outside in. Slaves learned that their self-preservation was contingent upon their ability to change their customary way of looking at the logistics of an issue.

Clearly in the above analysis Brer Rabbit is the community's moral symbol of playful versatility. He demonstrates the freedom to act from within himself for at least three reasons. First because he enjoys life and the world around him. The question must rightly be asked: how could this be the case for persons in slavery? It must be seen as wishful thinking, as well as vicarious participation. While it is not the intent here to make them synonymous, it is important to note that "enjoyment" and "playfulness" are closely connected, although enjoyment can exist without playfulness. The slaves make it clear that Brer Rabbit's primary objective is to enjoy life; to fulfill what philosophers have called the primordial relationship with the world. With this in mind it is not surprising that most of the stories about Brer Rabbit have to do with food and family. Second, Brer Rabbit has the courage to say "yes" to life. Through Brer Rabbit, slaves were able to express a feeling of at-homeness in the world that was the opposite of the escapism that permeated the evangelical language of Protestant Christianity. Natural obstacles of life did not intimidate the slave for the reason that they were thought to be a part of the at-homeness of the world. This is the point that is made in the "Brer Rabbit and the Briar Patch" story. In the story Brer Rabbit begs Brer Fox, when in the latter's grasp, *"please not to throw him in the briar patch."* Brer Fox violates Brer Rabbit's request only to find later that he has fulfilled Brer Rabbit's covert wish. In the end, Brer Rabbit rejoices in the fact that the briar patch was where he was born and reared. Third, Brer Rabbit has the courage to act from within himself. Brer Rabbit will not allow the stronger creatures to impose, from without, norms of behavior upon him to the point that they negate his capacity for playful versatility. It was by inverting the oppressor's rules of moral logic that Brer Rabbit creates the needed ethical elbow room (the ethical gap) to play with, what often was perceived to be, the permanently fixed social order of slavery.

God, Rabbit, and Play

The notion seemed to have prevailed in the slave community that even God recognized Brer Rabbit as having been made with a special capacity for playful versatility. It was for this reason that the community imagined God always reserving a marginal degree of suspicion of just what Brer Rabbit's motive was when they encountered each other.

The above truth is illustrated in the tale of "Brer Rabbit's Hankering for a Long Tail." It suggests that the community learned very early, perhaps in some mythic time, that God's gift to the individual for self-preservation was not a substitute for hard work. Brer Rabbit worked himself into a state of dissatisfaction over the way that God had made him for several reasons including the aggravation of pesky insects such as fleas and gnats in hot weather, and the aggravation over the thought that long-tail animals had a functional and an aesthetic advantage over short-tail animals. Perennial displeasure with himself provoked Brer Rabbit to go before God in person and petition for a long tail. The story goes that Brer Rabbit, *"with hat cocked on the side of his head and walking cane in his hand,"* went to God in request of a long tail. God is portrayed in the story anthropomorphically as the Great Ideal Observer of the cosmic order. In none of the Brer Rabbit stories, where God is mentioned, do the narrators ever say that God intervenes directly in human events to help the oppressed. On the contrary, there are accounts of Brer Rabbit going up to heaven to make appeals to God for personal empowerment against his oppressors. "Brer Rabbit's Hankering for a Long Tail" is a classical case in point. God's initial interrogative response to Brer Rabbit's arrival at the Big House of heaven reflects an irate mood on God's part at the sight of Rabbit: *"What do you want?"* God's second interrogative response explicitly reveals God's suspicion that was implied in the first question. God asks the clever Rabbit: *"What kind of trickery are you up to now?"* In the third question God implies full awareness of Brer Rabbit's nature as well as his case history: *"what is this thing that you want so badly that you have gotten bold enough to come way up here like this?"* The storyteller's description of God's anthropomorphic response to Brer Rabbit conveys expressed displeasure on God's part: *"God casted his eyes down at Brer Rabbit and squinched up his forehead and looked him over. Then he puckered up his mouth like he had been biting a green persimmon."* It is at this point that God states God's personal grievance against Brer Rabbit:

You are made like you are made. You have been contrary about that tail from the first day. Sister Nanny Goat did just as I told her, and she was kind to give you any tail at all. Even with all of the blessings you already have you come here to me to get a tail like the very best of creatures have. Hmm you are mighty little to have a long tail, brother horse, brother bull cow are big and stand off the ground, but your belly mostly drags in the dust. You can. You can jump around in the grass to keep those flies off.[53]

Rabbit reminds God that he has been *"jumping around in the grass"* all to no avail. God counters that the real reason why Brer Rabbit wants a long tail is that: *"You just want to be high fashion don't you?"* God gets at the heart of Brer Rabbit's vain nature although God's biting criticism does not discourage Brer Rabbit from persisting that he needs a long tail.

Finally, God agrees to grant Brer Rabbit's request on the condition that he accomplishes the following seemingly impossible feats: Get a tooth from the mouth of Brer Crocodile; Get a cup of tears from the eye of Brer Deer; Get some black birds and bring them back in a sack. In the face of what looked like an impossible and dangerous work assignment, Brer Rabbit expeditiously accomplished all three projects and brought the requested items back to God. God's response would suggest that God was somewhat vexed with the fact that Brer Rabbit was successful at doing the impossible so quickly. In a short time after God had given the assignment, Brother Rabbit appears back at the Big House door. The narrator says that: *"God looks out of the door of the Big House; seeing that it is Brer Rabbit God slams the door and goes back into the Big House."* Brer Rabbit, intimidated by God's response, takes cover under a tree in the yard of the Big House. While he is waiting for God to come out of the Big House a bolt of lightening sets the tree under which Brer Rabbit is taking cover on fire. In response, Brer Rabbit, with blinding speed, leaves the Big House. In the duration of his flight he hears God yell from the Big House window: *"You are so smart get your own long tail."*

The obvious moral of the story for the slave community was, perhaps that God in the primal act of Creation had given the oppressed the necessary intelligence for its own preservation. It was the responsibility of the oppressed to utilize the knowledge that God had already given them for their own liberation. The secular mentality of the community was that there was no need of the oppressed worrying God for what God had already provided them. Such notion constituted the very antithesis of the religious viewpoint that taught the oppressed to *"take it to the Lord in prayer."* Or, *"whatever you need ask God for it."* The point of the community was *"use the unusual gift of mind that God has already given you and free yourself."* This notion embodies the seed of what will later be called African-American humanism.

Brer Rabbit helped slaves redefine work psychologically by playing the spirit of work itself against the oppressive work structures (time and space) of the plantation world. As the playful worker, Brer Rabbit became for slaves the personification of the spirit of work itself. He knew how, as playful worker, to turn work into play and play into work. Slaves saw clearly how Brer Rabbit would work his clever mind to free his helpless fragile body; he would work his body and activate his mind. Applying this dialectical principle of work, in their daily activities of forced labor, slaves used their creative imaginations to relax their own fragile bodies.

By imagining Brer Rabbit as the bearer and expresser of their minds, slaves were able to reduce the negative impact that stress, caused by slavery, had upon their bodies. Stories about Brer Rabbit provided the slave community the medicine of therapeutic laughter for both the relaxation of their minds and bodies. Laughing at the capers of Brer Rabbit became their constructive means of releasing stress. Such entertaining laughter made it possible for creative play to take place between the mind and body. Entertaining laughter, also, released in the slave community a spirit of momentary triumph over those who had property right claims over their bodies. Brer Rabbit's genius was that he knew both privately and publicly the secret place of laughter.

Brer Rabbit most of the time would laugh in his innards, but then again when something touched his funny-bone, he would open up with a big ha-ha-ha that would make the other creatures take to the bushes.[54]

That is to say that Brer Rabbit would, via laughter, create a margin of spatial freedom for his own self-expression.

PHILOSOPHICAL IMPLICATIONS: THE MYTH ABOUT LAUGHTER

A principal point that the Brer Rabbit stories convey is that the slave community understood the gift of laughter to be humanly unattainable. The story of "Brer Rabbit's Laughing Place" clearly illustrates this fact. It takes place one day when all of the creatures of the woods were about to make war upon each other over an argument that started among them about which of them could laugh the loudest. All of them stopped to listen at Miss Squinch Owl, when she asked from the top of a tree: *"If they knew what laughter was?"* Her philosophical query induced them to cease making war upon themselves until they had had a laughing contest. All of the creatures showed up for the contest but Brer Rabbit, who had explained beforehand that he *"can laugh well enough for to suit hisself and his family, besides that, he don't care about laughing lessing there is something for him to laugh at."* Despite the begging from other creatures, Brer Rabbit refused to come saying that when he wants to laugh he has got a *"laughing place."* Rabbit explained that his *"laughing place"* was where he could go and get full release; go and play. Although curious as to how this could be, the creatures nevertheless agreed to go on with their laughing contest despite Brer Rabbit's scornful reminder that: *"anybody what got natural sense know that the monkey is a natural laughter just as Brer Coon is a natural pacer."*[55]

Humbled by Brer Rabbit's esoteric knowledge about laughter, the creatures agreed, rather than refute him, that it was better to ask Brer Rabbit certain questions regarding his professed secret laughing place. The first question was practical in nature: *"How did he know how to find it?"* The second question was more philosophical: *"How did you know it when you found it?"* Capitalizing on the opportune moment Brer Rabbit told them that he would only agree to take them to his laughing place one at a time. This meant that the group would have to vote on which one of them would be the first that Brer Rabbit would take to his mysterious laughing place. The group chose Brer Fox because he had more longevity status among all of the creatures, and he had an impeccable reputation among all of them. Brer Rabbit had Brer Fox to meet him the next day for the journey to his mysterious laughing place. This meant that Brer Fox had to behave according to Brer Rabbit's dictates, which the former was not used to doing. In the end Brer Rabbit takes Brer Fox to a place in the woods where he coaxed him to charge into a hornet's nest hanging from a tree. As Brer Fox is stung all over by the hornets, Brer Rabbit rolls on the ground in laughter. When Brer Fox makes an angry protest, Brer Rabbit quickly states that he said beforehand that this was his laughing place: *"I said that it was my laughing place. What do you reckon I have been doin' all of this time?"*[56]

Laughter derived from the Brer Rabbit stories gave slaves the necessary psychological distance from the mental stress caused by oppression. It became an alternative mode of response that allowed the body to save the mind from having to try and make sense out of the absurdities of life. The community created its own scenarios of the ridiculous in these evocative stories of laughter. Slaves' ability to create their own laughter-evoking resources gave them the last word, so to speak, in the master and slave relationship model. It symbolically amounted to them having the last card to play where the loss is gain. All rational responses to systemic evil requires that its victims respond ethically to the questions of human beings' inhumanity to each other. Victims are forced to deal ontologically with the unity relationship between the physical and the spiritual, the impersonal and the personal, the subjective and the objective dimensions of reality. Every individual is forced to deal with what it means to be an eccentric self in the world.

At this point I have found what the philosopher Helmuth Plessner has to say about the phenomenology of laughter and the body and mind relationship very instructive. Plessner notes that: *"It is to man only that his situation as body is given at once personally and impersonally."* How is this the case for the human being? Plessner says that it is because:

He experiences himself as a thing and in a thing: but a thing which differs absolutely from all other things because he himself is that thing, because he obeys his intentions or at least responds to them. He is borne by it, encompassed by it, developed to effectiveness with and by it, yet at the same time it forms a resistance never to be overcome. In this unity, of the relation to his physical existence as impersonally and personally given, a unity which he must constantly renew, a man's living body is disclosed to him as a means, i.e., as something he can utilize to move about, carry loads, sit, lie, grasp, strike, and so on. This adaptability, together with its independent, objective thinghood, makes the living body an instrument.[57]

We have tried to show from the beginning of our discourse in chapter one that slavery forced African-American slaves to struggle with the objective and the subjective sides of their bodies. The Brer Rabbit stories illustrate how slaves might have dealt with the issue of what it meant to objectify their minds in a nonthreatening way so as to protect their bodies. We saw that the slave community's ability to laugh at the capers of Brer Rabbit enabled them to relate creatively to their own bodies. Slaves' acts of spontaneous laughter released their bodies to act autonomously over their minds. I am very dependent here upon Plessner's theory in my own description of the relationship between the phenomenon of the slave's laughter and the slave's body. Let us first ask the question, what happens when we laugh? Plessner noted in his study that the activity of laughter might be described as a "falling into its power or breaking out laughing." He notes that in the laughing response:

Man responds—with his body as body, as if from the impossibility of being able to find an answer himself. And in the loss of control over himself and his body, he revels himself at the same time as more than a bodily being who lives in a state of tension with regard to his physical existence yet is wholly completely bound to it.[58]

If we accept Plessner's presupposition, slaves' capacity to laugh at Brer Rabbit enabled them to respond to their bodies as bodies. This was so crucial in a society where they were told that they were owned by another. That is to say that in the act of laughing slaves experienced bodily the losing of control over themselves. Existentially, they were autonomous of the master during this spontaneous moment of joy. It was another form of radical dissociation that was motivated more by a natural phenomenon than a spiritual one.

Plessner's theory of the phenomenology of laughing and crying helps us understand at a different level laughing as a behavior phenomenon among slaves. While it has been common knowledge that it helped slaves maintain their sanity, there has been no effort on the part of the students of the literature to tease out the theoretical structures of the phenomenon of laughter along with whatever implications that they may have. Plessner's theory helps us to appreciate the possible cooperation that the slave as person maintained with his or her body. It would be safe to say that the laughing itself was a conscious affirmation by the slave as being a body.

This was a way of countering the negative experiences of having a body for the master's exploitation. Answering directly with laughter, one is not implicated in the answer. In laughter one becomes anonymous, so to speak, a ground of infectious energy dwelling within the person.

The aim in this chapter has been to show that slaves created, via the animal stories, an alternative response to their oppressor's false doctrine of anthropology. They did so by projecting their minds into the body of Brer Rabbit. As they did, male slave storytellers became less of an embodied threat to the white male society. Through this art of storytelling, it might be concluded theoretically that slaves made several critical contributions to ethical discourse. First, they demonstrated the critical need to take seriously what constituted "the ethical boundary" of the oppressor's definition of "right and wrong" and "good and evil." Second, they demonstrated that an "ethical-gap" is always critical whenever there is an attempt at ethical discourse between oppressed and oppressors. Third, they demonstrated that "an ethic of playful versatility" has been essential for the survival of black Americans' moral sensibilities.

We sought to show in our presentation that Brer Rabbit symbolized for slaves, as opposed to Jesus, the personification of the ethic of self-preservation. It was shown that self-preservation is a constitutive element in the ethic of playful versatility. The bottom line was that the self dares play because it longs to preserve itself. In slavery, Brer Rabbit was just as essential for slaves' experiential understanding of the moral life and God, as was Jesus, in that the former saved them from their own moral naivete. Brer Rabbit's suspicion of his adversaries gives clarity to the slave community's hermeneutic of suspicion.

CHAPTER 7

Foundational Elements

Self, God, and Community

The primary intent of this study has been to: examine white masters'
false anthropological doctrine about their slaves; examine the slave community's constructive alternate response to the problem, and, examine the
implications of the varied types of response by slaves for the task of constructing an African-American theology and ethics. Our thesis has been a
complex one. First, we have claimed that the slave community responded
to the master's false anthropological doctrine out of more than one type of
genre. Second, we posited that slaves arrived at dialectical understandings
of the self, God, and community. Testimonies, song lyrics, trickster stories,
and autobiographies all were diverse types of discourse that African Americans both shaped, and allowed to shape, their vision of self, God, and
community. The four types of discourse have emerged out of what we
termed, in the beginning of this study, foundational African-American religio-moral language.

The primary intent of this chapter is to: identify and discuss the four
ideal types of the self that evolved out of the discourse genre; to discuss
the implications of these ideal types of the self for African-American theology and ethics; and to discuss conclusively the conceptual direction that
the sequel to this study must take us.

The conceptual phrase *ideal types*, as we have shown initially, has been
used theoretically to illustrate broad historical aspects of the slave experience. None of the ideal types is to be understood as having exposed every
complex dimension of the slave's experience. Conceivably, aspects of the
complex lived experiences of a Harriet Tubman or a Frederick Douglass
could be explained by more than one of these types. I have chosen to call
these "ideal types of narrative self" because of their value to our analytical
task. These ideal types have evolved out of our analysis of the religio-moral
language of the slave community. They clarify African-Americans' understandings of the self, God, and community. This study has shown that the

African-American self had its genesis in the complexities of the slave experience. Lack of an informed appreciation of this historical fact leads to a serious misunderstanding of the contemporary African-American self. Those who see the slave as merely having been determined by economic, political, and psychological variables cannot adequately comprehend the slave's genius. The slave, also, has to be understood from the perspective of religion and ethics since the master's false perception of his or her anthropological nature was informed by spurious interpretations of the Bible. Our use of the phrase ideal types of narrative self has emerged out of the study of the creative responses by slaves to their masters' false anthropological perspective of them.

FOUR IDEAL TYPES OF THE NARRATIVE SELF

Slaves wove out of the fabric of their own experience of slavery and their escape from it what I would term a mosaic portrait of the self, which shaped their complex views of self, God and community — and vice versa. Our theoretical claim here is that four ideal types of narrative self can be derived from the responses — testimonies or conversion stories, song lyrics, autobiographies, and trickster stories — that the slave community made to the soul and body and mind problems. The four ideal types are: the *soul* narrative self; the *rational* narrative self; the *playful* narrative self; and, the *dialogical* narrative self.

Conversion and the Soul Narrative Self

Conversion in this discussion has been viewed as foundationally critical for the task of African-American theological and ethical reflection for several reasons. African-American enslavement and Christian conversion were seen by many slave masters as complementary of one another. Conversion as a concept most adequately characterizes the moral phase of the narrative of the African-American self from slavery to the present. Conversion must be seen as a dialectical concept that shows, on the one hand, how whites have related Christianity to African Americans; on the other, it shows how African Americans have critically used the principles of Christianity to challenge the racist soul of America.[1] Conversion describes the theological and moral aspects of African-Americans' experience that cannot be adequately described by the sociological term "assimilation."

Slaves wisely borrowed the elements of the white community's conversion language to accommodate the theological and ethical questions elicited by their own experiences. The theological elements of the conversion language of white America consisted of fear, guilt, humiliation and helplessness, God's forgiveness, faith and love, personal consent. There were different opinions apparently among some New England whites and southern whites as to what was conversion. Slaves naturally were more influenced by the southern tradition of conversion than the New England one. A New England divine wrote in 1741 that conversion was more than being acted upon by the Spirit of God. He observed that the rational faculties of the converted were equally important:

> But let it be consider'd that the Spirit of God does no more in the Conversion of a Sinner, than bring him to the right Exercise of those rational Powers with which he was born; give him a just view of his greatest Concerns; and enable him to act worthy of reasonable Being.[2]

On the contrary, southerners viewed themselves as totally depraved before God.[3] They perceived God as too Holy to approach human beings, and human beings were too depraved to approach God. This dilemma was resolved in the incarnate life of Jesus Christ. Our study here has shown that if the slave had a problem of being totally depraved before God it was resolved in the visionary experience when God released the new self out of the convert's old self. Such a vision of conversion undoubtedly affected slaves' perception of nature and spirit.

That many oppressed people tend to internalize their masters' negative behavior is widely recognized. This point has been convincingly made by scholars from Hegel,[4] the philosopher, to Frantz Fanon,[5] the modern psychoanalyst. When such happens oppressed people can be guilty of subscribing to their oppressors' false doctrine of anthropology about themselves. Under such false doctrine the oppressed will see themselves as having only utility value. Conversion and the soul narrative self demands a critical response to the gnostic attitude of the self that requires the soul to be at war with the body. This is part of that nature and spirit phenomenon.

The Gnostic Self

Primary to the African-American theological and ethical task is the need of overcoming a gnostic view of the self that is very alive in the preaching and teaching of many black churches. I mean by a gnostic version of the self the evangelical belief that values the soul's sacredness at the expense of the body's social welfare. This view is often used as an opiate, allowing the oppressed to cope with poverty and persecution. A critical perspective of the soul narrative self might serve as a corrective of that black church ideology that minimizes the self as body. Christian teachings of those African-American churches that totally disregard the worth of the natural body contribute to the oppression of the oppressed. Such teachings do little, if anything, to counteract the homicide epidemic among blacks. It contributes very little to helping African-American males deal constructively with the social and political rights of their female counterparts. Such gnostic philosophy of the self minimizes the African-American women's claims of equality by appealing to Paul's principle of having genderless-status in

Christ where "there is neither male nor female." Tragically these leaders, like their white racist counterparts, have failed to see any correlation between Paul's principle of genderless-status in Christ and their unfair practices toward women in the African-American church. African-American church leaders, because of the subconscious influence of the gnostic attitude about nature itself, often find themselves unable to lead their followers in addressing survival issues that do not explicitly mention race.

Contrary to the African-American church's gnostic view is the African-American libertine street philosophy that values the African-American other only as a means to an end. Here the other as the means to my end must mean that the other only has value in relation to my need. The extreme of the libertine view is heard in African-American street language where the attempt of one interlocutor is to reduce the other to a zero sum value level. The language formula for this attempt at absolute negative reductionism is: "Nigger you ain't shit." Such acts of devaluing the worth of the other factors into the reason many African-American males, in the heat of anger, physically destroy each other easily. At the point of the physical annihilation of each other the oppressed have outdone their oppressors. Where and when the oppressed do not value themselves as sacred beings of God, it is futile to think that they will value each other.

The slave community's response to the body and soul phenomenon presents African-American theology with a different ontological challenge. It demands the refutation of the theological notion that the sacredness of the individual is in the soul alone. Instead, it calls for the affirmation of the sacred law of interdependence that must be recognized inevitably as existing between body and soul (as embodied phenomenon) in the social world. There is an urgent need for the African-American community to make this notion of sacredness an integral part of the consciousness of the community. Consequently slaves could celebrate what they called God's power to "kill them dead." They knew that only God could do this and bring forth out of them the new self who was previously repressed in the old self. God only has the right as Creator to dissolve the law of interdependence that exists between soul and body. Since this is the case, death as a natural phenomenon is considered the work of God.

Unfortunately given the premium placed on white skin color in the hierarchy of western values,[6] African-American theology must accent blackness as having ontological significance.[7] Denial of this fact means to admit that the self as body has only utility value. Also it means to take a gnostic attitude of the self. African-American theology must affirm the intrinsic worth of both the body and soul despite the tendency of modern culture to reduce individuals to an "it" status. Critical examination of the core experience of the African slave religion has much to teach our contemporary society about the sacredness of the human self. African Americans have a long tenure in this country of having been perceived by white racists in the following pathological ways: as invisible[8]; as aberrations of nature[9];

and, as bodiless minds. Some African Americans have sought to counter these notions of themselves, as they advance in the white corporate world, by pretending that whites do not see them as black. These African Americans become gullible to what we termed above the bodiless mind type theory.[10] Those of this type revel in the thought of being self-made. They present themselves to the society as model exhibits of those African Americans who achieved because of their mental finesse.

Self, God, and Jesus

God is perceived in the conversion language as the engager and the disengager of the self. God disengages the convert from the everyday world for the purpose of preparing him or her with the courage to engage it. Dream consciousness is the mode of experience that God, according to the convert, uses to dissociate the converted from the everyday world. Converts claimed that this God acts on the subject irrespective of their will, commissioning them with the power and courage to engage radically the world. Converts who experienced God's action believe themselves to be acting coterminously with God in the world. God is portrayed as the initiator and giver of redeeming freedom to the initiated of the conversion drama.

As disengager "from" and engager "of" everyday reality, God is perceived to act in two ways in relationship to the convert. First, God as radical disengager "of" the converted from the world must be experienced as *bodiless Other.* That is to say that God is initially experienced as the mysterious other. This perception of God, which is generally characterized as a disembodied voice, literally overwhelms the candidate for conversion. The experience of God as the disembodied Other could literally strike terror in the heart of the conversion candidate. It characterized for the conversion candidate God's transcendence; God's wholly Otherness. Converted slaves undoubtedly were consoled by the thought that God could disengage God's self from the world. They dared warn even their masters that: "My God is so high you can't get over Him; so wide you can't get around Him; so low that you can't go under Him. But you got to come in at the door." Understandably, God was understood by those experiencing conversion as wholly Other in relation to themselves and yet very near (symbolized by the metaphorical phrase of "you got to come in at the door") for those who were obedient.

God's actions as radical engager of the world take the form of the *embodied Other* in Jesus Christ. In Jesus, God personally engages all of the marginalized victims of the world. Jesus was viewed as having embodied in his person a creative tension between being a radical engager of the world and that of being critically able to disengage himself from it. This is heard in the claim that Jesus is in the world but not of it. Converted slaves believed that Jesus encouraged them to live on the same creative boundary, embodying in their persons both the priestly and prophetic roles of ministry.

African-American theology must recapture this dialectical method of being for God and Jesus in the world.

God as destroyer and redeemer. Converted slaves' primary perception of God was that God radically and personally engaged them in the salvation drama. They celebrated as a positive attribute God's power to "kill dead in order to make alive." No power was believed comparable to God's power to accomplish this feat. More so than the fact of God's power to create the world, God's power to kill an individual dead and make him or her alive suggested God's rare skill to use power delicately. Only God was perceived as having the power to reduce the person to a primordial awareness of being an irreducible "I."

God's power to "kill dead" and "make alive" gave birth to a radical awareness of double consciousness among converted slaves. The confessional statements "been struck dead by God" and having "awaken at old hell's dark door" meant that slaves had experienced seeing themselves from both the depth and the pinnacle of life. It meant, as well, that slaves had seen themselves through the eyes of the Jesus who becomes their Significant Other. This double consciousness of the self took the following scenario: First, God explained to the self who it had been before the vision and why. Second, God showed the self a vision of what it could become in God. Explanation was given for why the self's life had been unproductive before the conversion experience. The entire scenario is culminated with God transforming a purposeless, lethargic self into an energetic one for the cause of God. Life in Jesus for this self becomes the interpretative means for making constructive sense out of all past, present, and future chaos.

Slaves saw the Civil War as the historical stage on which God was involved as both destroyer and redeemer. They concluded that God was on the side of the Union Army as it marched through the South breaking the backbone of plantation owners' economic and political power. Many spiritual songs of the slave community are replete with imagery that portrays God as the Ultimate Warrior who fights on behalf of the oppressed. Seasoned faith warriors of the community constantly admonished the fainthearted among them to "be still and God will fight your battle." Fisher, Cone, and other scholars have identified and interpreted what were probably some theological implications of several of these songs for the slave community. All interpreters seem to be in common agreement that the slave community believed that God was using war to free them from bondage. This meant that slaves believed that God was equally as concerned about the welfare of their bodies as their souls. Even with this, slaves believed that the dialectic of God as Destroyer and Creator was best dramatized in Jesus's birth, death, burial, and resurrection.

Jesus as God's embodied self. Jesus Christ symbolized for slaves the radicalness of God's engagement of the world. This radicality might be referred to as God's hands-on-policy toward the world. Jesus, for the slave community, became the needed link to God. Those who were ambiguous about God's actions and nature were told to "come to Jesus" for its resolvability. On the one hand, slaves discovered in Jesus a soul-mate who also possessed a human body. On the other hand, they discovered God in whose "hands is the whole world." This explains, perhaps, why slaves became so apologetic and ashamed for not initially having recognized Jesus: "Lord, we didn't know who you was." They first saw the babe of the manger without having seen the Lord of history. The slaves' pivotal point of enlightenment for understanding Jesus' identity came when they saw the relationship between Jesus' status of victimization and their own. They saw that the world treated them with the same meanness that it treated Jesus. Subsequently, Jesus' common place of birth, *"in a manger Lawd,"* readily caught the attention of slaves. This fact about Jesus' place of lowly birth was a pleasant surprise to them. It caused them to ask: "What had Jesus done to cause the world to be so inhospitably cruel in its treatment of him?" Surprisingly they learned that Jesus had done nothing to merit such treatment. This fact became for them the key principle for understanding the real source of their own victimization. Like Jesus, slaves had done nothing to merit the cruel treatment of slavery. It makes sense that slaves would give graphic descriptions of the torturous treatment that Jesus' enemies rendered to his body before and during his crucifixion. Those of the world whipped Jesus "all night long." Although they could celebrate the divinity of Jesus' nature, slaves were realist enough to accept the fact that the world into which Jesus was born just had a natural proclivity to being mean. This realism is heard when they say to Jesus: "But that is the way things are down here Lord."

Also, it was because slaves saw Jesus as God's embodied self that they were acutely sensitive to the way that they treated strangers. There was always the hope that the incarnation of God could possibly take place in every human encounter. This belief about God made up one of the slave community's great theological and ethical tenets.

Jesus as witness and participator. Jesus' self was perceived by the slave community as the living embodiment of moral excellence. He was the normative self that all other selves were expected to emulate. Slaves saw Jesus as both God's witness and participator in humanity's behalf, that is, as God's sacrifice for its sins. They saw Jesus, also, as their mediator ("elder brother") who intercedes to God on their behalf. Jesus was qualified to serve in this role by virtue of the fact that he had fully participated in life as the Victimized One, that is, as both the Son of God and the Son of Man. This faith fact was the source of the community's confidence in Jesus' ability to substantiate in himself all of the needs of other embodied selves. It was Jesus' life that demonstrated to the community that there was no hiatus between word and deed. As the Son of Man Jesus became the first citizen of the new human family; as the Son of God, Jesus had always been the premier citizen of the kingdom of heaven. In the role of witness-participator, the community saw the subjective side of Jesus as the self-sacrificer and the objective side of Jesus as the one sacrificed for human sins. Said another way, Jesus was perceived as both the victim and the victor of the cross. He was praised as both God's passive and active agent in the salvific drama that was initiated and actualized by God.

Jesus as the victorious self over the suffering of this world was offered to the daily victimized as the antidote for self-pity. Suffering believers on the verge of falling into the trap of cynicism were warned to compare their situation with what the suffering Jesus experienced. The strong ones told the weak of the fellowship: "Just look how they done my Lord for me." The comparative test, when taken, showed every other human sufferer that in this world the experience of suffering does not always have to do with being guilty or innocent. It has more to do with the fact that human beings are sinful. In a sinful world the experience of Jesus clearly reveals that the one perfectly innocent is vulnerable. Slaves praised the fact that Jesus chose to love his persecutors; he chose silence when verbal protest would have seemed more appropriate. The slave community, despite the Bible's record of his last words from the cross, characterize Jesus as assuming the posture of silence on the cross: "He never said a mumbling word for me." It was as though Jesus' silence identified him both as participator and witness with the voiceless of history.

The Community as God's Social Body

All converts of Jesus, who had been slain in the Spirit, were considered members of God's social body. Having been ascribed godly status, members were expected to bear in their sable bodies the marks of the crucified Lord. We noted in a previous chapter that slaves used such somatic metaphors as the heart and ears to characterize their duties as God's social body. These organic symbols must be seen as vectors of meaning that have profound implications for the constructive task of African-American theology and ethics. As the social body of God, converted slaves were expected to carry out God's priestly and prophetic mission in the world. For the sake of brevity we will examine only two somatic metaphors — heart and ears.

The community as God's heart. Collectively and individually converted slaves desired that their hearts become the seat of God's rule. Daily the faithful cried "Lord I want to love everybody in-a my heart." Desirers of this ultimate state of moral fulfillment made up the community as God's social body. Such an ethical confession capsulized the converted community's core belief of what it meant to be both "in God" and "for God." It dramatized the tension between what John Lovell calls "being and behaving like a Christian."[11] Among true believers in the body of God there was no tolerance for surface operators when it came to their Christianity. Lovell thinks that the lyrical construction of the confession became the community's mask or symbol to wedge a protest against those who falsely represented Christianity:

What has probably happened is that the group, as individuals, have seen a lot of people who professed Christianity and did not behave as Christians are supposed to behave. As though it has held a discussion of the matter, it has concluded that it wants to make known its disgust with phoney, insincere Christians. It is tired for example of Christians who practice selfishness and brutality. It is tired of the so-called Christians who go to church on Sunday morning and come home and beat their slaves on Sunday afternoon. So using the mask of a song which seems to be praying for the Christian experience, it makes a commentary on the need for true religion, and the honest practice of the fine set of doctrines encompassed in Christianity. If this were not its intention, why does it phrase its poetic idea as it does, "I want to be a Christian . . . in-a my heart"?[12]

As the social body of God, every member has chosen to keep him- or herself wholesome through right Christian living. Failure of any one member of the social body to aspire for the fulfillment of this teleological and deontological objective was perceived as endangering the social harmony of the entire communion. Ideally it was expected that every individual would aspire to be "more loving" and "more holy" in his or her "heart." In the eyes of the community Judas epitomized the moral hypocrite whom they did not want to be like: "Lord I don't want to be like Judas in my heart." Why this passionate objection against being like Judas? The primary reason was that Judas was perceived as an enemy to the body of Christ. It was Judas' moral infraction of betraying Jesus to his enemies that created disharmony in the body of Christ.

The experience of what happened to Jesus on the cross is very vital to the community's understanding of what it means to be the body of God. Being like Jesus was thought to be more than an exercise of the human will itself. An individual's heartfelt response to what the community believed God was doing in the world was deemed imperative. Feeling identification with Jesus as embodied sufferer on the cross provided the community with the parameters for being God's social body.

The community as God's ears. Hearing God speak was perceived by the believing community as a corporeal responsibility. Although spoken of as personal, the experience of having heard God's call could not take place totally apart from the community of believers. This was due primarily to the fact that the community nurtured in the individual some idea of what it meant to hear God speak, and celebrated the individual who confessed to having heard God's voice. Believers believed that God often spoke loud enough via the thunder for all in the human community to hear, if they would. Those who heard and saw God in the natural elements became members of God's social body: "My Lord he calls me by the thunder." Thunder and lightening, viewed as more than mere natural phenomena, were heard and seen by believers to be God's revelatory sources. Believers became God's body when all could say, when having heard God in the thunder and seen God in the lightening, that: "The trumpet sounds within my soul."

As God's ears, the community was responsible for hearing God speak in the voices of one another. Hearers were to be God's hosts in the community of believers. This meant that hearers were ethically bound to ask: "Lord what is my duty to the human other?" Also, the hearer must always ask: "What is God saying and doing in the human other who speaks to me?" The hearer was expected, as well, to ask: "What is my response to what is going on in what I hear?"[13] Acute ethical sense of communal responsibility must be heard in the song lyrics: *"Hear the Lambs a Cryin'."* Claimers who confessed to having heard the cry of the innocent were reminded of their feeding responsibility: *"O Shepherd feed my sheep."* These instructive words regarding nurture, "shepherd feed my sheep," could very well suggest the belief of the priesthood of believers in the community. Seemingly every convert here is given shepherd status.

The theme of hearers' shepherding communal responsibility is best appreciated when the possible context for singing the lyrics is better understood. One significant context for teaching the shepherding responsibility of the "hearers" to that of the "criers" was that of the "mourners' bench" during the revival. The "mourners' bench" was where the ritual of dynamic pedagogical interaction took place between seasoned Christians (called "sheep") and young slaves (known as "lambs") who were potential converts. The latter were summoned by the former to present themselves unabashedly to God: *"Come on mourner and don't you be ashamed."* The mourner's responsive cry was always to be the desired ultimate fulfillment: *"I want to go to heaven when I die."* The shepherding community, responsible for helping them through this rite of passage, might assure young mourners that God anxiously wants the same thing for them. Believers raise the anxiety level of young mourners by telling them that: *"The angels waiting to write yo' name."* As God's social body, the shepherding community cannot be insensitive to *"God's cryin' lambs."* For to do so was to be insensitive to God. Another religious carrot that was held out before young slaves was that of the compensatory heavenly reward for all of their "ups and downs" on the earth: *"Angels waitin' for to give you a crown."* A final duty of the community was to warn young converts of the high cost of being disobedient to God. It was tantamount to gambling with one's soul: *"Mind out brother/ sister how you walk on the cross 'cause your foot might slip and your soul be lost."*

Contributions of the Soul Narrative Self

The soul narrative self makes significant contributions to the constructive task of African-American theology and ethics. First, it clearly challenges the current assumptions, spoken or unspoken, in African-American theological discourse about sin and race. The soul narrative self demands that

African-American scholars critically reexamine the notion of sin as an onto-logical phenomenon in the consciousness of the oppressed. Soul narrative self-reflection has introduced us to the slave community's consciousness of the origin of sin. It, nevertheless, is a root awareness of sin that grows out of the self's encounter with both God and human community. African-American theological and ethical discourse has been anemic in its inter-pretation of what constituted sin in the slave mind. Scholars such as James Cone and Gayraud Wilmore have rightly recognized that the sin of slavery and white racism was dominant in the slave's mind. They have failed, how-ever, to note that such symptomatic descriptions of sin do not adequately illuminate the depth structures of the slave mind regarding the sin question. Only a critical examination, as we have shown here, of slaves' religio-moral language will help us in answering this question. This study has shown that slaves, in their visionary encounters with God, experienced what we might theoretically term an existential and an ontological understanding of sin. It was the God of their visionary experience, rather than the slave master, who brought them to see that sin actually amounted to the fear of being-in-general. Whatever fear slaves had of the master and each other was rooted in this fundamental notion of fear.

Slaves' fear of being-in-general required that they, in the face of their masters, repress the original creative self with which God had endowed them. This fear demanded that slaves act according to the dehumanizing specifications of slave masters' image of the ideal slave. Slaves overcame this fear only when they had been what they termed "struck dead," or, "slain in the Spirit by God." Before this salvific experience the slave undoubtedly would not have been able to define the root source of his or her fear. This experience gave slaves the critical means of seeing why they had been fearful of being-in-general. It, also, gave them a new root defi-nition of sin, that is, the lack of the courage to be in the face of being itself.[14] In the conversion sources, sin must be defined as the converted's state of being rather than such unacceptable social conduct as drinking, dancing, and gambling. The genuine conversion experience brought slaves to an awareness of the true source and nature of their alienation from God and one another. Vertical alienation from God created horizontal aliena-tion from one another. Fear of being-in-general deluded many into believ-ing that they could placate their earthly masters.

Any statement of a theological and ethical nature that does not help oppressed people deal critically with their own language of the nature and origin of sin has little, if any, liberating value. The oppressed find them-selves in a hopeless situation if their definition of sin is limited to their oppressors' victimization of them. Such a notion of sin gives too much power to the oppressed.

Second, the soul narrative type self contributes to the radical theological notion that courage is God's gift to the fearful. Conversion sources make it clear that slaves equated the fear of having to confront the malevolent master with confronting the devil. They expressed this fear to God during that phase of their visionary experiences when God would command them to reenter the plantation world as a moral witness. God helps the convert to see that fear comes from within rather than the malevolent master. This is why God commands each transformed self to: "Go back into yonders world and fear no man for I will be with you." God's gift of courage gave the transformed self the sense of being radically free spiritually in the world of bondage. This meant that the master could only claim ownership of the slave's self as body.

The lack of the courage to be in the face of economic and psychological adversity seems to be the primary enemy of young African-Americans' upward mobility. Quick to grow faint of spirit and weak of heart, too many African-American youth are sacrificing themselves, body and soul, to the contemporary slave master of drugs and crime. It is a theological and moral challenge to help young African Americans recover the secret of courage that their ancestors once knew and displayed. When a people lose the courage to be, they become candidates for the endangered species list. There must be both a recovery of the intellectual virtues of African-Americans' heroes and heroines, as well as the secret of their spiritual tenacity. Robert Franklin's instructive study of the moral lives of African-American leaders such as DuBois, Washington, and King must be viewed as a prolegomenon of what needs to be done in future studies.[15] Peter Paris'[16] scholarly contribution on this subject has been invaluable. Katie Cannon's study of the moral contribution of Zora Neale Hurston has been of equal value for illuminating this issue.[17]

The third contribution of the soul narrative self is the dialectical construct of fact and fantasy. These constructs are foundational to every theological task. Critical consciousness of the soul narrative self is born out of the self's lived boundary existence between fact and fantasy. The whole corpus of the "God struck me dead" verbal constructions of the slave community are the product of slaves' collective, as well as, individual imagination. Religious language predicated on imaginary flights would understandably be viewed suspiciously and critically by scientifically influenced scholars of religion and theology. Such scholars have rightly questioned the authenticity of religious language that celebrates the invisible world of the spirit over that of everyday reality. Social scientists have viewed such religious rhetoric as being too otherworldly in character; being too subjective; and, being too abdicative of social responsibility. On the contrary, the soul narrative sources show that slaves' radical ethical sense of social responsibility was the consequence of having encountered God's revelatory self at the center of their imaginations. The slave's imagination became the conduit through which God made an alternate visionary world possible. Slaves of this visionary world claimed to have heard God commission them to be ethically responsible in an immoral world. The task of

African-American theology and ethics is to recover the value of the role of the imagination in reflection and action.

The fourth contribution of the soul narrative self is the dialectic of being both witness and participator of God's transforming power. This is another way of mapping the self's evolvement from a state of anomie to critical self-consciousness. If Jesus was God's exemplary model of witness and participator, African-American slaves came to see themselves as being God's witnesses and participators in the lived world by virtue of their association with Jesus. It was in this priestly and prophetic role of being witness and participator in God's salvation drama that slaves came to establish an identifying link with Jesus and one another. Converts believed that the God of their conversion experience had allowed them to see what happened during it. It was this God who brought the repressed ontologically-inhibited self out of the socially-fearful self. It amounted really to the dissociating of the ontological self from the socially-fearful self. The real self could only accomplish God's objective when this happened. Conversion amounted to God bringing the repressed self to be a witness of God's transformation of it. On the other side of the conversion equation God allows the convert to be a dialogical participator in every facet of the transformation process. Now the slave was able to ask God such an ontological question as: "Lord, what is this?" Or such a teleological question as: "Lord, what will thou have me to do?" Or such a deontological question as: "Lord, what is my duty?" Conversion means first that God frees the self for dialogue with God's self; second for the self's confirmation of God; and, third for the self's own right of self-confirmation with God.

Conversion as dialogical freedom meant that the converted of the community had a responsibility to be in dialogue with one another. It was believed that this notion of dialogue made the vision of liberated community a possibility. Members constantly reminded others of the therapeutic value of conversing with Jesus. Whatever the problem: "a little talk with Jesus makes it right." It put things in proper perspective. Conversation with Jesus has a way of minimizing the threatening power of "troubles of every kind." A "little talk with Jesus" was seen as the panacea for generic troubles. Before being converted, all cries to Jesus are of no use until the convert hears Jesus call. This encounter with Jesus becomes the testimony of every convert:

> My brother, I remember when I was a sinner lost, I cried, "have mercy Jesus," But still my soul was tossed. Till I heard King Jesus say, "Come here, I am the way."

The fifth contributive element of the soul narrative type is the dialectic of prophetical and priestly engagement and disengagement of the world. Prophetical disengagement of the world requires that the theologian get a critical reflective distance from the pious practices of the worshiping community. Besides critical reflection, the theologian of liberation must feel and be felt by the world. This dialectic method of doing African-American liberation theology must allow for the critical examination of all expressions of reality. The lived social world must be read as a text of God's action as well as the scriptures. Consequently our discussion has examined sources such as the Brer Rabbit stories in the slave community. The engagement-disengagement method of doing constructive theology might help African Americans overcome the identity crisis that comes with being a professional theologian of the church. This professional identity crisis is born out of the sense of alienation that the African-American scholar often senses in the white theological academy. The task of priestly engagement of the world means that the liberation theologian must see him- or herself as the spiritual and moral caretaker of the embodied soul of each individual, the world and the church. The reality of this alienation is exacerbated by the fact that traditional religious leaders of the African-American church are suspicious of professional theologians. Even many seminary-trained black preachers are inclined to condemn highly theoretical study about God as no more than an intellectual exercise of futility. Thus, even African-American theology, despite the efforts of a James Cone, suffers because of the hiatus between the church and the academy. African-American theology must find a way of engagingly communicating with the world of the African-American church.

The sixth contributive element of the soul narrative self is reflected in the creative tension between feeling and reason. This fact was seen in the discussion of ex-slaves' autobiographies (chapter 5). There we made the claim that ex-slave narrators of their own stories to the white world sought to present themselves as feeling selves. Ex-slave narrators of their escapes from slavery often used metaphorical expressions that came out of the Christian conversion experience idiom. Critical awareness of being a felt self was fundamental to the slave mind. It was important for the transformed slave to be able to say that: "I feel therefore I am." While the rational narrative self required that ex-slaves repress subjective feelings in the name of reason, the sentient narrative self required that they value subjective feelings as critical to genuine human expression. The articulation of subjective feelings was deemed just as important to being human as that of objective reasoning. Failure to understand the value of feelings in the human equation always runs the danger of affirming the oppressor's false distinction between mind and body. Ex-slaves made it clear in their autobiographies that it was just as important to reconstruct themselves into beings who were divinely endowed with feelings as it was to show that they were rational moral agents. This made freedom for them more than an abstract notion. Freedom for slaves, instead, was the object of their intentional feelings. Thus it can be said that "feelings are revealers of values."[18] That is to say that we might best know what slaves valued morally by trying to decipher what they felt. The main task of maverick narrators of their autobiographies, such as Frederick Douglass, was to show that freedom had always been the primary object of their feelings.[19]

Ex-slave autobiographies are lessons in how slaves moved from the status of negative to positive feelings about themselves. William Andrews classifies the narrative into what he termed the "ascent type" and the "immersion type." It is the "ascent type" that is the narrator's journey of ascending out of slavery into the land of freedom. On the contrary, the "immersion type" is the account of the slave reentering the territory of slavery to rescue other slaves such as close family members. In either case the narrator clearly shows that "feeling moods" were critical in each decision-making phase of the journey. Ex-slaves commonly refer in their narratives to freedom as "a feeling of desire" rather than an abstract notion upon which they first had to ponder greatly. It was perceived as an insatiable "feeling of desire" that was often implied to be inherent in the nature of the victim. Narrative scenes in most of the autobiographies commonly present portraits of the slave deducing from "intuitive feelings" alone that she or he was made for freedom. Basic to most of these scenes is the theme of communing with nature. The following quotation from Henry Bibb exemplifies the value slaves placed on communion with the natural order. It shows that communion with nature heightened his self-critical desire for freedom:

> The circumstances in which I was then placed, gave me a longing desire to be free. It kindled a fire of liberty within my breast which has never yet been quenched. This seemed to be a part of my nature; it was first revealed to me by the inevitable laws of nature's God. I could see that the All-Wise Creator, had made man a free, moral, intelligent and accountable being; capable of knowing good and evil.[20]

Another constructive task of the maverick narrator was to defend the feeling aspect of the self as a necessary aspect of moral agency. The self was really defended as the embodiment of "felt selfhood." Nowhere is this fact borne out more than in slaves' rationale for self-defense. The more slaves defied masters' authority in the name of freedom the closer they were to becoming autonomous moral agents. This was graphically illustrated in our treatment, in chapter 5, of Frederick Douglass with his overseer, Covey. Douglass makes it clear that he understands himself to be the embodiment of "felt selfhood." The slave who would feign his or her feelings for the pleasure of the sadistic master was considered the Sambo personality type. This type of slave felt through the master. This is heard in the old tale of where the slave was supposed to have asked his sick master: "Us sick master?" Douglass says that "Covey succeeded in breaking me — in body, soul, and spirit."[21] In defense of his own embodied felt presence Douglass resolved, in the face of Covey's physical assaults that "I was not afraid to die." He said that it was this spirit that gave him the sense of being half free. Douglass acknowledged that out of this undignified experience of physical encounter with Covey that he experienced a dignified self-transformation. This came about because he resolved to defend himself as a living, embodied, feeling self rather than wait for the master to defend him as the master's property.

The African-American self as "felt body" is one of the foundational principles in the constructive task of theology and ethics. It is the case primarily because it deals with the critical issue of self-identity. Subsequently every African-American scholar of any significance has cited it. In African-American theological studies, since the first published work of James Cone, scholars have repeatedly referred to W. E. B. Du Bois' double consciousness theory to summarize their identity crisis. Du Bois spoke of it as being that of "two selves in one dark body" pulling in opposite directions. DuBois thought these polar opposite selves to be of different cultural and ethnic origins: One was of European descent; the other was of African descent.[22]

Critical awareness of double consciousness, as we have tried to show in this study, does not begin de nova with Du Bois' brilliant analysis regarding color in the African-American experience as self. Although they do not mention color, slaves intuitively discover that their decisions to make the radical transition from being a slave to that of becoming a free moral agent creates double consciousness within them. It meant that they must, refocusing to see themselves through the eyes of the master, see themselves alternatively through the eyes of a significant other. In the conversion stories Jesus Christ becomes the Significant Other through whom slaves come to see themselves. It is because of God's conversion power, through Jesus and the Holy Spirit, that the converted slave is able to see the "old dead self" through the eyes of a "new revealed self." Brer Rabbit, the imaginary trickster in the folk stories, becomes slaves' significant other. In ex-slaves' autobiographies their significant other is the "imaginary free citizen" who transcends such variables as race and class.

This notion of critical double consciousness required that slaves alter their view of the "self as body." As property of the master, the slave was required to think of oneself only in relation to the master: "I belong to my master," which was another way of saying "I am my master's property." All of this was tantamount to saying that "I am my master's body." Such oppressive confessional formulas dictated that the slave was merely, at best, a subordinate extenuation of the master's being and will. This said in effect that the slave had no legitimate reason to be or think of being apart from the master. Critical double consciousness was born the moment the slave could emphatically say: "I am my body." Then the victim refused to see his or her body in a detached fashion.[23] The slave became the center of world experience. This means that the slave had to live between the creative tension that was derived from the dialectical awareness of "having a body" and "being body." The notion of "having a body" suggested that one's body was the master's property. It was recognizing the body's ability to make use of instruments and utensils as it inhabits the world. The slave came to accept his or her body as "myself in my lived concreteness." His or her body becomes a recognizable incarnate feeling, willing, and thinking project. The slave as the living embodiment of his or her experience is able to say "I can" as well as "I feel."

Self-consciousness of being the living embodiment of "I can" and "I feel" verbal constructions became slaves' way of overcoming oppressive anthropological dualism. It became their subjective way of declaring themselves in the world. This radical self-awareness of being a lived behavior project in the world means that the oppressed dared *be* in the face of *nonbeing.* One's embodied self is the center of his or her being. This analysis better explains why many slaves chose to dare their master to kill them rather than subject themselves to corporeal punishment. It was their way of saying that they would not accept the oppressive dichotomy that oppressors had made between body and soul. Such classical display of the courage of human dignity in the face of the master's power was conveyed by a slave named James Roberts. He witnessed the hanging of a slave named Joe, accused of using a hoe to kill an overseer who was severely whipping another slave. First, Roberts confessed the crime because he did not want other slaves to "be whipped around." Second, when addressing his friends Joe's last words before his hanging were:

> Don't one of you grieve after me; I die an honorable death. Do not grieve after me my friends. I bid you adieu. Here is an end to Joe in this life. Though I die with a sore back I die a man's death. Let no white man kill you but you kill him.[24]

Other commonly cited examples of slaves acting in the true sense of being embodied social selves must be seen in the rebellious actions of Frederick Douglass and Nat Turner. On the contrary the master might maintain a false gap between the slave perceiving himself as "I can" and "I feel" by only ceasing to punish the slave physically when the slave asked the punisher, and not God, for mercy. The objective being to drive home the point to slaves that God ruled heaven and the master ruled earth.[25]

Oppression creates such an unnecessary oppressive dichotomy between the body and the mind; the "self as felt selfhood" and the "self as willing and thinking selfhood." African-American theology and ethics must make constructive use of the insights that come from the language of the slave experience. It is from these sources that we come to see what can be said about a notion of being that is shaped by the ethos of oppression. A crucial problem facing African Americans at this point in our struggle is the tendency by the western world to devalue the worth of the body as a "feeling self" amid the world of high technology. African-American theology and ethics has the challenge of helping oppressed people understand what it means *to be* in the face of modern forms of oppression. In addition, it must help the oppressor see what it means to relate to the creation of their own hands. This might explain why African Americans have tended to influence America greatly in the creative arts. Urban poverty and all of its negative consequences have thrown us into an era where African Americans fear being annihilated by the violent behavior of each other more than they do the racist attacks of the Ku Klux Klan. Is it the case that too many African Americans suffer from the lack of the courage *to be* in the face of nonbeing?

The soul narrative self type challenges African-American theology to construe a doctrine of being out of the primary language of African Americans' notion of redemptive suffering. It must be a doctrine of ontology that critically addresses more than the issue of skin color. There is the need for an ontological understanding of the self that illuminates the creation itself as God's body. This is needed if the African-American church would respond both prophetically and priestly on such issues as sexism, global resources, and the military industrial complex. Also, it is needed to keep African Americans from becoming victims of the oppressive view of mind and body and the body and soul dualism of white America. This ideal type of soul narrative self complements what we have termed the ideal type rational narrative self. It does this by defying the oppressor's false rational reduction of the slave's being to the status of a thing.

The Autobiographic Genre and the Rational Narrative Self

The rational narrative self has its formal genesis in ex-slaves' autobiographies that delineate their escape from the plantations to the free land of the North. When I use the phrase rational narrative self in this discussion I mean the formal way in which ex-slaves sought to reconstruct themselves as rational beings. They used the structures of time and place from their own memory of the story of their captivity to restructure a formal image of themselves as free persons.[26] To do this, however, ex-slaves had to restructure themselves in the very act of telling their stories of how they found their freedom.[27] Thus I have chosen the phrase rational narrative self first to show that many slaves sought to prove that they were equal to whites by construing themselves in the formal literary image of white America; and second, to show that slaves' use of this formal literary image automatically created tension with the traditional slave community's notion of faith and reason.

Contributions of the Rational Narrative Self

What does the concept of rational narrative self contribute to the constructive task of African-American theology and ethics? First, it contributes the notion of the slave's potential for self-autonomy. The rational narrative self celebrates the fact of being created in the image of God and created with a need for freedom and literacy. The rational narrative self really reflects God as the Great Ideal Observer.

For those slaves, like Frederick Douglass, God was perceived more as the Rational Principle that illuminated the mind of the oppressed. This God, it was believed, helped befuddled slaves make the right decision, at the right time, in their quest for freedom. In my reading of these autobiographies I sense that God is viewed more as the Disembodied Mind than as the Disembodied Spirit such as portrayed in the conversion stories.

Ex-slave autobiographies help us to see how some of those slaves who escaped to freedom secularized the conversion idiom. Literal escape from the plantation was construed as a conversion experience of a secular kind. Many claimed that crossing into the land of freedom caused them to experience a great self-transformation. Contrary to the traditional conversion model's ethic of selfless devotion to Jesus Christ, slaves who literally escaped from the plantation subscribed to the ethic of self-preservation, "by any means necessary." It was not a crude selfishness, but a belief that "I can only help free others by freeing myself first." How could the world outside know what slaves were enduring unless someone escaped to be a witness on their behalf? Escaped slaves often viewed themselves as forerunners, interpreters, and intercessors for those left in captivity. The escaped slave could not afford to wait for God to come down in some apocalyptic manner and deliver the oppressed, though, every escaped slave believed she or he was working in partnership with God. Ex-slaves lived with the axiom that "If God endowed me with the capacity to think freedom, I am capable of initiating my own freedom project."

"Reason" and "self-autonomy" are two concepts from the slave experience that have been overlooked. African Americans have been hard-pressed to keep reason separated from the influence of race, class, and caste. Autobiographical discourse assumed the burden of presenting to white America a rational self.

In an earlier chapter it was shown how white editors and publishers sought to control the minds and thoughts of African-American ex-slaves. The problem must be seen as being of both a theological and ethical nature. It is theological because it deals with the question of being; and, it is ethical because it begs the question of human choice. African Americans must ask: How does our oppressors' so-called formal literate notion of being add to our own informal perception of being? Another way of asking the question is: When I choose to make myself in the white man's so-called formal literate image in what sense do I give up a more inclusive criteria for being? Or, the question can yet be asked in another way: Can authentic being be had outside the parameters of the oppressor's formal definition of rational culture? These questions have haunted African Americans since they started to make the transition from slavery to citizenship.

The other side of the reason and self-autonomy dilemma involves the issue of coexistence with the oppressor versus that of rebellion against an oppressive culture and values. Total disregard for the value of a formal knowledge of American culture leaves the oppressed with inadequate tools to wedge a civil protest against its demonic impact. In short, the oppressed lack the adequate literary tools for prophetical and priestly engagement of the oppressor. The real issue becomes: Does rebelling against the oppressor's culture and values assure the oppressed of their autonomy? Asked another way: Is not the very right to rebel itself acknowledged by the oppressor as being one of America's basic ideals of democracy?

The above questions of reason and autonomy ought to challenge us to make the critical distinction between informed and uninformed rebellion. Informed rebellion requires the light of rational inquiry and exploration. Uninformed rebellion is motivated by the heat of raw emotions. Thousands of poor black youth fall prey to the latter. African-American theology and ethics are faced with the constructive priestly task of helping poor black youth redefine themselves in relationship to the larger society. This does not minimize the prophetic task of working for social justice in that world. We are ever faced with the undeniable fact that the internal change of individuals and the change of the social world must complement one another. This means that the "work ethic of struggle" must be placed at the heart of the constructive task of African-American theology and ethics.

The rational narrative self, skewed in the oppressor's literary image, requires that the oppressed live with the burdensome challenge of the question: "How can we unmake the oppressor's image of us so as to remake ourselves in our own image and likeness?" Ex-slave autobiographies manifest the way in which escaped slaves understood the unmaking and the remaking of themselves in their own self-image. These stories portray the making of a linear image of the self in contrast to the spiritual narrative accounts that present the self as having both linear and vertical dimensions. The linear element of the self must be seen in the way that escaped slaves described their own radical transitions from servile status to that of self-autonomous beings. It is the narrator, who as creator of the escape story, has the right to unmake the oppressors' Sambo image in order to remake the self into a being divinely endowed with the capacity for rational autonomy. Successful escape from the plantation to the free land of the North was generally described by the narrator as an anthropological evolutionary ascent from subhuman to human status. It was for the narrator a rite of passage from the state of being less than human to that of becoming fully a rational human being. For the narrator of the rational narrative self the acquisition of full citizenship rights in America was what affirmed that one was an autonomous rational being. It must be noted that for the rational narrative type there is always the effort of the oppressed to gain their rights or to have the oppressor recognize them. Unfortunately the rights of those of this type are always dependent upon the charitable nature of the oppressor. This means that the oppressor is always "taking from" the oppressed rather than "sharing with" them.

The rational narrative self is valuable for showing how African Americans saw the political expediency of reconstructing themselves in the more inclusive civil religion language of the American society. It, also, helps to sharpen the focus of the soul narrative self. These two notions of the narrative selves must be seen in the light of the playful narrative self.

The Trickster Genre and the Playful Narrative Self

This notion of the self arises from the slave community's version of the Brer Rabbit stories. The adjective "playful" suggests that the slave community deemed Brer Rabbit's behavior, which whites called "trickery," as of positive rather than negative value. It was shown earlier in the discourse that slaves celebrated Brer Rabbit as the symbolic liberator of their own imaginations from the servile moral structures of the slave society. Belief in the efficacy of this imaginary animal symbol freed slaves to respond creatively in an alternate way to the closed moral system of the plantation. The presupposition was that the oppressed could sanely cope with the oppressor's closed system of morality only from the perspective of moral ambiguity. This perspective allowed the oppressed to live in creative awareness of the oppressor's definitions of conceptual categories such as "moral" and "immoral." An oppressive system always dictates that the oppressed make decisions regarding "right" and "wrong" according to the language logistics of the oppressor. Our interpretation of the Brer Rabbit stories revealed clearly how slaves countered their masters' definition of what made up the "good" and the "right." Ethical matters were often further complicated by those masters who required that their slaves practice in word and deed the servile morality of the plantation. The playful narrative self type, on one level, is the antithesis of the soul narrative self type, yet on a more critical level, it complements the soul narrative self theory.

The playful narrative self, antithetical to the soul self, makes it possible for the agent to assume an ambiguous moral posture in "moral" versus "immoral" situations. Categories such as "moral," "immoral," and "amoral" are not deemed as absolutely binding upon those of this type. They, instead, can only be endowed with creative meaning when the agent dares play creatively with them. Subscribers of this type perceive moral categories as a means to the end rather than the end itself. An example is the playful disregard that the trickster (or player) agent has for the moral boundaries permanently established by the oppressor. Playfully mixing up the oppressor's moral boundaries becomes the way that the victimized learns to cope with the oppressor's society of closed morality. The victimized player knows that in the oppressor's world it is "might" rather then "right" that really decides what is ethical and godly. Therefore the victimized must make a radical distinction between "playing the game" of morality and ethics, and "playing the rules" of the moral game itself. The oppressed are always afraid of the latter because the "rules of the moral game" are always defined by oppressors.[28]

The difference between "playing the game" of morality and ethics and "playing the moral rules" of the game can best be illustrated by an analogue from America's racist history of organized sports. Particular reference here is being made to such sports as football, basketball, and baseball. An American racist society prohibited African Americans from playing with white Americans in any organized sport. White America justified its racist exclusion from the start of African Americans on the false premise that they were both genetically and mentally inferior. It was taken for granted that African Americans did not have the mental aptitude to learn the rules necessary for playing any of these sports. Meeting this challenge head on, African Americans proved that they could play the respective sport in such a dramatic way that rule and record books had to be rewritten. It was their graceful style of skillful play that they brought to each sport that demanded whites' attention. Consequently African Americans eventually revolutionized white America's traditional way of playing all such major sports as baseball, basketball, and football. The introduction of the dunk shot in basketball, the Willie Mays' basket catch in baseball, and the swivel hipped runner in football all contributed to a new style of playing the game itself. It was a style of play that even encouraged white players themselves to abandon the old rules that once dictated how the game ought to be played. This is analogous to what the playful narrative self does to the oppressor's rules of ethical and moral discourse. It has required a rewriting of the public policy.

Contributions of the Playful Narrative Self

The playful narrative self type makes an invaluable contribution in several ways to African-American theology and ethics. First, it provides a humanist critique of masters' spurious verbal constructions about the slave's being. One such construction denounced the slave as being both "black of body and blacker of soul." In an earlier chapter we called this construction the double self-negation theory, that is, the self's propensity to deny that it has any spiritual or material worth. The objective of the makers of this theory was to unmake the being of the slave. Since slave masters accented stringent Puritan demands of self-denial, slaves undoubtedly found the activities of play and laughter, derived from the Brer Rabbit stories, invaluable therapy for their bodies and minds. It must have provided them self-release in the face of oppressive psychosocial structures. Graceful free play in the face of these oppressive structures became the way slaves subtly embraced the law of self-preservation. It provided a moral deterrent against slaves becoming innocent victims of their masters' skewed teachings about such Christian virtues as humility, self-denial and love.

Graceful free play kept the oppressed from idolizing their own acts of Christian piety. The experience of oppression itself taught slaves that only genuine Christian piety made for an authentic moral self and vice versa. False piety results from the self taking itself so seriously that it prevents God's grace of free play from transforming it into a creative moral agent.

The second contribution of the playful narrative self to the constructive task of African-American theology and ethics is its illumination of the notion of hospitality. This concept of playfulness helps us understand how African-American worshipers have responded to the activity of the Spirit of God in their lives. It is the playful nature that allows the self to remain open to the coming of the Spirit of God. This openness to the Spirit of God presumes that the ultimate duty of the self is to serve God's Spirit rather than vice versa. Although God comes into the world to be its host, the playful narrative self receives God as the royal guest. The playful narrative self theory requires that we read the gospel with the conviction that it is impossible to be God's guests without first learning to be God's hosts, that is, God's servants in the world. Being spiritual players of God must be viewed as essential to what it means to be Christians for African Americans. This means that God has the final say about the destiny of humankind. It also means that a guest is embodied in every host and vice versa.

Third, the playful narrative self theory makes a hermeneutical contribution to the African-American interpretative task of theology and ethics. It does this by freeing the interpreter to value the spirit of the law over the letter of the law. Tutored in the school of oppression itself, sensitive African Americans have learned not to take any one interpretation of scripture as absolutely definitive of God's actions in human community. Violent disagreement about the meaning of scripture has not been the primary focus of African-American churches. Their leaders, instead, have tended to value "fellowship in the Spirit of God" over interpretational differences about doctrinal beliefs relating to God's action and nature. "Fellowship in the Spirit of God" has been the major theological and ethical focus of African-American churches. Given this fact, many earlier social scientists, such as E. Franklin Frazier,[29] have superficially concluded that the church mainly served the social needs denied its members in the larger white society. This superficial reduction of African-Americans' practice of Christianity to a mere social variable ignored the fact that they were living heirs of a rich African religious tradition of communal hospitality.[30] Joseph Washington, an African-American social ethicist, made a similar kind of mistake when he concluded that "Black Religion" was, at best, no more than a "folk religion."[31] Washington's radical condemnation of African-American religion was motivated by the church's lack of prophetic effectiveness in the civil rights movement. While the African-American church must be judged for these failures, it ought not be seen as totally void of theological doctrine — as Washington would have us believe. Its doctrinal richness must be seen in the way African-American worshipers have embraced the ideal belief of Christian hospitality. This has been the community's way of affirming the biblical doctrine of being reconciled in God through Jesus Christ. Hospitality to the human or the Divine Other means that the self has the courage to play riskfully, knowing that the Significant Other tends to appear always in an insignificant form to us. Subsequently, hospitality generates a dialectical posture of free play on the part of believers. On one side of the dialectic the community believes that it becomes God's host in the world; on the other side, the community believes that it is made to be God's guest in the world. This dialectical function of being both host and guest of the Holy Spirit in the lives of believers suggests that God is never to be taken for granted. It, also, means that the "other" in human encounter must always be perceived as the potential bearer of the Ultimate Significant Other. This says that the African-American community remains sensitive to the fact that the localization of God is always unpredictable. Those of the traditional African-American belief have always believed that it is impossible to program the activity of the Holy Spirit in the lives of human beings. Worship itself is only viewed as genuine when the "Holy Spirit is allowed to play ("operate" and "move" are the terms commonly used) upon the main altars of their hearts." Worshipers are always aware that they only can plan the liturgy to a point. Beyond that they must act as host to the Holy Spirit who does not play by the logistical rules of human beings. Rather the Holy Spirit plays "above," "within," "before," and "behind" human hosts. The community's attitude is always that "God moves in mysterious ways, God's wonders to perform."

Jesus is seen as the exemplary model of the playful narrative self. The African-American folk preacher[32] construed an image of Jesus who demonstrated, in his encounter with others, skillful play in interpreting truth. Worshipers celebrate with the preacher the fact that even the devil cannot trap Jesus in a conversation. This perception of Jesus' playful method of hermeneutically surviving the verbal attacks of his adversaries is always consoling to the oppressed, especially since the oppressed live in a society where they are having to daily defend both what they say and think. It is for this reason that the oppressed still celebrate the fact that Jesus' hermeneutical genius must be seen in the way that he inverts his adversaries' logic back upon them. Also, Jesus transforms the death methods and symbols of his enemies, such as the cross, into a means *to* and symbol *of* eternal life. African Americans have heard the same kind of player (trickster) motif in the crucifixion and resurrection drama of Jesus that they heard in the "Brer Rabbit and the Briar Patch" story. The community can rejoice when the mob crucifies Jesus in the same way that it can when Brer Fox throws Brer Rabbit in the briar patch because it knows that Jesus, as with Brer Rabbit, is capable of surviving the land of death. In refusing to play by the devil's rule Jesus beats him at his own game. This way of understanding the scenario of Jesus was at the very heart of black preaching and singing in the slave community.

The Spiritual Song and the Dialogical Narrative Self

The dialogical narrative self is another type of theory involving self, God, and community that emerges out of the slave sources. It is a product of what has been termed above the primordial "call and response" communication structure (see chapter 4) that is indigenous to the conversion sources of the slave community. In actuality, it became the bedrock upon which converted slaves reconstructed their own radical notion of both double consciousness and community, that is, "I," "you" and "we" consciousness among each other.

This notion of the dialogical narrative self evolves out of the slave community's mutual understanding of the primordial "call and response" phenomenon that it believed to be a part of all human and divine encounters. Cultural anthropologists and ethnomusicologists have all rightly noted that this style of communication among slaves in the United States has its antecedents in the culture of Africa. Plantation slaves deemed the "call and response" method of communication invaluable to their survival of the oppressive conditions of slavery. The convert, in using it, before and after conversion, was able to communicate both with God and the community. What this means is that the "call and response" communication structure must be perceived to have both theological and ethical implications. God's revelation takes place to the oppressed through this vital structure. It must be assumed that every dialogic self has its social genesis in the structured "call and response" phenomenon. In addition, this "call and response" communication structure must be viewed as the foundational means via which God's self-disclosure is made to humankind.

Slaves' understanding of the phenomenon of "I," "You," and "we" consciousness was made possible because of their faithful response to the radicality of God's call in their lives. By virtue of having responded to it, slaves' experience of having been called to new being equaled being endowed with the gift of positive double consciousness. This call to positive from negative double consciousness initiated within them a dialectical notion of selfhood. Having experienced the call of God, every slave could speak dialectically of having been made a new creature in Jesus Christ. The confessional formula for acknowledging this new state of being was that "I have done died one time and I ain't gonna die no more." This meant that the slave could claim spiritual freedom in God despite the reality of physical bondage. Experiences of having been called by God gave slaves the needed critical framework from which to critique both the society in which they lived and each other.

Contributions of the Dialogical Narrative Self

The first structure of "call and response" communication, as reflected in the slave community's primary sources, portrays God as having both transcendent and immanent attributes. This is illustrated in the fact that the converted community understood God as both the primordial creator and respondent (both the caller and the answerer). Therefore slaves often described the experience of God's call as having been that of "hearing a small voice inside themselves talking back to God." God, as caller was perceived as transcendent; and God, as answerer was portrayed as very immanent in the life of the hearer. Slaves constantly referred to their own futile efforts of trying to initiate a conversation with God before ever having heard God call them. In the divine salvation drama Jesus becomes the exemplary model of God's obedient son who answers the call of his heavenly parent. To say that Jesus talked to God, his father, is the equivalent of saying that God talked to God's self.

Second, the acts of speaking and thinking about God are inextricably linked in the "call and response" structure. The experience of suffering itself makes no allowance for distinguishing between the act of speaking about God and that of thinking about God. It demands an ontology of world experience, an ontology of embodied behavior and life styles in which thinking and speaking are not juxtaposed and externally related entities but reciprocating ways of existing in the world.[33] African Americans are very sensitive to white theologians' tendencies to dismiss their talk about God as amounting, at best, to sermonic rhetoric. The assumption is that real thinking assumes the posture of silent colloquy. African-American theology must insist that dialogue provides the experiential basis for speaking and thinking alike. Liberation theology can never be perceived as merely the sterile monologue of a solitary thinker within the theological academy. Instead, it is a dialogue between the "I and thou." The point being made is that in the existential act of speaking thought is copresent.

Third, this "call and response" communication structure (comprised of "I," "you," and "we" elements) is foundational for developing an ethic of reciprocity between the individual and the community. Inherent in this primary structure of "I," "you," and "we" consciousness is the notion that "to be oneself means to be the other, and to be the other is to be oneself." The reality of oppression generally tends to make the oppressed community more sensitive to "the mystery of interhuman encounter." Scholarly statements of African-American theology and ethics have scarcely addressed this issue. Nowhere is it our intention to contend that slaves dealt with this problem abstractly. It, instead, is to show that this primordial communication structure is foundational for constructing a theological and ethical statement about the African-American experience. It helps us value the way the oppressed perceived their encounters with one another. Contemporary theorists of social philosophy, from Martin Buber to Martin G. Plattel,[34] all have contributed to a clearer understanding of the phenomenon of interhuman encounter. The person becomes genuinely an "I" only when she or he discovers the other as a "you," and together they form the "we."

In chapter 4 above we cited how the phenomenon of interhuman encounter among slaves was played out in the singing drama itself. Via ritualized singing, slaves expressed their social, psychological, and spiritual needs. "I" and "we" consciousness is formed as a result of interhuman encounters between the "I" and "you." The slave community's ritualized singing acts gave them that communal sense of being a transcendent "we." It, also, gave them the radical sense of having been created free moral agents.

Fourth, the "call-and-response" primordial communication structure is foundational for evaluating the reciprocal relationship between the andro-gogical and pedagogical methods of education. Contrary to the common practice of valuing one over the other, practitioners of African-American theology and ethics need to see how these different methods of education might reciprocate in the liberation project of the oppressed. This must be the case although these two methods are predicated on different value assumptions. A set of paternalistic values is presumed to be behind the pedagogical method of instruction. On the contrary a set of egalitarian values is presumed to be behind the androgogical method of instructions. It makes sense that the oppressed would rebel against the oppressor's ped-agogical method of instruction. We have yet to give scholarly attention to the issue of whether indigenous leaders of the oppressed might not find the paternalistic style of leadership more effective at certain stages of the liberation project. This is not an easy issue for African-American acade-micians to resolve since the majority of indigenous religious leaders in the community find the paternalistic leadership style to be the norm. It might be that a benevolent, paternalistic style of leadership is necessary to bring oppressed people to that level of maturity where they will be receptive of a more democratic style of leadership. A classical example would be the positive impact that the Honorable Elijah Mohammed's paternalistic lead-ership style had on the life of Malcolm X and thousands of other followers. In his autobiography, Malcolm notes the transforming impact that the life and ideas of the Honorable Elijah had on him both while in prison and after having been released.[35]

IMPLICATIONS FOR FURTHER STUDY

It can be concluded that the religio-moral language of the slave com-munity provides its own dialectical norm for African-American theological and ethical discourse. The dialectical norm of the language must be held in creative tension between the cultural polarities of the nonliterate and the literate. This is the case for at least two basic reasons. First, the religio-moral language provides a dialectical view of the African-American self, God, and community that was forged in the crucible of suffering collectively and individually. Slaves' religio-moral language showed that they, even in the face of mandated illiteracy, reflected meaning structures of lived expe-rience that have profound theological and ethical implications. This view emerges out of the folk language of a people who existed marginally to the master class. Any emergence of such a dialectical view would have been readily denounced by slave masters as contradictory of their one-dimen-sional explanations of the slave's understanding of self, God, and commu-nity. In their one-dimensional explanations, masters deemed the slave theologically and ethically an anthropological aberration of God's created order.

Slaves' experience of this God, who was marginal to slave masters' cultural norms, empowered them with a radical vision that defied slave masters' so-called normative religion. While it was not as much the case with ex-slaves, slaves of the conversion experience caught a normative vision of the self, God, and community apart from their masters. Since masters prohibited slaves from access to literacy, they could always speak of their experiential encounters with God as outside of the control of whites. Mandated illiteracy undermined the presumptuous authority of the slave master in that it forced slaves to recover a primordial sense of religious freedom that made literacy unnecessary.

Second, the religio-moral language provides us with a normative vision of beloved community that is based on spiritual kinship in God. Consequently, slave masters' demonic structures of cultural marginality symbolized by race, caste, and class could not abort slaves' vision. Slaves employed this normative vision of community to critique all forms of human institutions and relationships. Radical obedience to God was deemed by those in God's beloved community to be the fulfillment of the highest ethical imperative, even in the face of danger. Nowhere in slaves' religio-moral language does God tell them to obey their masters.

It is the literate contribution that ex-slaves, via the autobiographical genre, contribute to the discourse of religio-moral language that accents the other side of the dialectic. To make such a contribution, ex-slaves had to master skillfully the formal language of the oppressor. The question becomes one of moral integrity: To what extent must they compromise the slave community's normative vision of the self, God, and community? Will the adoption of the formal language of American freedom mean that African-American leaders following the Civil War must sacrifice radical obedience to the conversion God for acceptance into America's kingdom of ideal citizenship?

Questions such as those raised above must inform the sequel inquiry to our present study. The African-American quest for literacy, particularly following the Civil War, has critical theological and ethical implications. It will invariably impact the way African Americans view the self, God, and community. We might end this discussion with two questions: Did educated African Americans' adoption of the freedom language of American individualism cause them to abandon the nonliterate community's vision of beloved community and ethnic loyalty? Have African Americans' fusion of the visions of the nonliterary and the literary traditions of religio-moral language better enabled them to affect the majority culture's vision of the self, God, and community?

Notes

INTRODUCTION: REVALUING THE SLAVE EXPERIENCE

1. John W. Blassingame, "Using the Testimony of Ex-Slaves," in *The Slave's Narrative*, ed. Charles T. Davis and Henry Louis Gates, Jr. (New York: Oxford University Press, 1985), 94.

2. Ibid.

3. Ibid., 94.

4. Ronald Potter, a former student and constant intellectual sparring partner, teaches at a community college in New Jersey. Professor Potter challenged me some years ago to think of the slave folk sources as really comprising the religio-moral language of the African-American experience.

5. Lawrence Levine, *Black Culture and Black Consciousness: Afro-American Folk Thought From Slavery to Freedom* (New York: Oxford University Press, 1975). Levine delineates his methodology in chapter one of the book.

6. Mechal Sobel, *Trabelin' on: The Slave Journey in America to an Afro-Baptist Faith* (Westport, Conn.: Greenwood Press, 1979). See also, Sobel, *The World They Made Together* (Princeton, N.J.: Princeton University Press, 1987).

7. Eugene Genovese, *Roll, Jordan, Roll: The World the Slaves Made* (New York: Vintage Books, 1972).

8. Ibid., pp. 6, 18.

9. Albert J. Raboteau, *Slave Religion* (New York: Oxford University Press, 1978), has deepened my appreciation for possible correlations between African-American slaves' religious beliefs and practices and their African derivations. In a descriptive analysis of the slave sources Raboteau gives a very helpful introductory background to antecedents of certain African religions. The first chapter is very helpful for understanding Raboteau's methodological presuppositions. In addition to Raboteau's book see Roger Bastide, *The African Religions of Brazil: Toward a Sociology of the Interpretation of Civilizations*, trans. Helen Sebba. (Baltimore, Md.: Johns Hopkins University Press, 1978). Henry Mitchell's *Black Religious Beliefs* (New York: Harper & Row, 1975) has also been very informative on this subject.

10. Howard Harrod, *Renewing the World: Plains Indian Religion and Morality* (Tucson, Ariz.: University of Arizona Press, 1986). Harrod's use of this methodology has clearly informed his interpretation of the beliefs and practices of American Plains Indians.

11. Howard L. Harrod, *The Human Center: Moral Agency in the Social World* (Philadelphia: Fortress Press, 1981). Harrod makes a scholarly contribution in this book to the ways in which discourses about social reality illuminate our understandings about the self as moral agent.

12. Alfred Schutz, *The Problem of Social Reality: Collected Papers, Volume I.*

Edited and introduced by Maurice Natanson with a preface by H. L. Van Breda (The Hague, Netherlands: Martinus Nijhoff, 1967). Maurice Natanson, *The Journeying Self* (Santa Cruz, Calif.: University of California Press, 1970). Maurice Natanson, *Phenomenology, Role, and Reason: Essays on the Coherence and Deformation of Social Reality* (Springfield, Ill.: Charles C. Thomas Publisher, 1974). Aron Gurwitsch, *Human Encounters in the Social World*, ed. Alexandre Metraux, trans. Fred Kersten. (Pittsburgh, Pa.: Duquesne University Press, 1979). Calvin O. Shrag, *Experience and Being: Prolegomena to a Future Ontology* (Evanston, Ill.: Northwestern University Press, 1969). Stephan Strasser, *Phenomenology of Feeling: An Essay on the Phenomena of the Heart.* Foreword by Paul Ricoeur and translated with introduction by Robert E. Wood. (Pittsburgh, Pa.: Duquesne University Press, 1977). Max Scheler, *Formalism in Ethics and Nonformal Ethics of Value*, translated by Manfred S. Frings and Roger L. Funk (Evanston, Ill.: Northwestern University Press, 1973). Max Scheler, *Ressentiment*, translated by William W. Holheim (New York: Free Press, 1961). John Paul Sartre, *The Psychology of Imagination*, translated by Bernard Frechtman (New York: Philosophical Library, 1948).

13. Robert Wuthnow, *Meaning and Moral Order: Exploration in Cultural Analysis* (Berkeley, Calif.: University of California Press, 1987). Wuthnow has done an excellent job in this text of summing up the varied theoretical approaches to interpreting social reality.

14. Hans-Georg Gadamer, *Truth and Method* (New York: A Continuum Book/ Seabury Press, 1984). See also J. N. Findlay, *Hegel: A Re-examination* (New York: Oxford University Press/A Galaxy Book, 1958).

15. Gadamer, *Truth and Method*, 273f, 337f.

16. Shelton Smith, *In His Image, But . . . : Racism in Southern Religion, 1780-1910* (Durham, N.C.: Duke University Press, 1972).

17. Alfred Schutz, *The Phenomenology of the Social World* (Evanston, Ill., Northwestern University Press, 1967), pp. 187-88. The phrase *ideal type* is a theoretical construct that has been passed on from the eminent scholar Max Weber. Weber used this construct for the purpose of both simplifying and exaggerating concrete historical evidence. This is the sense in which I have used the Weberian construct known as ideal type. Moreover, my understanding of Weber's use of the concept has been illuminated by Alfred Schutz's appropriation of it in his study, *The Phenomenology of the Social World*. Schutz notes:

[T]here is something ambiguous about this concept of an ideal type of human behavior. It denotes at one and the same time ideal types covering (1) pre-given objective meaning-contexts, (2) products, (3) courses of action, and (4) real and ideal objects, whenever any of the above are the result of human behavior. Included also would be interpretations of the products of ideal-typical behavior. The latter are the interpretations to which we resort when we know nothing of the individual experiences of those who created these products. Whenever we come upon any ordering of past experience under interpretive schemes, any act of abstraction, generalization, formalization, or idealization, whatever the object involved, there we shall find this process in which a moment of living experience is lifted out of its setting and then, through a synthesis of recognition, frozen into a hard and fast "ideal type." Insofar as the term "ideal type" can be applied to any interpretive scheme under which experience is subsumed — as in Max Weber's early writings — it raises no special problem for the social scientist. We could speak in exactly the same sense of ideal types of physical objects and processes, of meteorological patterns, of evolutionary series in biology, and so forth. How useful the concept of ideal types would be in these fields is not for us to say, since we are concerned here with a specific group of problems in the social sciences.

The concept "ideal type of human behavior" can be taken in two ways. It can mean first of all the ideal type of another person who is expressing himself or has expressed himself in a certain way. Or it may mean, second, the ideal type of the expressive process itself, or even of the outward results which we interpret as the signs of the expressive process. Let us call the first the "personal ideal type" and the second the "material" or "course-of-action type." Certainly an inner relation exists between these two. I cannot, for instance, define the ideal type of a postal clerk without first having in mind a definition of his job. The latter is a course-of-action type, which is, of course, an objective context of meaning. Once I am clear as to the course-of-action type, I can construct the personal ideal type, that is "the person who performs this job." And, in doing so, I imagine the corresponding subjective meaning-contexts which would be in his mind, the subjective contexts that would have to be adequate to the objective contexts already defined. The personal ideal type is therefore derivative, and the course-of-action type can be considered quite independently as a purely objective context of meaning.

I. THE SLAVE: A CHILD OF GOD?

1. Eugene D. Genovese, *Roll, Jordan, Roll: The World the Slave Made* (New York: Vintage Books, 1972), pp. 3–7. See his discussion on paternalism.

2. Stanley M. Elkins, *Slavery: A Problem in American Institutional and Intellectual Life* (Chicago: University of Chicago Press, 1959), 82.

3. I am deeply indebted to the discussions set forth by both Alfred Schutz and Thomas Luckman on the typologies of social reality. See their book *The Structure of the Life-World*, trans. Richard Zaner and H. Tristram Engelhardt, Jr. (Evanston, Ill.: Northwestern University Press, 1973).

4. Morgan Godwin, *The Negro's Indian advocate: suing for their admission to the church: or A persuasive to the instructing and baptizing of the Negro's and Indians in our plantations. Shewing that as the compliance therewith can prejudice no man's just int.* . . . (London: Printed by the author, J. D., 1680), 13.

5. John Evrie, in the preface to Godwin, *Negro's Indian*, 1.

6. Joseph R. Washington, *Anti-blackness in English Religion* (New York: Mellen Press, 1984), xiii.

7. Ibid.

8. Ibid.

9. Evrie, 95.

10. Winthrop Jordan, *White Over Black: Attitudes Toward the Negro 1550–1812* (Baltimore, Md.: Penguin Inc., 1969).

11. Evrie, 105–106.

12. Elkins, *Slavery*, 84-86, 88-89.

13. Ibid., 81-82.

14. Earl E. Thorpe, "Chattel Slavery and Concentration Camps," *The Negro History Bulletin* 25, no. 8:174-175.

15. Kenneth Stampp, "Rebels and Sambos: The Search For the Negro's Personality in Slavery," *Journal of Southern History* 27, no. 3 (August 1971).

16. Ibid., 381.

17. Milton C. Sernett, ed., *Afro-American Religious History: A Documentary Witness* (Durham, N.C.: Duke University Press, 1985), 88. See also Gayraud S. Wilmore, *Black Religion and Black Radicalism: An Examination of the Black Experience in Religion* (Garden City, N.Y.: Doubleday, 1972).

18. See *The Southampton Slave Revolt of 1831: A Compilation of Source Material Including the Full Text of the Confessions of Nat Turner*, comp. Henry Irving Tragle (New York: Vintage Books, 1971), 64.

19. Ibid., 132.

20. H. Shelton Smith, *In His Image, But . . . : Racism in Southern Religion, 1780-1910* (Durham, North Carolina: Duke University Press, 1972).

21. Leigh Richmond, *The African Servant. An Authentic Narrative* (Published by the American Tract Society, And sold at their Depository, No. 144 Nassau Street, Near the City-Hall, New York; and by Agents of the Society, its Branches and Auxiliaries, in the Principal Cities and Towns in the United States), 1. (Found in the Schomburg Center for Research in Black Culture.)

22. Ibid., 1.

23. Ibid., 2.

24. Ibid., 5.

25. Thomas Bacon, *Four Sermons Upon the Great and Indispensable Duty of All Christian Masters and Mistresses to Bring up Their Negro Slaves in the Knowledge and Fear of God. Preached at the Parish Church of St. Peter in Talbot County, in the Province of Maryland* (London: Printed by H. Oliver, in Bartholomew-Clofe, near Weft-Smithfield, MDCCL), 437.

26. Ibid., xii.

27. Washington, *Anti-blackness in English Religion*, 503.

28. Ibid., 502.

29. "A Letter to an American Planter from His Friend in London." (London: Printed by H. Reynell, No. 21 Piccadilly, 1781).

30. Ibid., 9.

31. Ibid., 12-19.

32. Henry Pattillo, *The Plain Planter's Family Assistant . . . Address to Husbands and Wives, Children and Servants . . .* (Wilmington, 1787), 51-52.

33. George Whitfield, "A Letter to the Ten Inhabitants of Maryland" (London, 1771).

34. Washington, *Anti-blackness in English Religion*, 351–53.

2. DUTY, BONDAGE, AND PEDAGOGY

1. See Eugene D. Genovese, *Roll, Jordan, Roll: The World the Slaves Made* (New York: Vintage Books, 1972). Note the critical attention that Genovese gives to the idea of the social structure of the plantation in the first section of the text.

2. See W. P. Harrison, ed. *The Gospel Among Slaves; A Short Account of Missionary Operations Among the African Slaves of the Southern States* (Nashville: Publishing House of the M.E. Church, South Barbee and Smith, Agents, 1893).

3. Ibid., 14.

4. Ibid., 264.

5. See Erskine Clarke, *Wrestlin' Jacob* (Atlanta: John Knox Press, 1973).

6. Bishop Meade, *Pastoral Letter* (Richmond, Va.: H. K. Ellyson, 147 Main Street, 1853), 21. See also Harrison, *Gospel Among Slaves,* 255.

7. W. T. Hamilton, "The Duties of Masters and Slaves Respectively, or Domestic Servitude As Sanctioned By The Bible: A Discourse by Rev. W. T. Hamilton" (Published in 1845), 16.

8. Richard Nisbet, *The Capacity of Negroes* (Westport, Conn.: Negro Universities Press, 1970), 17.

9. Thomas V. Peterson, *Ham, Japheth: The Mythic World* . . . (Metuchen, N.J.: Scarecrow Press, 1978), 12-31, 109-122.

10. John Fairly, "The Negro in His Relations to the Church," *Historical Review* (Charleston: Walker, Evans & Cogswell Co., Printers, 1889), 1.

11. Ibid., 4.

12. Ibid., 5.

13. Ibid., 5, 6.

14. Ibid., 9.

15. Charles C. Jones, *The Religious Instruction of the Negroes in the United States* (Savannah: Published by Thomas Purse, 1842; reprint, New York: Kraus Reprint Co., 1969), 165.

16. Ibid.

17. Ibid., 159.

18. Ibid., 160.

19. Ibid., 160.

20. Ibid., 160.

21. Ibid., 160-61.

22. Ibid., 168.

23. Meade, *Pastoral Letter*, 5.

24. Ibid., 18.

25. James H. Thornwell, "Sermon: The Rights and Duties of Masters, preached on Sunday evening May 26, 1850." Second Presbyterian Church (Charleston, South Carolina), 11.

26. Ibid.

27. Ibid.

28. Meade, *Pastoral Letter*, 10.

29. Ibid., 21-22.

30. Bishop William Meade, "Duties of Christian Masters," 245-246.

31. Thomas Bacon, *Four Sermons* . . . *Duty of Masters*, 500-510.

32. E. T. Baird, "A Pastoral Letter," *Religious Instructions of Our Colored Population* (Starkville, Mississippi, April 16, 1859), 10.

33. Quoted in Harrison, *The Gospel Among Slaves*, 212.

34. Ibid.

35. Ibid.

36. Ibid., 251.

37. Ibid.

38. Ibid., 251.

39. Ibid., 273.

40. Ibid.

41. Ibid.

42. David B. Davis, *The Problem of Slavery in Western Culture* (Ithaca, N.Y.: Cornell University Press, 1966), 85.

43. Practically all of those who wrote instructions to those who were missionary-preachers on the plantations were of this disposition.

44. Charles C. Jones, *Religious Instruction of the Negroes*, 49.

45. Ibid., 10

46. Barnwell, Gadsden, and Tapier, *Easy Instructions for Coloured Persons* (Charleston: Printed and Published by A. E. Miller, No. 4 Broad Street, 1837), 10.

47. Francis Xavier Murphy, "Cathechesis: Early Christians," in *New Catholic Encyclopedia*, ed. William J. McDonald, D.D. (New York: McGraw-Hill Book Co., 1967), 3:208.

48. Susan Markey Fickling, *Slave Conversion in South Carolina 1830-1860* (Columbia, S.C.: University of South Carolina, 1924), 33.

49. Rev. A. F. Dickson, *Plantation Sermons* (Philadelphia: Presbyterian Board of Publications, No. 265, 1856), i-xi.

50. Ibid., xi.

51. Ibid.

52. Harrison, *Gospel Among Slaves*, 249.

53. John B. Adger, "Sermon on the Religious Instruction of the Coloured Population" (Preached in the Second Presbyterian Church, Charleston, South Carolina, May 19, 1847), 9-10.

54. Ibid.

55. Washington, *Anti-blackness in English Religion*, 508.

56. Ibid., 508.

57. Edmund Botsford, *The Spiritual Voyage* (London: Privately Printed, 1821; Charleston: W. Riley Reprinted for D. Barnes, 1828), 22.

58. Edmund Botsford, *Sambo and Toney: A Dialogue Between Two Slaves* (New York: American Tract Society, No Date), 6.

59. Ibid.

60. Ibid., 71.

61. Ibid., 12.

62. Ibid.

63. Ibid.

64. Frank Klingberg, *An Appraisal of the Negro in Colonial South Carolina* (Washington, D.C.: Associated Publishers, 1941), 13.

65. Ibid.

66. Arthur P. Hudson, "Some Curious Negro Names," *Southern Folklore Quarterly* 2, no. 4 (Dec. 1938): 183ff.

67. Barnwell, Gadsden, and Trapier, *Easy Instructions for Coloured Persons,* 17.

68. Ibid., 23.

69. Dean J. Epstein, *Sinful Tunes and Spirituals* (Urbana, Ill.: University of Illinois Press, 1977), 238.

70. Barnwell, Gadsden, and Tapier, *Easy Instructions for Coloured Persons*, 26-27.

71. Ibid., 78.

72. Ibid., 79.

73. Ibid., 78.

74. Ibid., 3.

75. Ibid.

3. THE SELF IN THE SELF RESPONSE

1. Charity Moore, *American Slave: A Composite Autobiography*, ed. George P. Rawick (1941; reprint, Westport, Conn.: Greenwood Publishing Company, 1972), 3:206.

2. Ibid., 205-207.

3. John B. Sale, *The Tree Named John* (Chapel Hill, N.C.: University of North Carolina Press, 1929).

4. Eli Shepherd, "Certain Beliefs and Superstitions" in Bruce Jackson, *The Negro and His Folklore* (Austin: University of Texas Press, 1969), 248.

5. *God Struck Me Dead*, vol. 19 of *The American Slave: A Composite Autobiography*, ed. George P. Rawick (1945; reprint, Westport, Conn.: Greenwood Publishing Co. 1972), 1. In the remainder of the discussion the title will be referred to as *God Struck Me Dead.*

6. See the introduction where I give credit to the historians and phenomenologists that have influenced my thinking and methodology.

7. Eugene D. Genovese, *Roll, Jordan, Roll: The World the Slave Made* (New York: Vintage Books, 1972). See Part 1 of the book where the author shows theoretically how the issue of compromise was informally worked out between slave and master.

8. *God Struck Me Dead*, 1.

9. Ibid., 3.

10. Ibid., 3.

11. Ibid., 4.

12. Ibid., 5.

13. Ibid., 5.

14. Ibid., 6.

15. Ibid.

16. Ibid., 1.

17. Ibid., 3.

18. Ibid., 20.

19. Ibid., 9.

20. Ibid., 67.

21. Ibid., 74.

22. Ibid., 99.

23. Ibid., 215.

24. Eli Shepherd, "Certain Beliefs and Superstitions," 260.

25. Ibid., 261.

26. Ibid., 260.

27. Ibid., 24.

28. Ibid., 39.

29. *God Struck Me Dead*, 65.

30. Ibid., 78.

31. Ibid., 11.

32. Ibid., 11.

33. Ibid., 16.

34. Ibid., 10.

35. Ibid., 88.

36. Ibid., 27.
37. Ibid., 29.
38. Ibid., 50.
39. Ibid., 34.
40. Ibid., 34.
41. Ibid., 88.
42. Ibid., 61.
43. Ibid., 34.
44. Ibid., 21, 82.
45. Ibid., 84.
46. Ibid., 33.
47. Ibid., 40.
48. Ibid., 40.
49. Ibid., 48.
50. Ibid., 90.
51. Ibid., 68.
52. Ibid., 64.
53. Ibid., 31.
54. Ibid., 57.
55. Ibid., 91.
56. "Story of Ex-Slave Isaiah Jeffries," in vol. 3 of *The American Slave*, 19.
57. *God Struck Me Dead,* 124.

4. THE SPIRITUALS: COMMUNITY IN SONG

1. John Lovell, Jr., *Black Songs: the Forge and the Flame* (New York: Macmillan, 1972).

2. See especially William Fisher, *Seventy Negro Spirituals* (Boston: Oliver Ditson Company, 1926) and James H. Cone, *The Spirituals and the Blues* (New York: Seabury Press, 1972; Maryknoll, N.Y.: Orbis Books, 1991).

3. Langston Hughes and Arna Bontemps, eds. *The Book of Negro Folklore* (New York: Dodd, Mead, 1958), 101.

4. Charity Bowery quoted in Dean J. Epstein, *Sinful Tunes and Spirituals* (Urbana, Ill.: University of Illinois Press, 1977), 385.

5. George P. Rawick, ed. *The American Slave: A Composite Autobiography*, vol. 18 (1945; reprint, Westport, Conn.: Greenwood Publishing Company, 1972), 125.

6. Olli Alho, *The Religion of the Slave* (Helsinki: Academia Scientarium Fennica, 1976), 120.

7. Ibid.

8. Rawick, *American Slave*, 19:171.

9. Lovell, *Black Songs*. See especially chapter twenty where the writer deals with the double meaning of the spiritual songs.

10. See Sidney Mead, *Lively Experiment: The Shaping of Christianity in America* (New York: Harper & Row, 1963).

11. Bruce Jackson, ed. *The Negro and His Folklore* (Austin, Tex.: University of Texas Press, 1967), 99.

12. James W. Johnson and J. Rosamond Johnson, *The Books of American Negro Spirituals* (New York: Viking Press, 1953), I:134-135.

13. Lovell, *Black Songs*, 328.

14. Miles Mark Fisher, *Negro Slave Songs in the United States* (New York, Citadel Press, 1953). See the section on the Civil War songs.

15. Lovell, *Black Songs*, 328.

16. Ibid., 312.

17. Ibid., 320.

18. Nicholas Ballanta, *St. Helena Island Spirituals* (New York: C. Scribner, 1925), 90.

19. *Jubilee Songs as Sung by the Jubilee Singers of Fisk University* (New York: Biglow & Main, 1872), 26.

20. Ibid., 31.

21. Thomas Fenner, Frederic G. Rathbun, and Miss Bessie Cleveland, arrang. *Cabin And Plantation Songs* (New York and London: Putnam, 1901), 181.

22. Ibid., 177.

23. See Theo Witvliet, *The Way Of The Black Messiah* (Oak Park, Ill.: Meyer Stone Books, 1987).

24. Fenner, et al., *Cabin and Plantation Songs,* 178.

25. Ibid., 187.

26. *Jubilee Songs*, 18.

27. Ibid., 33.

28. Ibid., 52.

29. Ibid., 53.

30. Ibid., 58.

31. Ibid.

32. Johnson and Johnson, *Negro Spirituals*, 164-65.

33. Hughes and Bontemps, ed. *Book of Negro Folklore*, 124-125.

34. James Weldon Johnson and J. Rosamond Johnson, Vol. I of *The Books of American Negro Spirituals* (New York: Viking Press, 1953), 158-159.

35. Ibid., 2:37-39.

36. Mary Allen Grissom, *The Negro Sings a New Heaven* (Chapel Hill, N.C. University of North Carolina Press, 1930), 88-89.

37. Ibid., 98-99.

38. Jackson, *The Negro and His Folklore*, 98.

39. Margaret W. Creel, *"A Peculiar People": Slave Religion and Community-Culture Among the Gullahs* (New York: New York University Press, 1988), 270.

40. Ballanta, ed. *St. Helena Island Spirituals*, 79.

41. Lovell, *Black Songs*, 307-308.

42. Ibid., 109.

43. Ballanta, ed. *St. Helena Island Spirituals*, 69.

44. Johnson and Johnson, *American Negro Spirituals*, 1:184-185.

45. Ibid., 155-157.

46. Ibid., 145-144.

47. *Jubilee Songs*, 30.

48. Ibid., 9.

49. Johnson and Johnson, *American Negro Spirituals*, Vol. I, 183-184.

50. Ibid., 50.

51. W.E.B. Du Bois, *The Souls of Black Folk* (New York: Signet Classic/New American Library, 1969), 5.

52. John Work, ed. *American Negro Songs and Spirituals* (New York: Bonanza Books, 1940), 170.

53. Ibid., 150.

54. Ibid., 130.

55. Jackson, *The Negro and His Folklore*, 92.

56. Johnson and Johnson, ed. *American Negro Spirituals*, 2:76.

57. Ibid., Vol. II, 84-85.

58. Bruce Jackson, *The Negro and His Folklore*, 55.

59. Work, *American Negro Songs and Spirituals*, 116.

60. Ibid., 91.

61. Ibid., 91.

62. Ibid., 97.

63. Ibid., 90.

64. Ibid., 60.

65. Ibid., 62.

66. Thomas L. Webber, *Deep Like the Rivers*, (New York: W. W. Norton and Company Inc., 1978) 127.

67. Paulo Freire, *Pedagogy of the Oppressed* (New York: Paulist Press, 1977).

68. Cone, *The Spirituals and the Blues*, 67-68.

69. Work, ed. *American Negro Songs and Spirituals*, 27.

70. Johnson and Johnson, ed. *American Negro Spirituals*, 21.

71. Ibid., 22.

72. Nathaniel Detts, *Religious Folk Songs of the Negro* (Hampton, Va.: Hampton Institute Press, 1927), 230.

73. Paul Ricoeur, *Freedom and Nature* (Evanston, Ill.: Northwestern University Press, 1966), 480.

74. Detts, *Religious Folk Songs*, 230.

75. See John Crossan, *In Parables: The Challenge of the Historical Jesus* (New York: Harper & Row, 1973) for a brilliant insight into the way that language is used in his interpretation of the parables in the New Testament.

76. Charles Stearns quoted in Olli Alho, *The Religion of Slaves*, 134.

77. Lovell, *Black Songs*, 272-273.

78. Edward P. Wimberly and Anne Streaty, *Liberation and Human Wholeness: The Conversion Experiences of Black People in Slavery and Freedom* (Nashville: Abingdon Press, 1986).

79. Sarah Bradford, *Scenes in the Life of Harriet Tubman* (Auburn: W. J. Moses, Printer, 1869), 27-29.

80. Ibid., 27-28.

81. Ibid., 29.

82. Lovell, *Black Songs,* 304.

83. Ibid., 304.

84. Ibid.

85. Dett, *Religious Folk Songs*, 78.

86. Rawick, *God Struck Me Dead*, vol. 19 of *The American Slave,* 7.

87. Ibid.

5. EX-SLAVES TELL THEIR STORIES

1. William Andrews, *To Tell a Free Story: The First Century of Afro-American Autobiography, 1760-1865* (Urbana, Ill.: University of Illinois Press, 1986).

2. Frederick Douglass, *The Life and Times of Frederick Douglass* (London: Collier-Macmillan, 1962); Jarena Lee, *The Life and religious experience of Jarena Lee* (Philadelphia: the author, 1836 [24 pp.]).

3. Andrews, *To Tell a Free Story*. See section on slaves becoming the authors of their own autobiographies.

4. Ibid., 110.

5. Ibid., 5.

6. Frederick Douglass, *The Life and Times of Frederick Douglass*, 358.

7. For a deeper theoretical insight see Hans-Georg Gadamer, *Truth and Method,* (New York: Seabury Press, 1985), 349.

8. Ibid., 353.

9. Paul Ricoeur, *Pastoral Care and Hermeneutics* (Philadelphia: Fortress Press, 1984), 192-198.

10. *Monthly Review* 80 (June 1789), 551-552.

11. "Life of a Negro Slave," in *Southern Quarterly Review* 23 (January 1853), 206-227.

12. Frederick Douglass, *The Liberator* (December 12, 1845).

13. "The Life and Venture of a Fugitive Slave," in *Quarterly Anti-Slavery Magazine* 5, no. 4 (1836), 375-393.

14. Ibid., 376.

15. Ibid.

16. Ephraim Peabody, "Narratives of Fugitive Slaves," in *Christian Examiner* 43, no. 1 (July-September 1849): 61.

17. Andrews, *To Tell a Free Story*, 11.

18. It was Ray Hart who, during my graduate studies at Vanderbilt University, first introduced me to the notion of first-order language. Hart notes the difference between the notions of first-order language and second-order language in his book *The Unfinished Man and the Imagination* (New York: Herder & Herder, 1968).

19. Among the few white scholars who have had the courage to address the topic of black liberation theology, one of the best constructive statements was done by Peter Hodgson. See the small treatise that he did called *Children of Freedom* (Philadelphia: Fortress Press, 1974). Here Hodgson used Douglass' clandestine quest as a slave to learn the art of reading to illustrate the role of language in the true liberation process.

20. Richard Wright came to an understanding of the power of literacy and the place that it had in shaping his own understanding of being. See especially his autobiography *American Hunger: The Compelling Continuation of Wright's Great Autobiographical Work Black Boy* (New York: Harper & Row, 1977), 111.

21. Walter J. Ong, *Interfaces of the Word: Studies in the Evolution of Consciousness and Culture* (Ithaca, N.Y.: Cornell University Press, 1977), 1.

22. Ibid., 18.

23. Michael Polanyi, *The Tacit Dimension* (Garden City, N.Y.: Anchor Books, Doubleday & Co., Inc., 1966), 15.

24. Austin Steward, *Twenty-Two Years a Slave, and Forty Years a Freeman* (New York: New American Library, 1969), Preface xii.

25. Again Polanyi's theoretical insight has been of value. See *The Tacit Dimension*, 15-16.

26. Harriet Tubman gives a graphic description of how she felt when she first

set foot on free territory. Sarah H. Bradford, *Scenes in the Life of Harriet Tubman* (Auburn: W.J. Moses, Printer, 1869).

27. See books by Alice Walker, *In Search of Our Mothers' Gardens*, (San Diego: Harcourt Brace Jovanovich, 1983); Jacquelyn Grant, *White Women's Christ, Black Women's Jesus* (Atlanta: Scholars Press, 1989); and Katie Cannon, *Black Womanist Ethics* (Atlanta: Scholars Press, 1988).

28. Michele Wallace, *Black Macho and the Myth of the Superwoman* (New York: Dial Press, 1979), 107.

29. Deborah Gray White, *Ar'n't I a Woman: Female Slaves in the Plantation South* (New York: Norton, 1985), 28-29.

30. Ibid., 46.

31. Ibid., 49.

32. Ibid., 61.

33. Andrews, *To Tell a Free Story*, 15.

34. Ibid., 15.

35. Amanda Smith, *An Autobiography* (New York: Oxford University Press, 1988), 81.

36. Charles L. Perdue, Thomas E. Barden, and Robert Phillips, eds. *Weevils in the Wheat: Interviews with Virginia Ex-slaves* (1976; reprint, Bloomington, Ind.: Indiana University Press, 1980), 221.

37. Zilpha Elaw, *Memoirs of the Life, Religious Experience, Ministerial Travels and Labours of Mrs. Zilpha Elaw, An American Female of Colour; Together with Some Account of the Great Religious Revivals in America* (London: Published by the Authoress, and Sold by T. Dydley and Mr. B. Taylor, 1846), 7.

38. Ibid., 33.

39. Ibid., 64.

40. Ibid., 79.

41. Ibid., 79.

42. Ibid., v. Characterizing herself as a female servant of the cross, Elaw considered herself "the poor and weak instrumentality in the Gospel of Jesus Christ. . . ."

43. Ibid., 127.

44. Ibid., 135.

45. Ibid., 135.

46. Smith, *An Autobiography*, 23.

47. Ibid., 23.

48. Ibid., 46.

49. Ibid., 46.

50. Ibid., 78.

51. Ibid., 80.

52. Ibid., 111.

53. Ibid., 118.

54. Ibid., 205.

55. Douglass, *The Life and Times of Frederick Douglass* (London: Collier-Macmillan Ltd., 1962), 90.

56. Ibid., 90.

57. Ibid., 91.

58. Ibid., 126.

59. Ibid., 125.

60. Ibid., 131.

61. Ibid., 143.

62. Ibid., 143.

63. Ibid., 143.

64. Ibid., 144.

65. Ibid., 202.

66. Ibid., 202.

67. H. C. Bruce, *The New Man* (New York: P. Amstadt and Sons, 1895), 51; Bethany Veney, *A Slave Woman* (Worcester, Mass.: A. P. Bicknell, 1890), 10.

68. Douglass, *Life and Times*, 186.

69. See John Navone, *The Jesus Story: Our Life as Story in Christ* (Collegeville, Minn.: Liturgical Press, 1979).

70. John W. Blassingame, ed. *Slave Testimony: Two Centuries of Letters, Speeches, Interviews, and Autobiographies* (Baton Rouge, La.: Louisiana State University Press, 1977), 586.

71. James Watkins, *Narrative of the Life of James Watkins, Formerly A Slave in Maryland, US: Containing An Account of His Escape From Slavery, and His Subsequent History, With Notices of the Fugitive Slaves Law, The sentiments of American Divines on the Subject of Slavery and the Labours of the Fugitive in England, etc.* (Manchester: Printed for James Watkins, 1859), 21-22.

72. Ibid.

73. Blassingame, ed. *Slave Testimony*, 461.

74. Charles Nichols, *Many Thousand Gone: The Ex-Slaves' Account of their Bondage and Freedom* (Bloomington, Ind.: Indiana University Press, 1963), 73.

75. Blassingame, ed. *Slave Testimony*, 276.

76. Ibid., 277-279.

77. Ibid., 50-51.

78. Ibid., 48-49; William Grimes, *The Life of William Grimes* (New Haven, Conn., 1855), 99.

79. Gilbert Osofsky, ed. *Puttin' On Ole Massa: The Slave Narratives of Henry Bibb, William Wells Brown, and Solomon Northup* (New York: Harper & Row, 1969), 101.

80. Ibid., 206.

81. James Pennington, "The Fugitive Black Smith," quoted in Thomas L. Webber, *Deep Like the River* (New York: Norton, 1978), 12-13.

82. Osofsky, ed. *Puttin' On Ole Massa*, 213.

83. Ibid., 213.

6. BRER RABBIT STORIES

1. Melville J. Herskovits, *The Myth of the Negro Past* (Boston: Beacon Press, 1941); Sterling Stuckey, *Slave Culture: Nationalist Theory and the Foundations of Black America* (New York: Oxford University Press, 1987), 1-97.

2. Zora Neale Hurston, "Sometimes in the Mind" in Langston Hughes and Arna Bontemps, eds. *The Book of Negro Folklore* (New York: Dodd, Mead, 1958), 93.

3. Ibid., 94.

4. Ibid., 95.

5. Ibid., 95.

6. Ibid., 96.

7. William Faulkner, *The Days When Animals Talked* (Chicago: Fowlett, 1977), 6.

8. Joel Chandler Harris, *Nights With Uncle Remus* (Boston: Houghton-Mifflin, 1917), 547.

9. Ibid., 584.

10. Ibid., 551-552.

11. Ibid., 552.

12. Ibid., 552.

13. *Plato's Republic*, trans. G. M. A. Grube (Indianapolis, Ind.: Hackett Publishing Co., 1974), 47.

14. Harris, *Nights with Uncle Remus*, 48.

15. Ibid., 560.

16. Ibid.

17. Ibid., 561.

18. Ibid., 563.

19. Ibid., 607.

20. Ibid., 186.

21. Ibid., 186.

22. Ibid., 6.

23. Ibid., 8.

24. Ibid., 18.

25. Ibid., 488.

26. Ibid., 273.

27. Ibid., 271.

28. Ibid., 274.

29. Ibid., 468-469.

30. Ibid., 679.

31. Ibid., 665.

32. Ibid., 252.

33. Faulkner, *The Days When Animals Talked*, 3.

34. Ibid., 15.

35. Ibid., 39.

36. Ibid., 19.

37. Ibid., 116.

38. Ibid., 117.

39. Ibid., 118.

40. Ibid., 121.

41. Edward C. L. Adams' book, *Nigger to Nigger* (New York: Scribners, 1928) was republished as *Tales of the Congaree*, edited with an Introduction by Robert G. O'Meally (Chapel Hill, N.C.: University of North Carolina Press, 1987).

42. Ibid., 235.

43. Ibid., 240.

44. Ibid.

45. Ibid.

46. Harold Courlander, *A Treasury of Afro-American Folklore*, (New York: Columbia University Press, 1963), 92.

47. Ibid., 92.

48. Ibid., 478-479.

49. Ibid., 405.

50. Ibid., 497.

51. Lawrence W. Levine, *Black Culture and Black Consciousness*, (Oxford: Oxford University Press, 1977). See the section on trickster stories, 102-135. Here Levine gives an excellent account of the way that the trickster motif has worked in the mind of African-American slaves as well as contemporary urban dwellers.

52. Faulkner, *The Days When Animals Talked*, 81-84.

53. Roger D. Abrahams, *African Folktales: Selected and Retold by Abraham Rogers* (New York: Pantheon Books, 1983), 55.

54. Harris, *Nights With Uncle Remus*, 647.

55. Ibid., 609.

56. Ibid., 613.

57. Helmuth Plessner, *Laughing and Crying. A Study of the Limits of Human Behavior*, trans. James Spencer Churchill and Marjorie Grene (Evanston, Ill.: Northwestern University Press, 1970), 41.

58. Ibid., 31.

7. FOUNDATIONAL ELEMENTS

1. Orlando Patterson, *Slavery and Social Death: A Comparative Study* (Cambridge: Harvard University Press, 1982), chap. 2.

2. "Theology of the New Birth: Jonathan Dickinson, True Scripture-Doctrine, 1776," in *The Great Awakening Documents on the Revival of Religion 1740-1745*, ed. Richard Bushman (New York: Atheneum, 1970), 78.

3. John Boles, *The Great Revival, 1787-1805: The Origins of the Southern Evangelical Mind* (Lexington, Ky.: University Press of Kentucky, 1972). See 125-141. John Boles' study throws a needed light upon the way that Southerners understood this phenomenon.

4. G. W. F. Hegel, *Phenomenology of Mind*, trans. J. B. Baillie (New York: Harper Torchbook, 1967). See chapter on master/slave relationship.

5. Frantz Fanon, *Black Skin and White Mask*, trans. Charles Lam Markmann, (New York: Grove Press, 1982).

6. Cornel West, *Prophesy Deliverance! An Afro-American Revolutionary Christianity* (Philadelphia: Westminster Press, 1982).

7. Dwight N. Hopkins, *Black Theology USA and South Africa: Politics, Culture, and Liberation* (Maryknoll, N.Y.: Orbis Books, 1989), 41-46.

8. Ralph Ellison, *Invisible Man* (New York: Random House, 1952).

9. See Charles Johnson, *Being and Race: Black Writing Since 1970* (Bloomington, Ind.: Indiana University Press, 1988).

10. See the characters in Gloria Naylor's *Linden Hills* (New York: Ticknor & Fields, 1985), who graphically illustrate this type.

11. John Lovell, Jr., *Black Songs: The Forge and the Flame* (New York: Macmillan, 1972), 191.

12. Ibid., 191-192.

13. H. Richard Niebuhr, *The Responsible Self: An Essay in Christian Morals* (San Francisco: Harper & Row, 1963).

14. Paul Tillich, *The Courage To Be* (New Haven: Yale University Press, 1952).

15. Robert Franklin, *Liberating Visions* (Minneapolis, Minn: Fortress Press,

1990); Samuel Proctor, *My Moral Odyssey* (Valley Forge, Pa.: Judson Press, 1989).

16. Peter Paris, *Black Leaders in Conflict: Joseph H. Jackson, Martin Luther King, Jr., Adam Clayton Powell and Malcolm X* (New York: Pilgrim Press, 1978).

17. Katie G. Cannon, *Black Womanist Ethics* (Atlanta: Scholars Press, 1988).

18. See Thomas W. Ogletree, *Hospitality to Strangers: Dimension of Moral Understanding* (Philadelphia: Fortress Press, 1985); Calvin Shrag, *Experience and Being* (Evanston, Ill.: Northwestern University Press, 1969); William Earle, *The Autobiographical Consciousness: A Philosophical Inquiry into Existence* (Chicago: Quadrangle Books, 1972); Emmanuel Levinas, *Totality and Infinity: An Essay on Exteriority*, trans. Alphonso Lingis (Pittsburgh, Pa.: Duquesne University Press, 1969).

19. William Andrews, *To Tell a Free Story: The First Century of Afro-American Autobiography, 1760-1865* (Urbana, Ill.: University of Illinois Press, 1988).

20. Gilbert Osofsky, ed. *Puttin' On Ole Massa: The Slave Narratives of Henry Bibb, William Wells Brown and Solomon Northup* (New York: Harper & Row, 1969), 66.

21. Frederick Douglass, *The Life and Times of Frederick Douglass* (London: Collier-Macmillan, 1962), 124.

22. William E. B. Du Bois, *Souls of Black Folk* (New York: A Signet Classic/ New American Library, 1969).

23. Gabriel Marcel, *The Mystery of Being*, vol. 2, *Faith and Reality* (South Bend, Ind.: Gateway Editions, 1951).

24. Cited in Thomas L. Webber, *Deep Like the River,* (New York: Norton, 1978), 233.

25. B. A. Botkin, ed. *Lay My Burden Down: A Folk History of Slavery* (Chicago: The University of Chicago Press, 1945), 6.

26. Andrews, *To Tell a Free Story.* See where Andrews discusses how slaves used their own memory of the story of their captivity to restructure a formal image of themselves having become free.

27. See Paul Brockelman, *Time and Self: Phenomenological Explorations* (Decatur, Ga.: Scholars Press, 1985).

28. Robert Pelton, *The Trickster Tradition in West Africa* (Berkeley, Calif.: University of California Press, 1980). See trickster theories.

29. E. Franklin Frazier, *The Black Bourgeoisie* (London: Collier-Macmillan, 1962).

30. Sullivan Challenor, William A. Shack and Elliot P. Skinner, *The Stranger in African Societies* (Berkeley: University of California Press, 1979).

31. Joseph R. Washington, *Black Religion in America* (Boston: Beacon Press, 1964).

32. African American biblical scholars have yet to do a critical study of the biblical imagination of the African-American folk preacher. See Henry Mitchell, *Black Preaching* (Philadelphia and New York: Lippincott, 1970).

33. Calvin Shrag, *Experience and Being* (Evanston, Ill.: Northwestern University Press, 1969), 177ff.

34. See Martin G. Plattel, *Social Philosophy* (Pittsburgh, Pa.: Duquesne University Press, 1965).

35. *Autobiography of Malcolm X,* ed. Alex Haley (New York: Grove Press, 1965; New York: Ballantine Books, 1987). Here I have reference to Malcolm's recall of his first encounter with the prominent religious leader and father figure.

Bibliography

BOOKS

Abrahams, Roger D. *African Folktales.* Selected and Retold by Abraham Rogers. New York: Pantheon Books, 1983.

Adams, Edward C. L., *Tales of the Congaree.* Robert G. O'Meally, ed. Chapel Hill, N.C.: University of North Carolina Press, 1987.

Alho, Olli. *The Religion of the Slave.* Helsinki: Academia Scientarium Fennica, 1976.

Andrews, Williams L. *To Tell a Free Story.* Urbana, Ill.: University of Illinois Press, 1986.

Apte, Mahadev L. *Humor and Laughter.* Ithaca, N.Y.: Cornell University Press, 1985.

Aptheker, Herbert, ed. *From Colonial Times Through the Civil War.* Vol. 1 of *A Documentary History of the Negro People in the United States.* New York: Citadel Press, 1971.

Ball, Charles. *Fifty Years in Chains.* New York: Cover Publications, 1970.

Ballanta-(Taylor), Nicholas George Julius, ed. *Saint Helena Island Spirituals.* Recorded and Transcribed at Penn Normal, Industrial and Agricultural School, St. Helena Island, Beaufort County, South Carolina, 1924. New York: Scribners, 1925.

Baltazar, Eulalio P. *The Dark Center: A Process Theology of Blackness.* New York: Paulist Press, 1973.

Bastide, Roger. *The African Religions of Brazil: Toward a Sociology of the Interpretation of Civilizations.* Translated by Helen Sebba. Baltimore, Md.: Johns Hopkins University Press, 1978.

Blassingame, John W., ed. *Slave Testimony: Two Centuries of Letters, Speeches, Interviews, and Autobiographies.* Baton Rouge, La.: Louisiana State University Press, 1977.

Blassingame, John W. *The Slave Community: Plantation Life in the Antebellum South.* New York: Oxford University Press, 1972.

Boles, John B. *The Great Revival, 1787-1805.* Lexington, Ky.: University Press of Kentucky, 1972.

Bontemps, Arna., comp. *Great Slave Narratives.* Boston: Beacon Press, 1969.

Bontemps, Arna. *Five Black Lives.* Middleton, Conn.: Wesleyan University Press, 1971.

Botkin, B. A., ed. *Lay My Burden Down: A Folk History of Slavery.* Chicago: The University of Chicago Press, 1945.

Breeden, James O., ed. *Advice Among Masters: The Ideal in Slave Management in the Old South.* Westport, Conn.: Greenwood Press, 1980.

Brockelman, Paul. *Time and Self: Phenomenological Explorations.* Atlanta: Scholars Press; New York: Crossroad, 1985.

Buber, Martin. *I and Thou*. A new translation with a prologue "I and You" and notes by Walter Kaufman. New York: Scribners, 1970.

Bushman, Richard L., ed. *The Great Awakening: Documents on the Revival of Religion, 1740-1745*. New York: Atheneum, 1970.

Butterfield, Stephen. *Black Autobiography in America*. Amherst, Mass.: University of Massachusetts Press, 1974.

Cannon, Katie. *Black Womanist Ethics*. Atlanta: Scholars Press, 1988.

Chancellor, Sullivan, William A. Shack and Elliott Skinner. *The Stranger in African Societies*. Berkeley, Calif.: University of California Press, 1979.

Chase, Arabella V. *A Peculiar People*. Washington, D.C.: W. C. Chase, Jr. printer, 1905.

Clarke, Erskine. *Wrestlin' Jacob: A Portrait of Religion in the Old South*. Atlanta: John Knox Press, 1979.

Cleague, Albert. *Black Messiah*. New York: Sheed & Ward, 1968.

Cone, Cecil Wayne. *The Identity Crisis in Black Theology*. Nashville: African Methodist Episcopal Church, 1975.

Cone, James H. *The Spirituals and the Blues*. New York: Seabury Press, 1972.

Cone, James H. *Black Theology and Black Power*. New York: Seabury Press, 1969.

Cone, James H. *God of the Oppressed*. New York: Seabury Press, 1974.

Courlander, Harold. *A Treasury of Afro-American Folklore*. New York: Crown, 1976.

Courlander, Harold. *Negro Folk Music, U.S.A.* New York: Columbia University Press, 1963.

Cox, Harvey. *The Feast of Fools: A Theological Essay on Festivity and Fantasy*. Cambridge, Mass.: Harvard University Press, 1969.

Creel, Margaret Washington. *"A Peculiar People": Slave Religion and Community-Culture Among the Gullahs*. New York: New York University Press, 1988.

Crossan, John Dominic. *In Parables: The Challenge of the Historical Jesus*. New York: Harper & Row, 1973.

Davis, Charles T. and Henry Louis Gates, Jr., ed. *The Slave's Narrative*. Oxford: Oxford University Press, 1985.

Davis, David B. *The Problem of Slavery in Western Culture*. Ithaca, N.Y.: Cornell University Press, 1966.

Detts, Nathaniel. *Religious Folk Songs of the Negro*. Hampton, Va.: Hampton Institute Press, 1927.

Douglass, Frederick. "A Slave Catechism, June 2, 1854" Reprinted in *The Negro American: A Documentary History*. Leslie H. Fishel, Jr. and Benjamin Quarles. Glenview: Scott, Foresman and Company: 1967.

Douglass, Frederick. *Life and Times of Frederick Douglass*. London: Collier-Macmillan, 1962.

Drake, St. Clair. *The Redemption of African and Black Religion*. Chicago: Third World Press, 1970.

DuBois, W. E. B. *Darkwater Voices from Within the Veil*. 1920; reprint New York: Schocken Books, 1969.

DuBois, W. E. B. *Souls of Black Folk*. New York: A Signet Classic/New American Library, 1969.

Dunbar, Paul Laurence. *The Complete Works of Paul Laurence Dunbar*. New York: Dodd, Mead, 1913.

Dundes, Alan. *Mother Wit from the Laughing Barrel*. Englewood Cliffs, N.J.: Prentice-Hall, 1973.

Eames, Wilberforce. *Early New England Catechisms*. Worcester: Press of Charles Hamilton, 1898; Reissued by Singing Tree Press, Book Tower, 1969.

Earle, William. *The Autobiographical Consciousness: A Philosophical Inquiry into Existence*. Chicago: Quadrangle Books, 1972.

Elkins, Stanley M. *Slavery: A Problem in American Institutional and Intellectual Life*. Chicago: University of Chicago Press, 1959; 3rd ed. 1976.

Ellison, Ralph. *Invisible Man*. New York: Random House, 1952.

Epstein, Dean J. *Sinful Tunes and Spirituals*. Urbana, Ill.: University of Illinois Press, 1977.

Fanon, Frantz. *Black Skin and White Mask*. Translated by Charles Lam Markmann. New York: Grove Press, 1982.

Faulkner, William J. *The Days When The Animals Talked: Black American Folktales and How They Came To Be*. Chicago: Fowlett Publishing Company, 1977.

Fenner, Thomas P., Frederic G. Rathbun, and Miss Bessie Cleveland, arrangers. *Cabin and Plantation Songs*. New York and London: Putnam's, 1901.

Fickling, Susan M. *Slave-Conversion in South Carolina, 1830-1860*. Columbia: University of South Carolina, 1924.

Findlay, J. N. *Hegel: A Re-examination*. New York: Oxford University Press, 1958.

Fishel, Leslie H. Jr., and Benjamin Quarles. *The Negro American: A Documentary History*. Atlanta: Scott, Foresman, 1967.

Fisher, Miles Mark. *Negro Slave Songs in the United States*. New York: Citadel Press, 1969.

Fogel, Robert W. and Stanley L. Engerman. *Time on the Cross: The Economics of American Slavery*. Boston: Little Brown, 1974.

Franklin, Robert. *Liberating Visions*. Minneapolis, Minn.: Fortress Press, 1990.

Franklin, V. P. *Black Self-Determination*. Westport, Conn.: Hill, 1984.

Frazier, E. Franklin. *Black Bourgeoisie: The Rise of a New Middle Class*. London: Collins-Macmillan, 1962.

Freire, Paulo. *Pedagogy of the Oppressed*. New York: Paulist Press, 1977.

Friedman, Maurice. *The Confirmation of Otherness in Family, Community and Society*. New York: Pilgrim Press, 1983.

Gadamer, Hans-Georg. *Truth and Method*. New York: Seabury Press, 1975.

Genovese, Eugene D. *Roll, Jordan, Roll: The World the Slaves Made*. New York: Vintage Books, 1976.

Genovese, Eugene D. *The Political Economy of Slavery: Studies in the Economy and Society of the Slave South*. New York: Vintage Books, 1967.

Goss, Linda and Marian E. Barnes, ed. *Talk That Talk*. New York: Simon & Schuster, 1989.

Grant, C. David. *God the Center of Value Theory in the Theology of H. Richard Niebuhr*. Fort Worth, Tex.: Texas Christian University Press, 1984.

Grant, Jacquelyn. *White Women's Christ, Black Women's Jesus*. Atlanta: Scholars Press, 1989.

Grissom, Mary Allen. *The Negro Sings a New Heaven*. Chapel Hill, N.C.: University of North Carolina Press, 1930.

Groome, Thomas H. *Christian Religious Education: Sharing our Story and Vision*. San Francisco: Harper & Row, 1982.

Gurwitsch, Aron. *Human Encounters in the Social World*. Pittsburgh: Duquesne University Press, 1977.

Haley, Alex. *The Autobiography of Malcolm X.* 1965; reprint New York: Ballantine Books, 1987.

Halling, Steen. "The Implications of Emmanuel Levinas' Totality and Infinity for Therapy," in *Duquesne Studies in Phenomenological Psychology,* ed. A. Agiorgi, et al. Pittsburg: Duquesne University Press, 1975.

Harper, William. "Memoir on Slavery Read Before the Society for the Advancement of Learning of South Carolina, at its Annual Meeting at Columbia, 1837." Reprinted in *The Negro American: A Documentary History.* Leslie H. Fishel and Benjamin Quarles. Glenview: Scott, Foresman and Company, 1967.

Harris, Grace. "Inward-Looking and Outward-Looking Symbols." *The Realm of the Extra-Human Ideas and Actions: Agents and Audiences,* Agehananda Bharati, ed. Paris: Mouton Publishers, World Anthropology Series, 1976 pp. 301-335.

Harris, Joel Chandler. *Nights With Uncle Remus.* Boston: Houghton Mifflin, 1917.

Harris, Joel Chandler. *The Complete Tales of Uncle Remus.* New York: Houghton, Mifflin, 1955.

Harrod, Howard L. *Renewing the World: Plains Indian Religion and Morality.* Tucson, Ariz.: University of Arizona Press, 1987.

Harrod, Howard L. *The Human Center: Moral Agency in the Social World.* Philadelphia: Fortress Press, 1981.

Hart, Ray. *Unfinished Man and the Imagination.* New York: Herder & Herder, 1968.

Hegel, G. W. F. *The Phenomenology of Mind.* Translated by J. B. Baillie. New York: Harper Torchbooks, 1967.

Herskovits, Melville. *The Myth of the Negro Past.* Boston: Beacon Press, 1941.

Hodgson, Peter C. *Children of Freedom.* Philadelphia: Fortress Press, 1974.

Hopkins, Dwight N. and George Cummings. *Cut Loose Your Stammering Tongue: Black Theology in the Slave Narratives.* Maryknoll, N.Y.: Orbis Books, 1991.

Hopkins, Dwight N. *Black Theology USA and South Africa: Politics, Culture and Liberation.* Maryknoll, N.Y.: Orbis Books, 1989.

Hughes, Langston and Arna Bontemps, eds. *The Book of Negro Folklore.* New York: Dodd, Mead, 1958.

Hurston, Zora Neale. *Their Eyes Were Watching God.* Urbana, Ill.: University of Illinois Press, 1937.

Jackson, Bruce. *The Negro and His Folklore.* Austin, Tex.: University of Texas Press, 1967.

Johnson, Charles S. *Being and Race.* Bloomington, Ind.: Indiana University Press, 1988.

Johnson, Charles S. *Shadow of the Plantation.* Chicago: University of Chicago Press, 1934.

Johnson, Clifton H., ed. *God Struck Me Dead* with a foreword by Paul Radin. Philadelphia: Pilgrim Press, 1969.

Johnson, James Weldon and J. Rosamond Johnson. *The Books of American Negro Spirituals.* Vols. I and II. New York: Viking, 1953.

Jones, William R. *Is God a White Racist?* Garden City, N.Y.: Anchor Press/Doubleday, 1973.

Jordan, Winthrop. *White Over Black: White Attitudes Toward the Negro, 1550-1812.* New York: Norton Library, 1977.

Jung, Hwa Yol, ed. *Existential Phenomenology and Political Theory: A Reader.* Chicago: Henry Regnery Co., 1972.

Keiser, R. Melvin. *Recovering the Personal Religious Language and the Post-Critical*

Quest of H. Richard Niebuhr. Atlanta: Scholars Press, 1988.

King, John Owen III. *The Iron of Melancholy: Structures of Spiritual Conversion in America from the Puritan Conscience to Victorian Neurosis.* Middletown: Wesleyan University Press, 1983.

Klingberg, Frank J. *An Appraisal of the Negro in Colonial South Carolina: A Study in Americanization.* Washington, D.C.: Associated Publishers, 1941.

Knowles, Malcolm S. *The Modern Practice of Adult Education.* Chicago: Association Press/Follett Publishing Co., 1980.

Kwant, Remy C. *Encounter.* Translated by Robert C. Adolfs, O.S.A. Pittsburgh: Duquesne University Press, 1960.

Levi-Strauss, C. *Tristes Tropiques.* Translated by John Russell. New York: Criterion Books, 1961.

Levine, Lawrence W. *Black Culture and Black Consciousness.* Oxford: Oxford University Press, 1977.

Lide, R. W. *Loyalties in Black and White.* Columbia, S.C.: Bryan, 1940.

Long, Charles H. *Significations: Signs, Symbols, and Images in the Interpretation of Religion.* Philadelphia: Fortress Press, 1986.

Loveland, Anne C. *Southern Evangelicals and the Social Order 1800-1860.* Baton Rouge, La.: Louisiana State University Press, 1979.

Lovell, John Jr. *Black Song: The Forge and the Flame.* New York: Macmillan, 1972.

Marcel, Gabriel. *Faith and Reality.* Vol. 2 of *The Mystery of Being.* Gabriel Marcel, trans. Chicago: Henry Regnery, 1960.

Martin, Waldo E. *The Mind of Frederick Douglass.* Chapel Hill, N.C.: University of North Carolina Press, 1984.

May, Herbert G. and Bruce M. Metzger, eds. *The New Oxford Annotated Bible.* New York: Oxford University Press, 1962.

Mead, Sidney. *The Lively Experiment: The Shaping of Christianity in America.* New York: Harper & Row, 1963.

Merquior, J. G. *The Veil and the Mask: Essays on Culture and Ideology.* London: Routledge & Kegan Paul, 1979.

Mitchell, Henry H. *Black Religious Beliefs: Folk Beliefs of Blacks in America and West Africa.* New York: Harper & Row, 1975.

Mitchell, Henry H. *Black Preaching.* Philadelphia and New York: Lippincott Company, 1970.

Moyd, Olin P. *Redemption in Black Theology.* Valley Forge, Pa.: Judson Press, 1979.

Murphy, Francis Xavier. "Catechesis, I (Early Christian)" in *New Catholic Encyclopedia,* ed., William J. McDonald, D.D., Vol. 3. New York: McGraw-Hill Book Co., 1967, 3:208.

Natanson, Maurice. *Phenomenology, Role, and Reason: Essays on the Coherence and Deformation of Social Reality.* Springfield, Ill.: Charles C. Thomas Publisher, 1974.

Natanson, Maurice. *The Journeying Self.* Santa Cruz, Calif.: University of California, Santa Cruz, 1970.

Navone, John, S.J. *The Jesus Story: Our Life as Story in Christ.* Collegeville, Minn.: Liturgical Press, 1979.

Naylor, Gloria. *Linden Hills.* New York: Ticknor & Fields, 1985.

Nichols, Charles H. *Many Thousand Gone: The Ex-Slaves' Account of Their Bondage and Freedom.* Bloomington, Ind.: Indiana University Press, 1963.

Niebuhr, H. Richard. *The Responsible Self: An Essay in Christian Morals.* San Francisco: Harper & Row, 1963.

Nisbet, Richard. *The Capacity of Negroes.* Westport, Conn.: Negro Universities Press, 1970.

Northup, Solomon. *Twelve Years a Slave.* 1854; reprint New York: Dover Publications, 1970.

Ogletree, Thomas W. *Hospitality to the Stranger: Dimension of Moral Understanding.* Philadelphia: Fortress Press, 1985.

Ong, Walter J. *Interface of the Word: Studies in the Evolution of Consciousness and Culture.* Ithaca, N.Y.: Cornell University Press, 1977.

Osofsky, Gilbert, ed. *Puttin' On Ole Massa: The Slave Narratives of Henry Bibb, William Wells Brown, and Solomon Northup.* New York: Harper & Row, 1969.

Osofsky, Gilbert. *The Burden of Race: A Documentary of Negro-White Relations in America.* New York: Harper & Row, 1968.

Paris, Peter J. *The Social Teaching of the Black Churches.* Philadelphia: Fortress Press, 1985.

Paris, Peter J. *Black Leaders in Conflict: Joseph H. Jackson, Martin Luther King, Jr., Malcolm X and Adam Clayton Powell.* New York: Pilgrim Press, 1978.

Patterson, Orlando. *Slavery and Social Death: A Comparative Study.* Cambridge, Mass.: Harvard University Press, 1982.

Pelton, Robert D. *The Trickster in West Africa: A Study of Mythic Irony and Sacred Delight.* Berkeley, Calif.: University of California Press, 1980.

Perdue, Charles L., Jr., Thomas E. Barden, and Robert Phillips, eds. *Weevils in the Wheat: Interviews with Virginia Ex-slaves.* 1976; reprint Bloomington: Indiana University Press, 1980.

Peterson, Thomas V. *Ham, Japheth: The Mythic World.* Metuchen, N.J.: Scarecrow Press, 1978.

Phillips, Ulrich B. *Life and Labor in the Old South.* Boston: Little Brown, 1963.

Plattel, Martin G. *Social Philosophy.* Pittsburgh, Pa.: Duquesne University Press, 1965.

Plessner, Helmuth. *Laughing and Crying: A Study of the Limits of Human Behavior.* Translated by James Spencer Churchill and Marjorie Grene. Evanston, Ill.: Northwestern University Press, 1970.

Polanyi, Michael. *The Tacit Dimension.* Garden City, N.Y.: Anchor, Doubleday, 1966.

Porter, Dorothy, ed. *Early Negro Writing, 1760-1837.* Boston: Beacon Press, 1971.

Proctor, Samuel D. *Samuel Proctor: My Moral Odyssey.* Valley Forge, Pa.: Judson Press, 1989.

Proctor, Samuel D. *Preaching About Crises in the Community.* Philadelphia: Westminster Press, 1988.

Puckett, Newbell Niles. *The Magic and Folk Beliefs of the Southern Negro.* New York: Dover, 1969.

Raboteau, Albert J. *Slave Religion: The "Invisible Institution" in the Antebellum South.* New York: Oxford University Press, 1978.

Radin, Paul. *The Trickster: A Study in American Indian Mythology.* With Commentaries by Karl Kerenyi and Carl G. Jung and Introduction by Stanley Diamond. New York: Schocken Books, 1972.

Rawick, George P., ed. *The American Slave: A Composite Autobiography,* Vols. 1, 3, 18, 19. Westport, Conn.: Greenwood Publishing Company, 1972.

Richardson, Harry V. *Dark Salvation: The Story of Methodism as It Developed Among Blacks in America*. Garden City, N.Y.: Anchor Press/Doubleday, 1976.

Ricoeur, Paul. *Hermeneutics and the Human Sciences*. New York: Cambridge University Press, 1981.

Ricoeur, Paul. *Freedom and Nature*. Evanston, Ill.: Northwestern University Press, 1966.

Roberts, J. Deotis. *Black Theology and Reconciliation: A Black Theology*. Philadelphia: Westminster Press, 1946.

Roberts, John W. *From Trickster to Badman*. Philadelphia: University of Pennsylvania Press, 1989.

Rose, Willie Lee., ed. *A Documentary History of Slavery in North America*. New York: Oxford University Press, 1976.

Rosengarten, Theodore. *Tombee: Portrait of a Cotton Planter*. New York: Morrow, 1986.

Ruchames, Louis, ed. *Racial Thought: A Documentary History*. Amherst: University of Massachusetts Press, 1969.

Sale, John B. *The Tree Named John*. Chapel Hill, N.C.: University of North Carolina Press, 1929.

Scarry, Elaine. *The Body in Pain: The Making and Unmaking of the World*. New York: Oxford University Press, 1985.

Scheler, Max. *The Nature of Sympathy*. Translated by Peter Heath. London: Routledge & Kegan Paul, 1954.

Schutz, Alfred. *Collected Papers*. Vol. 1, *The Problem of Social Reality*. Edited by Maurice Natanson. The Hague, Netherlands: Martinus Nijhoff, 1973.

Schwartzman, Helen B. *Transformations: The Anthropology of Children's Play*. New York: Plenum Press, 1978.

Sernett, Milton C., ed. *Afro-American Religious History: A Documentary Witness*. Durham, N.C.: Duke University Press, 1985.

Shrag, Calvin O. *Experience and Being*. Evanston, Ill.: Northwestern University Press, 1969.

Smith, Amanda. *An Autobiography*. New York: Oxford University Press, 1988.

Smith, H. Shelton. *In His Image, But . . . : Racism in Southern Religion, 1780-1910*. Durham, N.C.: Duke University Press, 1972.

Snowden, Frank M. *Before Color Prejudice: The Ancient Views of Blacks*. Cambridge, Mass.: Harvard University Press, 1983.

Sobel, Mechal. *The World They Made Together*. Princeton, N.J.: Princeton University Press, 1987.

Sobel, Mechal. *Trabelin' On: The Slave Journey to an Afro-Baptist Faith*. Westport, Conn.: Greenwood Press, 1979.

Sommers, Christina and Fred Sommers. *Vice and Virtue in Everyday Life*. San Diego: Harcourt Brace Jovanovich, 1989.

Spengemann, William C. *The Forms of Autobiography Episodes in the History of a Literary Genre*. New Haven, Conn.: Yale University Press, 1980.

Stampp, Kenneth M. *The Peculiar Institution: Slavery in the Ante-Bellum South*. New York: Vintage Books, 1956.

Stanner, W. E. H. "Dreaming" in *Reader in Comparative Religion: An Anthropological Approach*. Evanston, Ill.: Row, Peterson, 1958.

Stemons, James Samuel. *As Victim to Victims: An American Negro Laments With Jews*. New York: Fortuny's, 1954.

Stepto, Robert B. *From Behind the Veil: A Study of Afro-American Narrative.* Urbana, Ill.: University of Illinois Press, 1979.

Steward, Austin. *Twenty-two Years a Slave, and Forty Years a Freeman.* New York: New American Library, 1969.

Stuckey, Sterling. *Slave Culture: Nationalist Theory and the Foundations of Black America.* New York: Oxford University Press, 1987.

Thomas, Latta R. *Biblical Faith and the Black American.* Valley Forge, Pa.: Judson Press, 1976.

Thurman, Howard. *Jesus and the Disinherited.* New York: Abingdon-Cokesbury Press, 1949.

Thurman, Howard. *Luminous Darkness.* New York: Harper & Row, 1965.

Tragle, Henry Irving. *The Southampton Slave Revolt of 1831: A Compilation of Source Material.* Including the Full text of the "Confessions" of Nat Turner. New York: Vintage Books, 1973.

Walker, Alice. *In Search of Our Mothers' Gardens.* San Diego: Harcourt Brace Jovanovich, 1983.

Wallace, Michelle. *Black Macho and the Myth of the Superwoman.* New York: Dial Press, 1979.

Washington, Joseph R. *Black Religion and the Negro.* Boston: Beacon Press, 1964.

Washington, Joseph. *Anti-Blackness in English Religion.* New York: Mellen Press, 1984.

Webber, Thomas L. *Deep Like the Rivers.* New York: Norton, 1978.

Welsch, Roger. *Omaha Tribal Myths and Trickster Tales.* Chicago: Sages/Swallow Press, 1981.

West, Cornel. *Prophesy Deliverance! An Afro-American Revolutionary Christianity.* Philadelphia: Westminster Press, 1982.

White, Deborah Gray. *Ar'n't I a Woman?* New York: Norton, 1985.

Whitten, Norman E. Jr. and John F. Swed, eds. *Afro-American Anthropology: Contemporary Perspectives.* Toronto: Free Press/Macmillan, 1970.

Wilmore, Gayraud S. *Black Religion and Black Radicalism.* Garden City, N.Y.: Doubleday, 1972.

Wilson, Harriet E. *Our Nig: or Sketches from the Life of a Free Black.* New York: Vintage Books, 1983.

Wimberly, Edward P. and Anne Streaty. *Liberation and Human Wholeness: The Conversion Experiences of Black People in Slavery and Freedom.* Nashville: Abingdon Press, 1986.

Witvliet, Theo. *The Way of the Black Messiah.* Oak Park, Ill.: Meyer-Stone Books, 1987.

Work, John W. ed. *American Negro Songs and Spirituals.* New York: Bonanza Books, MCMXL.

Work, John W. *Folk Song of the American Negro, 1871-1925.* 1915; reprint New York: Negro University Press, 1969.

Wright, Ellen and Michel Fabre, eds. *Richard Wright Reader.* New York: Harper & Row, 1978.

Wright, Richard. *American Hunger: The Compelling Continuation of Wright's Great Autobiographical Work Black Boy.* New York: Harper & Row, 1977.

Wuthnow, Robert. *Meaning and the Moral Order: Explorations in Cultural Analysis.* Berkeley, Calif.: University of California Press, 1987.

ARTICLES

Armstrong, A. MacC. "Objectivity in Historical Writing." *The Monist: An International Quarterly Journal of General Philosophical Inquiry* 62, no. 4 (October 1979):429-445.

Baier, Kurt. "Action and Agent." *The Monist: An International Quarterly Journal of General Philosophical Inquiry* 49, no. 2 (April 1965):183-195.

Beck, Lewis E. "Agent, Action, Spectator, and Critic." *The Monist: An International Quarterly Journal of General Philosophical Inquiry* 49, no. 2 (April 1974):167-182.

Bellot, Leland J., "Evangelicals and the Defense of Slavery in Britain's Old Colonial Empire." *Journal of Southern History* 37, no. 1 (February 1971): 19-40.

Bossert, Phillip. "The Explication of 'the World' in Constructionalism and Phenomenology." *Man and World: An International Philosophical Review* 6, no. 3 (September 1973):231-251.

Botkin, B. A. "The Slave as His Own Interpreter." *The Library of Congress Quarterly Journal of Current Acquisitions* 2, no. 1 (July, August, September, 1944):37-63.

Braybrooke, David. "Our Natural Bodies, Our Social Rights: Comments on Wheeler." *Nous Nihil philosophicum a nobis alienum putamus* XIV, no. 2 (May 1980):195-202.

Burke, Richard. " 'Work' And 'Play'." *Ethics: An International Journal of Social, Political, and Legal Philosophy* 82, no. 1 (October 1971):33-47.

Byrum, Charles Stephen. "Philosophy as Play." *Man and World: An International Philosophical Review* 8, no. 3 (August 1975):315-326.

Dauner, Louise. "Myth and Humor in the Uncle Remus Fables." *American Literature* 97 (1948-49):129-143.

Donald, David. "The Proslavery Argument Reconsidered." *Journal of Southern History* 37, no. 1 (February 1971):3-18.

Dunn, Richard S. "A Tale of Two Plantations: Slave Life at Mesopotamia in Jamaica and Mount Airy in Virginia, 1799 to 1828." *William and Mary Quarterly* 34 (1977):32-65.

Earl, Riggins R., Jr. "The Genius of Douglass' Moral Understanding While a Slave." *The Interdenominational Theological Center Journal* 9, no. 1 (Fall 1981):19-28.

Edie, James M. "The Genesis of a Phenomenological Theory of the Experience of Personal Identity." *Man and World: An International Philosophical Review* 6, no. 3 (September 1973):322-340.

Edwards, Rem B. "Agency Without A Substantive Self." *The Monist: An International Quarterly Journal of General Philosophical Inquiry* 49, no. 2 (April 1965):273-289.

Epps, Archie C. III. "The Christian Doctrine Of Slavery: A Theological Analysis." *Journal of Negro History* 46, no. 4 (October 1961):242-249.

Erickson, Stephen A. "Views and Perspectives." *Man and World: An International Philosophical Review* 7, no. 2 (May 1974):103-117.

Ernst, Robert. "Negro Concepts of Americanism." *Journal of Negro History* 39, no. 2 (April 1954):206-219.

Finley, M. I. "Myth, Memory, and History." *History and Theory: Studies in the Philosophy of History* 4, no. 3 (1965):281-302.

Fredrickson, George and Christopher Lasch. "Resistance to Slavery." *Civil War History: A Journal of the Middle Period* 13, no. 4 (December 1967):315-329.

Genovese, Eugene D. "Rebelliousness and Docility in the Negro Slave: A Critique of the Elkins Thesis." *Civil War History: A Journal of the Middle Period* 13, no. 4 (December 1967):293-313.

Gottfried, Paul. "On The Social Implications and Context of the Hegelian Dialectic." *Journal of the History of Ideas* 41, no. 3 (July-Sept. 1980):421-432.

Harris, N. G. E. "On Seeing Everything Upside Down." *Analysis* 33, no. 1 (October 1972):28-31.

Herskovits, Frances and Melville. "Sibling Rivalry, The Oedipus Complex and Myth" *Journal of American Folklore* 71, 1958:1-15.

Hinman, Lawrence M. "On Work and Play: Overcoming a Dichotomy." *Man and World: An International Philosophical Review* 8, no. 3 (August 1975):327-346.

Hudson, Arthur P. "Some Curious Negro Names." *Southern Folklore Quarterly* 2, no. 4 (December 1938):179-193.

Inscoe, John C. "Carolina Slave Names: An Index to Acculturation." *Journal of Southern History* 49, no. 4 (Nov. 1983):527-54.

Jones, Jerome W. "The Established Virginia Church And The Conversion of Negroes And Indians, 1620-1760." *Journal of Negro History* 46, no. 1 (January 1961):12-23.

Kelly, George Armstrong. "Notes on Hegel's 'Lordship and Bondage'." *Review and Metaphysics Exploration* 19 (June 1966):780-802.

Klingberg, Frank J. "The Making of a Paradox: The Despicable Other in the Consciousness of Europeans." *Anglican Humanitarianism in Colonial New York.* Publication No. 11. Philadelphia: The Church Publication Society, 1940.

Kolchin, Peter. "Reevaluating the Antebellum Slave Community: A Comparative Perspective." *Journal of American History* 70 (December 1983):579-601.

Kraditor, Aileen S. "A Note on Elkins and the Abolitionists." *Civil War History: A Journal of the Middle Period* 13, no. 4 (December 1967):330-339.

Kyles, L. W. "The Contribution of the Negro to the Religious Life of America." *Journal of Negro History* 11, no. 3 (1926):8-16.

Loury, Glenn C. "The Moral Quandary of the Black Community." *The Public Interest* 79 (Spring 1985):9-22.

MacIntyre, Alisdair. "Pleasure As A Reason For Action." *The Monist: An International Quarterly Journal of General Philosophical Inquiry* 49, no. 2 (April 1965):215-233.

McDade, Jesse N. "Towards An Ontology of Negritude." *The Philosophical Forum* 20, nos. 2-3 (Winter-Spring 1977-78):161-168.

McKeon, Richard. "Person and Community: Metaphysical and Political." *Ethics: An International Journal of Social, Political and Legal Philosophy* 88, no. 3 (April 1978):207-217.

Mandelbaum, Maurice. "Subjective, Objective, and Conceptual Relativisms." *The Monist: An International Quarterly Journal of General Philosophical Inquiry* 62, no. 4 (October 1979):403-428.

Matthews, Gareth B. "On Being Immoral in a Dream." *Philosophy: The Journal of the Royal Institute of Philosophy* 56, no. 215 (January 1981):47-54.

Miller, Randall. "When Lions Write History: Slave Testimony and the History of American Slavery." *Washington State University Research Studies* 44, no. 1 (1976):13-23.

Moore, Harold, Robert Neville, and William Sullivan. "The Contours of Responsibility: A New Model." *Man and World: An International Philosophical Review* 5, no. 4 (November 1972):392-421.

Moseley, James G., Jr. "Conversion Through Vision: Puritanism and Transcendentalism in the Ambassadors." *Journal of the American Academy of Religion* XLIII, no. 3 (September 1975):473-484.

Munk, Arthur W. "The Self As Agent and Spectator." *The Monist: An International Quarterly Journal of General Philosophical Inquiry* 49, no. 2 (April 1965):273-289.

Olson, Carl. "The Human Body as a Boundary Symbol: A Comparison of Merleau-Ponty and Dogen." *Philosophy East and West* 36, no. 2 (April 1986):107-120.

Paskins, Barrie. "Some Victims of Morality." *The Aristotelian Society* 76 (1975-76):89-108.

Read, Allan W. "The Speech of Negroes in Colonial America." *Journal of Negro History* XXIV, no. 3 (July 1939):247-258.

Rempel, Henry David. "On Forcing People to be Free." *Ethics: An International Journal of Social, Political, and Legal Philosophy* 87, no. 1 (October 1976):18-34.

Riddel, William Renwick. "Baptism of Slaves in Prince Edward Island." *Journal of Negro History* 6, no. 3 (1921):307-309.

Sekora, John. "Slavery: Language and Personal History in Douglass' Narrative of 1845." *C. L. A. Journal* 29, no. 2 (1985):157-170.

Simpson, Evan. "Objective Reason and Respect for Persons." *The Monist: An International Journal of General Philosophical Inquiry* 62, no. 4 (October 1979):457-469.

Stafford, John. "Patterns of Meaning in Nights With Uncle Remus" *American Literature* 18 (January, March and May 1946-47):87-108.

Stampp, Kenneth. "Rebels and Sambos: The Search for the Negro's Personality in Slavery. *Journal of Southern History* 37, no. 3 (1971):367-392.

Stebbins, Robert A. "Putting People On: Deception of Our Fellowman in Everyday Life." *Sociology and Social Research: An International Journal* 59, no. 3 (April 1975):189-200.

Szabados, Bela. "Wishful Thinking and Self-Deception." *Analysis* 33, no. 6 (June 1973):201-205.

Thorpe, Earl E. "Chattel Slavery and Concentration Camps." *The Negro History Bulletin* 25, no. 8 (May 1962):171-175.

Turner, Ralph H. "The Real Self: From Institution to Impulse." *American Journal of Sociology* Vol. 81, no. 5: 982-1016 .

Vasile, Peter. "Cooper's *The Deerslayer*: The Apotheosis of Man and Nature." *Journal of the American Academy of Religion* XLIII, no. 3 (September 1975):485-507.

Weber, Eugene "Fairies and Hard Facts: The Reality of Folktales." *Journal of the History of Ideas* 42, no. 1 (January-March 1981):93-113.

Wellbourne, Michael. "My Body and I — A Reply to Fahrnkopf." *Analysis* 42 (March 1982):86-88.

Wheeler, Samuel C. "Natural Property Rights as Body Rights." *Nous Nihil philosophicum a nobis alienum putamus* 14, no. 2 (May 1980):171-194.

Williams, Donald C. "The Past and the Historical Past." *Journal of Philosophy* 52, no. 10 (January-December 1955):253-277.

Wilshire, Bruce. "Self, Body and Self-Deception." *Man and World: An International Philosophical Review* 5, no. 4 (November 1972):422-451.

Wojtyla, Karol. "The Person: Subject and Community." *Review of Metaphysics* 33, no. 2 (December 1979):273-308.

ARCHIVAL RESOURCES

Adams, J. "The Relation of Christianity to Civil Government in the United States: A Sermon, Preached in St. Michaels Church, Charleston, Feb. 13, 1833 before The Convention of the Protestant Episcopal Church of the Diocese of South Carolina." Charleston: Printed by A. E. Miller, No. 4 Broad Street, 1833.

Adger, John B. *My Life And Times*. Published possibly in 1896 or 1897.

Adger, John B., ed. "The Collected Writings of James Henley Thornwell, D.D., LL.D.," *Theological and Ethical* Vol. II, Richmond: Presbyterian Committee of Publication, 1871. ·

Alexander, McGill T. *The Hand of God With Black Race: A Discourse delivered before the Presbyterian Colonization Society*. Philadelphia: William F. Geddes, Printer, 320 Chestnut Street, 1862.

Bacon, Thomas. *Four Sermons Upon The Great and Indispensible Duty of all Christian Masters and Mistresses to bring up their Negro Slaves in the Knowledge and Fear of God. Preached at the Parish church of St. Peter in Talbot County, in the Province of Maryland*. London: Printed by H. Oliver, in Bartholomew-Clofe, near Weft-Smithfield, MDCCL.

Bacon, Thomas. *Sermons to Masters and Servants*. 1813.

Bacon, Thomas. *Two Sermons to a Congregation's Black Slaves*. 1749.

Bailey, Rufus William (of South Carolina). *The Issue, Presented in a Series of Letters on Slavery*. New York: Published by John S. Taylor, 1837.

Baird, E. T. "A Pastoral Letter," *Religious Instruction of the Coloured Population*. Starkville, Mississippi, April 16, 1859.

Barnwell, Gadsden and Tapier. *A Catechism to be Used by the Teachers in the Religious Instruction of Persons of Colour: To Which Are Prefixed, Easy Instructions for Coloured Persons young or adult, who are not yet baptized, intended to prepare them for that sacrament, and for further instruction according to the Catechism*. Charleston: Printed and Published by A. E. Miller, No. 4 Broad Street, 1837.

Barton, William E. *Old Plantation Hymns*. Boston, New York, London: Lamson, Wolffe and Company, MDCCXCIX.

Beaty, Leroy. *"Work of South Carolina Methodism Among the Slaves" An address delivered before the Historical Society of the South Carolina Annual Conference of Methodist Episcopal Church, South, at Columbia, S. C.*, November 26, 1901.

Benedict, David. *A General History of the Baptist Denomination in America and Other Parts of the World*. Boston: Printed by Manning & Loring, No. 2 Cornhill for the Author, 1813.

Berry, Philip. *A Review of The Bishop of Oxford's Counsel To The American Clergy, with reference to The Institution of Slavery. Also Supplemental Remarks on the Relation of the Wilmot Proviso to the interests of the Colored Class*. Washington: William M. Morrison; Richmond, Drinker & Morris; Baltimore, Jos. Robinson; Philadelphia, Herman Hooker; New York, Stanford & Swords; Boston, C. Stimpson, 1848.

Billings, Edward C.(of New Orleans). "The Struggle Between the Civilization of

Slavery and that of Freedom, Recently and now going on in Louisiana," An address delivered by Edward C. Billings. Hatfield, Massachusetts, October 20, 1873.

Botsford, Edmund. *The Spiritual Voyage Performed in the ship convert, under the command of Captain Godly-Fear from the Port of Repentance-Unto-Life, to the haven of felicity on the continent of glory, An Allegory.* London: Privately printed, 1821; Charleston: W. Riley, reprinted for D. Barnes, 1828.

Botsford, Edmund. *Sambo and Toney: A Dialogue Between Two Slaves.* New York: American Tract Society, No Date.

Bowen, Nathaniel. *A Pastoral Letter on the Religious Instruction of the Slaves of Members of the Protestant Episcopal Church in the State of South Carolina.* Prepared at the Request of the Convention of the Churches of the Diocese, Charleston: Printed by A. E. Miller, No. 4 Broad Street, 1835.

Brantly, Benjamin. "Slavery, A Treatise, Showing That Slavery is Neither A Moral, Political, Nor Social Evil." Printed by Benjamin Brantly in 1844, Penfield, GA.

Bruce, J. G. "A Sermon on the Duty of Instructing Slaves." Published in 1846.

Bullock, F. W. B. *Evangelical Conversion in Great Britain 1516-1695.* Sussex: Printed by Budd & Gillatt, North Street, St. Leanards-on-Sea, 1966.

Cluskey, Michael W., compiler, "Buchanan and Breckinridge. The Democratic Hand-Book." Washington (Recommended by the Democratic Committee), 1856.

Cobbs, John B., James T. Laney, Thomas F. O'Dea and George W. Webber. *The Nature of the Conversion Experience — The Report of the 1967 Theological Consultation of the Methodist Board of Missions.* New York: Joint Commission on Education and Cultivation, 1968.

Daniel, Canon. *"How To Teach the Church Catechism" Together With a Complete Set of Notes of Lessons (Religious Knowledge Manuals For Sunday and Day School Teachers).* London: National Society's Depository, 19 Great Peter Street, Westminster, no date.

Davenport, Frederick Morgan. *Primitive Traits in Religious Revivals: A Study in Mental and Social Evolution.* London: MacMillan & Co., Ltd., 1917.

DeLeon, Edwin. *An Address Delivered Before The Two Literary Societies of The South Carolina College.* Columbia: Printed by A. S. Johnston, 1845.

Dickson, A. F. (of Charleston, South Carolina). *Instruction of the Unlearned.* Philadelphia: Presbyterian Board of Publications, No. 265 Chestnut Street, 1856.

Dickson, A. F. *Plantation Sermons.* Philadelphia: Presbyterian Board of Publications, 1856.

Douglass, Frederick. *Liberator.* Boston, December 12, 1845.

Dunwoody, Samuel. "Sermon Upon The Subject of Slavery." Columbia: Printed by S. Weir, State Printer, 1837.

Fairly, John S. *The Negro in His Relations to the Church: Letter.* Historical View. Charleston: Walker, Evans & Cogswell Co., Printers, 1889.

Fawcett, Benjamin. *A Compassionate Address to the Christian Negroes in Virginia.* London: Reprinted from an original copy in the collections of the Virginia State Library, from the edition of 1756.

Ferguson, J. B. *Address on the History, Authority and Influence of Slavery.* Nashville: John T. S. Fall, Book and Job Pr-Ben Franklin Office, College St., 1850.

Furman, Richard. *The Pleasure of Piety and Other Poems.* Charleston, S.C.: S. G. Courtenay & Co., 1859.

Glennie, Alexander. *Sermons Preached on Plantations.* Freeport, New York: The

Black Heritage Library Collection, Books for Libraries Press, 1971. (First published in 1844, Charleston: Published and sold by A. E. Miller, No. 4 Broad Street, 1844).

Godwin, Morgan. *The Negro's Indian advocate: suing for their admission to the church: or A persuasive to the instructing and baptizing of the Negro's and Indians in our plantations. Showing that as the compliance therewith can prejudice no man's just int.* . . . London: Printed by the author, J. D., 1680. (microform)

Griffin, Edward D. *A Plea for Africa A Sermon preached October 26, 1817 in the First Presbyterian Church in the City of New York, Before the Synod of New York and New Jersey, at the Request of the Board of Directors of The African School established by the Synod.* New York: Published by Request of the Board, 1817.

Grimes, William. *The Life of William Grimes, the runaway slave, brought down to the present time.* New Haven, Conn.: Author, 1855.

Hamilton, W. T. *The Duties of Masters and Slaves Respectively* or *Domestic Servitude As Sanctioned By The Bible: A Discourse by Rev. W. T. Hamilton.* Published in 1845.

Hammond. "Letter to His Excellency Governor Hammond, To The Free Church of Glasgow on the Subject of Slavery." Columbia: A. J. Pemberton, 1814.

Hammond, J. H. *Two Letters on Slavery In The United States, Addressed to Thomas Clarkson, Esq.* Columbia: Allen, McCarter & Co. The South Carolina Press, 1845.

Harrison, W. P., ed. and compiler. *The Gospel Among The Slaves: A Short Account of Missionary Operations Among The African Slaves of the Southern States.* Nashville: Publishing House of the M. E. Church, South Barbee & Smith, Agents, 1893.

Hart, Albert B., ed. *Liberty Documents with Contemporary Exposition and Critical Comments Drawn from Various Writers selected and prepared by Mabel Hill.* New York: Longman's, Green and Company, 1907. (1) "Emancipation of the Slaves (1862-1863)" Chapter XXII and (2) "The Reconstruction Amendments (1863-1870), Chapter XXIII.

Jay, William. *Miscellaneous Writings on Slavery.* Boston: John P. Jewett & Co.; Cleveland: Jewett, Proctor and Worthington; London: Sampson Low, Son and Co., 1853.

Jones, Charles C. *The Religious Instruction of the Negroes in the United States.* Savannah: Published by Thomas Purse, 1842; New York: Kraus Reprint Co., 1969.

Jones, Charles C. *Address To the Senior Class in the Theological Seminary of The Synod of South Carolina and Georgia, On the Evening of the Anniversary* (July 10, 1873 in Columbia). Savannah: Thomas Purse & Co., 1837.

Jones, Charles C. *A Catechism For Colored Persons.* Charleston: Observer Office Press, 1834.

Jones, Charles C. *Annual Reports of the Association for the Religious Instruction of the Negroes in Liberty County, Georgia*, Vol. 1-13.

Klingberg, Frank Joseph. "The Society for the Propagation of the Gospel Program For Negroes In Colonial New York." *Anglican Humanitarianism in Colonial New York.* Philadelphia: Church Historical Society, 1940, pp. 121-185.

Knox, William. "Of The Negro Slaves in the Colonies" (Second Tract), no date.

Knox, William. "Of The Indians in the Colonies" (First Tract). Three Tracts Respecting the Conversion and Instruction of the Free Indians, and Negro slaves in the Colonies, addressed to the Venerable Society For The Propagation of the Gospel in Foreign Parts.

Lafon, Thomas Dr. "The Great Obstruction to the Conversion of Souls at Home and Abroad." (an address) New York: Published by the Union Missionary Society, 1843.

Laurens, Edward R. (of St. Philip's and St. Michael's) "A Letter to the Hon. Whitemarsh B. Senbrook of St. John's Collection: In Explanation and Defense of 'An Act To Amend The Law In Relation To Slaves and Free Persons of Color.' " Charleston: Observer Office Press, 1835.

Lee, Jarena. *The life and religions of Jarena Lee, a coloured lady, giving an account of her call to preach the gospel.* Revised and corrected by herself. Philadelphia: the Author, 1836.

Magee, J. H. (Pastor of the Union Baptist Church, Cincinnati), *The Night of Affliction and the Morning of Recovery: An Autobiography.* Cincinnati: Published by the author, 12 Rittenhouse Street, 1873 (Excerpts).

Mather, Cotton. *Rules For the Society of Negroes, 1693.* New York, 1888.

Meade, William. "Pastoral Letter of the Right Rev. William Meade," (Assistant Bishop of Virginia) To the Members, Ministers and Friends of the Protestant Episcopal Church in the Diocese of Virginia, on the "Duty of Affording Religious Instruction To Those In Bondage," delivered in the year 1834. Reprinted by the Convocation of Central Virginia in 1853. Richmond: H. K. Ellyson, 147 Main Street.

Morrow, Honore Willsie. *I Learned About God from A Negress.* An advance printing from the March issue of *Cosmopolitan* (Fisk University):2-21.

Murphy, John. (originally published in 1844, Baltimore, MD) *Letters of the Late Bishop England.* New York: Negro Universities Press, Reprinted in 1969.

Quarterman, Robert. "Ninth Annual Report of the Association for the Religious Instruction of the Negroes in Liberty County, Georgia" together with the address to the association by the President. Savannah: Printed by Thomas Purse, 1844.

Palmer, B.M., moderator. *Address of the General Assembly of the Presbyterian Church in the Confederate States of America.* Augusta, Georgia, December 1861.

Pattillo, Henry. "The Plain Planters' Family Assistant . . . Address to Husbands and Wives, Children and Servants. . . ." Wilmington: James Adams (1787):51-52.693

Peabody, Ephraim. "Narratives of Fugitive Slaves" in *Christian Examiner*, Vol. XLVII, no. 1 (July-September, 1849).

Richmond, Leigh. *The African Servant: An Authentic Narrative.* Published by the American Tract Society, And sold at their Depository, No. 144 Nassau-Street, Near the City-Hall, New York: and by Agents of the Society, its Branches and Auxiliaries, in the Principal Cities and Towns in the United States (Found in the Schomburg Center for Research in Black Culture).

Ross, Fred A. (Pastor of the Presbyterian Church, Huntsville, AL) *Slavery Ordained of God.* New York: Negro University Press, A Division of Greenwood Publishing Corporation, 1969; Published by J. B. Lippincott & Company in 1859.

Segar, Joseph. "Speech of Mr. Joseph Segar on the Wilmot Proviso." Printed in 1849.

Smith, William A. *Lectures on the Philosophy and Practice of Slavery as Exhibited in the Institution of Domestic Slavery in the United States: with Duties of Masters to Slaves.* Edited by Thomas O. Summers. Nashville: Stevenson and Evans 1856.

Stoddard, Solomon. *Guide To Christ, Or, The Way of Directing Souls That Are Under the Work of CONVERSION.* Compiled for the Help of Young Ministers, and May be Serviceable to Private Christians Who Are Inquiring With an Epistle Prefixed, by the Rev. Dr. Increase Mather. To Which is added, Sixteen Short Sermons, by a Clergyman of the Church of England. Northhampton: Printed by Andrew Wright, 1816.

Thompson, George and Henry Wright. *The Free Church and Her Accusers: The Question at Issue.* A Letter from George Thompson, Esq. to Henry Wright; and one from Henry Wright to Ministers and Members of the Free Church of Scotland. Glasgow: George Gallie, Buchanan Street, W. & R,. Smeal, 161 Gallowgate; Quintin Dalrymple 29, Frederick Street, Edinburgh, 1840.

Thornwell, James H. *Judgements, A Call To Repentance. A Sermon Preached by Appointment of the Legislature in the Hall of House of Representatives.* Columbia: R. W. Gibbes & Co., State Printers, 1854.

Thornwell, Dr. James. "Sermon: The Rights and Duties of Masters" preached on Sunday evening May 26, 1850. Second Presbyterian Church, Charleston, South Carolina.

Thornwell, J. N. "Review of Paley's Moral Philosophy." 1858.

Thornwell, J. N. *A Review of Rev. J. B. Adger's Sermon on the Religious Instruction of the Coloured Population.* Charleston: Burges, James and Paxton, Printers, 1847.

Van Evrie, John H. *Negroes and Negro "slavery": the first an inferior race, the latter its normal condition.* Baltimore, Md.: J. D. Troy Printer, 1853.

Vassa, Gustavus. "The Life of Olaudah Equiano, or Gustavus Vassa, the African." In *Great Slave Narratives.* Selected and Introduced by Arna Bontemps. Boston: Beacon Press, 1969. First published in London, 1789 as "The Interesting Narrative of the Life of Olaudah Equiano, or Gustavus Vassa, the African."

Veney, Bethany. *The Narrative of Bethany Veney, a slave woman.* Worcester, Mass: A. P. Bicknell, 1890.

Washington, Joseph. *Black Religions: The Negro and Christianity in the United States.* Boston: Beacon Press, 1964.

Watson. "Sermon." West Indies.

Watson, Richard. *The Religious Instruction of the Slaves in the West India Colonies Advocated and Defended A Sermon preached before The Wesleyan Methodist Missionary Society, in the New Chapel, City Road, London, April 28, 1924.* London: Sold by Butterworth and Son, Fleet-Street and Kershaw, Paternoster-Row, 1924.

Wellwisher. *A Letter to An American Planter from His Friend in London.* London: Printed by H. Reynell, No. 21, Piccadilly, 1781.

Whitfield, George. "A Letter To The Ten Inhabitants of Maryland . . ." 6 Vols. London, 1771.

Wright, Henry C. *No Rights, No Duties; or Slaveholders, as Such, Owe No Duties.* An Answer to a Letter From Hon. Henry Wilson, Touching Resistance to Slaveholders being the Right and Duty of the Slaves, and of the People and States of the North. Boston: Printed for the Author, 1860.

(No author noted) *Jubilee Songs: as sung by the Jubilee Singers of Fisk University.* New York: Biglow & Main, 1872.

(No author noted) *"Letters on Slavery,"* originally published in the Christian Mirror, 1835-1837.

(No author noted) *The Converted Negro To Which Are Added The History of Babay;*

and the Conversion of Certain Indians. London: Printed by G. Auld, Breville Street, for William and Smith, Stationers Court.

(No author noted) *The Praying Negro.* Andover: Printed for the New England Tract Society by Flagg and Gould, 1818 (Fisk University Library).

(No author noted) *Duties of Christian Masters to Their Servants.* Nashville: No publisher, Feb. 10, 1859.

(No author noted) "Religion Among Slaves." *The London Methodist Magazine, Antigua-Extracts from Mr. Hyde's Journal, dated Parham, May 7, 1821.*

(No author noted) *An Appeal To The Good Sense of A Great People.* Charleston: Dan J. Dowling, Printer, 1835.

(No author noted) *The Convert's Guide.* Entered according to Act of Congress, in the year 1841, by George Lane, in the Clerk's Office of the District Court of the Southern District of New York.

(No author noted) *The Mediator Between the North and South.* Seven Pointers of the North Star. Washington, 1862.

(No author noted) *"View of The Subject of Slavery."* The Biblical Repertory Pittsburgh (April, 1836), 1-36.

(No author noted) *A Letter from An Elder In An Old School Presbyterian Church to His Son At College.* New York, 1863.

(No author noted) *Proceedings of the Meeting in Charleston, S.C. May 13-15, 1845, on the Religious Instruction of the Negroes, together with The Report of the Committee and the Address To the Public.* Charleston: Printed by B. Jenkins, 100 Hayne-Street, 1845.

(No author noted) *The American Missionary.* Vol. LVIII No. 8, New York: Published by the American Missionary Association, Monthly, Except July and August (October, 1904), 239-258.

DISSERTATIONS

Cannon, Katie. *Resources for a Constructive Ethic for Black Women with Special Attention to the Life and Work of Zora Neale Hurston.* Ann Arbor, Michigan: University Microfilm International, 1983.

Cobb, Jimmy Gene. *A Study of White Protestants' Attitudes Toward Negroes in Charleston, South Carolina, 1790-1845.* (A Dissertation submitted to the Faculty of Baylor University in Partial Fulfillment of the Requirements for the Degree of Doctor of Philosophy) Waco: Baylor University, 1976.

Cornelius, Janet Duitsman. *God's Schoolmasters: Southern Evangelists To the Slaves, 1830-1860.* (Submitted in partial fulfillment of the requirements for the degree of Doctor of Philosophy in History in the Graduate College of the University of Illinois at Urbana-Champaign) Urbana: University of Illinois at Urbana-Champaigne, 1977.

Iverson, Vincent Albert. *Memory and the Past.* (Ph.D. Dissertation done at Yale University Ann Arbor) Ann Arbor: University Microfilms, Inc., 1968.

Loring, Edward N. *Charles C. Jones: Missionary To Plantation Slaves, 1831-1847.* Dissertation submitted to the Faculty of the Graduate School of Vanderbilt University for the Degree, Doctor of Philosophy in Religion, May 1976, Nashville, Tn. (1-200).

Thomas, Arthur D. *The Second Great Awakening in Virginia and Slavery Reform.* Pt. 2. University Microfilm International, Ann Arbor, Mich., 1981.

Van Horne, John. *"Pious Designs": The American Correspondence of the Associates of Dr. Bray, 1731-1775.* (A Dissertation Presented to the Graduate Faculty of the University of Virginia in Candidacy for the Degree of Doctor of Philosophy) Virginia: Corcoran Department of History, University of Virginia, May 1979.

BOOKLETS

Bradford, Sarah H. *Scenes in the Life of Harriet Tubman.* Auburn: W. J. Moses, Printer, 1869.

Brown, Henry Box. *Narrative of the Life of Henry Box Brown.* Written By Himself. Manchester: Printed by Lee and Glynn, 8, Cannon Street, 1851.

Browne, Martha. *Autobiography of a Female Slave.* New York: Redfield, 34 Beekman St., 1857. Reprinted by Mnemosyne Publishing Co., Inc., Miami, Florida.

Elaw, Zilpha. *Memoirs of the Life, Religious Experience, Ministerial Travels and Labours of Mrs. Zilpha Elaw, An American Female of Colour; Together With Some Account of the Great Religious Revivals in America.* London: Published by the Authoress, and Sold by T. Dudley, 19, Charter-House Lane; and Mr. B. Taylor, 19, Montague-St., Spitalfields, 1846.

Proctor, C. H. *The Life of James Williams, Better known as Professor Jim for a Half Century Janitor of Trinity College.* Hartford: Case, Lockwood & Bainard, Printers, 1873.

Ward, Samuel Ringgold. *Autobiography of A Fugitive Negro: His Anti-Slavery Labours in the United States, Canada & England.* London: John Snow, 35, Paternoster Row, 1855.

Watkins, James. *Narrative of the life of James Watkins, Formerly A Slave In Maryland, US: Containing An Account of His Escape From Slavery, and His Subsequent History, With Notices of the Fugitive Slaves Law, The Sentiments of American Divines on the Subject of Slavery and the Labours of the Fugitive in England, etc.* Manchester: Printed for James Watkins, 1859.

Williams, Peter Jun. *An Oration on The Abolition of the Slave Trade; Delivered in The African Church, in the City of New York, January 1, 1808.* New York: Printed by Samuel Wood, No. 362 Pearl Street, 1808.

Author Unknown (By a Lady in Boston). *Memoir of Mrs. Chloe Spear, A Native of Africa, Who Was Enslaved In Childhood, and Died In Boston, January 3, 1815 . . . Aged 65 Years.* Boston: Edited by James Loring, 1815.

Index

Abolitionists: ex-slaves' autobiographies and, 8, 105-6, 109
Abuse: of Douglass, Frederick, 120-23; physical, 22, 70, 125, 175; of power, 31; psychological, 46, 70
Adam: slave's relationship to, 28-29
Adams, Edward C. L., 140, 143-44
Adger, J. B., 40
African Servant, The (Leigh), 17
Alho, Olli, 74
Alienation, 70, 78, 127, 169
Anansi myth, 132
Andrews, William, 68, 105-7, 109-10, 115
Anthropological theory, 1, 5, 21, 23, 129-30, 158-61
Antiblackness/anti-blackness mindset, 12, 41
Ascending metaphor, 75
Assimilation, 160
At-homeness of the world, 152
Autobiographical narratives: authenticity of, 108; body-soul dichotomy and, 7, 102, 122; control of, 177; embodied selves theme in, 110-13; escape and, 178; "feeling moods," 173; first-order language of, 111; fugitive period in, 104; Jezebel stereotype, 113-19; literary assessment of, 105; as literary text, 107; mammy stereotype, 113-19; metaphorical language, 121; mirror metaphor, 108-9; purpose of, 3, 8, 104, 173-74; rational narrative self, 176-79; reason dilemma, 177; sanctification myth, 114-19; second-order language of, 111; self-autonomy dilemma, 176-77; strong woman myth, 113-14; styles of, 120-30; as symbolic statement,

106; testimonial letters and, 108; white readers' responses to, 108-10; white sponsors of, 8, 105-6; as womanist statement, 119
Autonomy: autobiographical narrative themes, 110-19, 176; as spiritual theme, 73. *See also* Self-autonomy
Bacon, Thomas, 18-19, 34
Baptism: ceremony, 126; symbolism of, 43-45
Bard, E. T., 34
Bibb, Henry, 128
Black Culture and Black Consciousness, 2
Black Religion, 181
Blassingame, James, 1-2
Body-soul dichotomy: in autobiographical narratives, 122; in Brer Rabbit stories, 7, 102, 136; ideal Christian master type response and, 16; interdependence and, 162; significance of, 4-8; value and, 15-16; worth and, 162, 175
Bondage, and Christian duty: biblical authority and duty, 29-32; Christian apologists, 27-34; marginal servant class, 25-27; twice-fallen theory, 29
Botsford, Edmund, 42-43
Bowery, Charity, 73
"Brer Rabbit and the Briar Patch," 152, 182
"Brer Rabbit and the Tar Baby," 148-49
"Brer Rabbit Seeks Wisdom," 147-48
"Brer Rabbit's Hankering for a Long Tail," 153-54
"Brer Rabbit's Laughing Place," 155-56
Brer Rabbit stories: anthropological